Blue Sky
Warriors

This book is dedicated to every one of the men and women of Britain's armed forces; ordinary people doing extraordinary things on a daily basis.

'Anyone who fights, even with the most modern weapons, against an enemy who dominates the air, is like a primitive warrior who stands against modern forces, with the same limitations and the same chance of success.'
Field Marshal Erwin Rommel

Blue Sky Warriors

THE RAF IN AFGHANISTAN IN THEIR OWN WORDS

Antony Loveless

Foreword by
Air Chief Marshal Sir Stephen Dalton
KCB, ADC, BSc, FRAeS, CCMI, RAF
Chief of the Air Staff

Haynes Publishing

The views and opinions expressed in this book are those of the contributors alone and do not necessarily represent those of Her Majesty's Government, the MoD, the RAF or any Government agency.

© Antony Loveless 2010

First published in 2010

A catalogue record for this book is available from the British Library

ISBN 978 1 84425 633 4

Library of Congress control no 2009936938

Published by Haynes Publishing,
Sparkford, Yeovil, Somerset BA22 7JJ, UK
Tel: 01963 442030 Fax: 01963 440001
Int. tel: +44 1963 442030 Int. fax: +44 1963 440001
E-mail: sales@haynes.co.uk
Website: www.haynes.co.uk

Haynes North America Inc.
861 Lawrence Drive, Newbury Park,
California 91320, USA

Printed and bound in Great Britain

CONTENTS

To the RAF

Never since English ships went out
To singe the beard of Spain,
Or English sea-dogs hunted death
Along the Spanish Main,
Never since Drake and Raleigh won
Our freedom of the seas,
Have sons of Britain dared and done
More valiantly than these.

Whether at midnight or at noon,
Through mist or open sky,
Eagles of freedom, all our hearts
Are up with you on high;
While Britain's mighty ghosts look down
From realms beyond the sun
And whisper, as their record pales,
Their breathless, deep, Well Done!

© Alfred Noyes

FOREWORD

Air Chief Marshal Sir Stephen Dalton
KCB, ADC, BSc, FRAeS, CCMI, RAF

When the RAF was forged in the crucible of the First World War, its formation was revolutionary and highly innovative. Yet more than 90 years on, not only does it have the unique distinction of being the oldest independent air force in the world, but it has also demonstrated its ability to adapt and deliver distinct and invaluable operational capability in defence of the UK and its global interests. The Royal Air Force has more potent capability than ever, and after around 20 years of operations in and over Iraq, it is Afghanistan that dominates its operations, for it is here that the RAF is most heavily engaged.

Much has been written about the lives and roles played by our front-line personnel over the years. But what of the modern-day successors to those Battle of Britain pilots of whom Churchill said, 'Never in the field of human conflict was so much owed by so many to so few'? What of the engineers, the operations support staff, the medics, the Forward Air Controllers, and the RAF Regiment? What of the Chinook, Merlin, and Puma crews on whom the Army are so heavily reliant in Afghanistan and recently Iraq; or the Hercules crews who have so effectively revitalised and honed their airdrop capabilities to resupply otherwise isolated forward-operating outposts? What of the Tornado GR4 and the Harrier aircrew who provide vital, often life-saving Close Air Support and those crews providing airborne surveillance? And what of the essential, but often unsung movers, chefs and administrative staff who keep the machine oiled and in working order?

What follows, on the pages of this book, are the voices and personal accounts of RAF men and women who have travelled thousands of miles from home, to an environment where the expeditionary nature of warfare is at its strongest and most demanding.

A book like this can only ever be a snapshot of a particular time frame in the war. People, aircraft, places – and indeed, the tide of battle – can all change over time. Those serving in Afghanistan come from all ranks, from SAC to Air Commodore. They encompass men and women of diverse background, skills and age but who are united in their motivation, ethos and bravery. Their stories are as individual as their characters, but each is compelling in its own way.

There are many books about, and by, pilots, and their heroic deeds in the air. Yet it's those who work alongside them, support them, and enable them to fly that often have some very interesting and compelling stories to tell. They are a modest bunch, unassuming, but who work with a quiet confidence born of their training, teamwork and ethos.

The unwavering professionalism, dedication, courage and commitment of these motivated and highly trained people are the key to how successfully the Royal Air Force operates today, and they are fundamental to how it will develop for the future. I am very proud of them all and the sacrifices they and their families make in the service of their country.

ACKNOWLEDGEMENTS

No book is ever the work of a single person; as the duck swimming gracefully across the surface of the water masks the frenetic activity beneath, so an author's name on the cover stands as testament to the industriousness and efforts of a whole team of people, each of whom is essential to the project's existence.

First and foremost, I'd like to thank every member of the RAF who made this work possible – the countless men and women who gave up their time to talk to me. I'd like to thank Squadron Leader Brian Handy, whose inspiration and support saw this project given wings, and to my friend Squadron Leader Al Green at the MoD who accompanied me in theatre; Al, you went far and beyond the call of duty in tirelessly responding to my every query, often at short notice. You also made an eventful trip unforgettable and gave me 'wings' at RAF Shawbury. For all that you've done, thank you.

Special thanks to Carol; for your patience, believing in me, putting up with the inconvenience, and for the endless support and countless long nights transcribing the hours of interviews I recorded in theatre. I couldn't have done it without you. To Betty, too; happily retired from audio typing, but still willing to don those headphones one last time for me; your help was invaluable.

Thanks too, to Jonathan Falconer, Christine Smith, and all at Haynes Publishing, who saw the potential in this book from the very beginning and shared my belief that the stories of those unsung heroes of the RAF needed to be told. I can't thank you enough for your support, enthusiasm, and sheer hard work.

I'm indebted to the Ministry of Defence and its staff for supporting and believing in this project, helping me to identify and locate the interviewees, and for getting me into theatre to talk to them. At KAF, thank you Squadron Leader Al McGuinness – for going without sleep to set everything up at such short notice and track down so many willing volunteers for me. Also, to Captain Andy Whitehead at Camp Bastion for doing the same there. And Moggy; thanks for 'shooting' so many people for me.

A great many people worked behind the scenes to make my numerous visits to Afghanistan possible, including the pilots who flew me there and back and invited me into their world; thank you. Wing Commander Sophy Gardner and Squadron Leader Stuart Balfour at the MoD both took ownership of issues whenever I encountered obstacles, made strenuous efforts to smooth the path for me and I am enormously grateful to you both for your assistance. Also, to Mala, for staying late on several Fridays waiting for me to finish interviews in the MoD main building. I'm indebted to Wing Commander Simon 'Spoons' Edwards and everyone at 99 Squadron for their generous help and for moving mountains to make things happen.

Huge thanks to my friends and family who have supported me throughout.

The final word must go to all those men and women who contributed their experiences and time to create this book. Meeting them all was a humbling, moving, and rewarding experience and I will always remember the time I spent listening to their remarkable accounts of life on the front line. I heard so many extraordinary stories from so many of those I met in Afghanistan who took part in Operation Herrick 8, that it simply hasn't been possible to include all of them here. Perhaps the most difficult aspect of this whole project was deciding which stories to include and which ones to leave out; I could have written this book several times over. I am enormously grateful to every single one of the men and women I met for their candour and trust. This is not my book; my name is on the front cover only because someone's had to be. All I did was sit and listen to them recount their experiences. These are their words, their stories, and this is *their* book.

INTRODUCTION

Born of Britain and the US response to the terrorist attacks on the World Trade Center on 11 September 2001, as I write, the war in Afghanistan is now in its eighth year; 150 members of British forces have lost their lives in the conflict and if current estimates are to be believed, it could be several decades before the last British forces finally leave for good. To put things in perspective, many of the British men and women now deployed to Afghanistan in the fight against the Taliban were just ten years old when the Twin Towers fell.

The Army may dominate in terms of column inches, and in the countless books that this conflict has given birth to, but this is most definitely a tri-service operation. Of the 8,300 or so British forces currently in theatre, only around 1,500 are front-line soldiers. These are predominantly drawn from the infantry regiments of the Army and the Royal Marines, but they don't operate in isolation; for each soldier living at a Forward Operating Base and engaging with Taliban forces, a whole team of others is required to support his day-to-day existence. From the Army, Royal Navy, and RAF chefs who cook his meals, to the Royal Navy and RAF pilots that provide Close Air Support, a whole army of RAF personnel supports, directs and controls operations in theatre.

Between June and December 2008, I talked with countless members of the RAF about their role in Afghanistan. They told me, often with astonishing candour, of their experiences living in theatre, away from families and loved ones, working punishing hours in one of the most hostile environments on the planet. We talked in myriad places: from the hot, dusty air of the Afghanistan desert, the cockpits of countless jets and helicopters on sorties in theatre, and in tents and kitchens to the rarefied air of Dukes Hotel in London's St James' and the MoD, a world away.

Almost every single Briton deployed to Afghanistan will be in harm's way countless times during their four-month tour of duty. And many of the men and women I talked with have faced death and moved forward in its face.

For many, talking to me was the first time they had recounted their experiences. A few told me they found the experience cathartic; a few had tears in their eyes; several have struggled emotionally to readjust since returning from theatre. For my part, the whole exercise was humbling, rewarding and moving, in equal part. All of those I talked to, however, shared one feature which dominated their personalities: modesty. None thought of themselves as heroes, none requested inclusion in this book and none regarded anything they'd done as 'out of the ordinary'. All expressed a similar sentiment: 'I was just doing my job.' Their modesty speaks volumes about the sort of people they are. There is no ego there, no desire for recognition. Few expressed any personal thoughts or feelings about the rights or otherwise of the war they were involved in. Overwhelmingly, they seemed possessed of a commonly held belief that they had a job to do and it wasn't for them to question why or where they were sent. Their professionalism was evident.

I was privileged enough to spend time in theatre with most of the men and women I interviewed for this book. I joined them on patrols outside the wire, flew with them, ate with them, and shared the same accommodation. I took cover with them as rockets and mortars rained down from the night-time sky and I saw and experienced at first hand the conditions in which they had to work. It was not a quiet time; sadly, I saw first-hand the fallout following not one, but 12 deaths of British servicemen and women in just a single ten-day period. First, a suicide bomber killed three Paras; a well-planned ambush accounted for another two. A bomb attack left a further four soldiers dead – including Corporal Sarah Bryant, 26, the first female British soldier to die in Afghanistan. Four more died in the following four days: one Para died in a firefight, two more were killed by land mines, and one more when his vehicle overturned while on patrol.

There is only one way into theatre for the countless servicemen and women deployed there: via the ageing TriStar fleet of airliners operated by Brize Norton-based 216 Squadron. The faded decals in the aircrafts' toilets and galleys hint at their previous, rather more glamorous life, from a time when people dressed to fly. Now, they wear desert combats, Kevlar helmets, and body armour for a night-time descent made in total darkness. Each passenger deals with the darkened approach differently, but there can't be a man or woman aboard who doesn't momentarily dwell on the fact that there is a better than even chance that one or more of their fellow passengers won't be coming home the same way. For those destined to make the news while increasing the British casualty list, the route home is rather more high profile: a ramp ceremony at Kandahar usually at sunset, a C17 Globemaster into RAF Lyneham, a private repatriation service there for the family, followed by a procession through the centre of Wootton Bassett lined by locals who turn out to honour every fallen soldier repatriated back to Britain.

Helmand Province is unforgiving territory. It can take over three weeks to acclimatise on arrival. The temperature while I was there in June and July rarely dropped below 48°C and reached as high as 55°C with humidity consistently around 9 per cent; it is arid, hot, and dusty. Heatstroke is almost as much of a threat as the Taliban, so too is the dreaded D&V (Diarrhoea and Vomiting), which can strike down a whole patrol within days. You need to take in ten litres of water a day just to stay hydrated and there is almost no shelter from the sun. That is the landscape among which our forces live and work, uncomplaining. Watching them as they went about their business with typical good humour, one thought kept coming back to me: the men and women who make up Britain's armed forces have frequently been described as 'ordinary people doing extraordinary things', but there is nothing ordinary about them. They are, without exception, a credit to our country.

Theirs is an asymmetric war; in Afghanistan, the old rules of warfare no longer exist and have been replaced by one-sided rules. It's an environment where medics and doctors carry weapons for self-defence and may use them in accordance with the Geneva Conventions; where, to work within the accords of the Hippocratic axiom, *Primum Non Nocere* – 'above all, do no harm' – they may be forced into taking a life to preserve one. It's an environment where the Taliban's desire to 'down' a Chinook extends to their planting Improvised Explosive Devices (IEDs) in civilian markets, because they know that the Chinook-borne Medical Emergency

Response Team (MERT) will be scrambled to help. British airmen, medics and soldiers risk their lives to recover and treat enemy wounded; the best they could expect were they to be wounded and captured by the Taliban would be inhumane treatment and torture followed by a painful, protracted death.

It's a war where enemy forces masquerade as civilians; where insurgents will place mortar tubes in crowds of women and children and launch attacks on ISAF and ANF forces, knowing that our moral and ethical code prevents us from returning fire. Where a man will take his five-year-old along as cover on a mine-laying expedition. The Rules of Engagement that dictate how and when we open fire on the Taliban prevent us from fighting on an equal footing, yet our troops continue to risk their lives on a daily basis and fight fair, within the rules and without complaint. It's a thin line to tread; a 500lb bomb dropped from a Harrier on a lone Taliban gunman could be construed as disproportionate, yet using the same weapon on a group of enemy wouldn't. In the heat of battle, these are the things that our troops have to consider, even while the Taliban show blatant disregard for the rules.

Viewed from afar, our role in Afghanistan appears straightforward. But that received wisdom masks a reality that is far from clear. For one, few outside of the military and the press seem to have a clear understanding of the pressures facing our men and women in theatre. This was a conflict that, in its early days, received widespread public support compared to our role in Iraq. Yet as our numbers in that latter conflict wound down, so too has public sympathy for our role in Afghanistan. Every new reported fatality of another young British soldier has the potential to erode what remains of support for our presence in Afghanistan still further. And anti-war demonstrations, such as that which took place in March 2009, when Islamist protesters held up banners labelling soldiers returning from Iraq as 'killers, cowards, and butchers' serve only to muddy the waters still further. One of the potential problems with fighting a war on two fronts is that those members of the public who are uninterested and uninformed confuse one conflict with another. As General Sir Richard Dannatt said while Chief of the General Staff, 'I think the Army is at war; the nation is not at war.'

And who are the Taliban anyway? Those described as 'Tier one' fighters – the committed, diehard Islamic fundamentalists who believe they are fighting a *jihad* – are far from representative. There are also a large number of 'Tier two' fighters – farmers mostly, young, disenfranchised Afghan men with a sense of resentment and antipathy to authority, happy to fight for money as and when they can. There are the countless numbers of Afghanistan's young men pressed into fighting for the Taliban at gunpoint. And there are a large number of foreign *Jihadis* from outside of Afghanistan's borders, mostly schooled in Madrassas, happy to take up arms at what they see as an 'infidel' occupation of a Muslim country – the Pakistanis, Iranians, Chechens, Saudis and even British fighters. Taliban mullahs are more than happy to let foreign fighters seeking *shaheed,* or martyrdom, die on their behalf.

All of this takes place in Afghanistan, a land that is only a country by virtue of a political map that defines its borders. A land whose border with Pakistan is so porous, there is no effective governmental influence from either country on it, and through which the Taliban can move about freely. Indeed, as I write, Pakistan is in turmoil and US strategy for the region is switching under President Obama to integrate policy on Afghanistan and Pakistan. The thinking now is that we can't solve the problems in one without doing so in the other. Those people we know generically as Afghanis or Afghans hail from at least five different ethnic groups and countless different tribes, many of which are spread across Pakistan's Federally Administered Tribal Areas. More than 30 languages are spoken within the country's borders, in addition to the three official tongues of Dari, Farsi, and Pashto. Perhaps the only common thread to tie the country's people together is their Muslim religion. The average Afghan feels little sense of loyalty to Harmid Karzai; it is in the nature of many to support whoever looks likely to be the victor of any given argument, battle or confrontation. A deep-rooted system of tribal and ethnic loyalty overrides any sense of nationality such as that possessed by the average Briton.

Are we storing up problems in the long term? Possibly; the intensity of fighting in Afghanistan is unprecedented for British forces in modern times and many of the troops returning home have suffered emotionally as a result of what they've seen or been involved in while in theatre. And long term, there remains the vexing question of how to motivate pilots who are heavily combat experienced right at the beginning of their careers. Before Operation Herrick, it wasn't unusual for pilots to serve 20 or 30 years and never see active service. Now, many deploy straight to Helmand Province and intensive combat ops when they complete their training. I met junior aircrew in theatre who are flying on their tenth tour of duty in Afghanistan, so what can the service do to keep them motivated when they return to the UK and a life of training and exercises? People develop a frame of reference for combat and can become blasé about it very quickly. What next for those people?

And yet we are making progress. When the Taliban fell from power eight years ago, there were only 900,000 children in school, all of them boys. Last year saw over 330,000 girls start school for the first time, a figure unprecedented in Afghanistan's history. The combined figure is now six million and rising. Five million refugees have returned home and 82 per cent of the population has access to healthcare, some nine times the figure in 2002. The GDP of Afghanistan has tripled since 2001 and we are achieving some notable successes in training the Afghan National Army to eventually take over security. A new policy is likely to see a greater focus on utilising new counter-insurgency doctrine pioneered in Iraq, with a focus on embedding troops more closely with the local population and working harder to engage them. There is clearly a long way still to go and the long-term solution to Afghanistan's problems has to be political – militarily, we can only ever hope to stabilise the security situation to allow that to take place.

It's a thankless task, but provided our forces receive the support they need, it's one that they are more than ready to take on. Army, Navy and RAF – one of our key strengths lies in the fact that ours is a military force of volunteers, drawn from the civilian population that strives with professionalism and dedication to serve and defend that community wherever they may be required. Those members of the RAF that I met while in Afghanistan were a disparate bunch, from all sorts of backgrounds and with differing motivations, but they were representative; from London, the Home Counties and the South West, to the Midlands, the North, Scotland, Wales, and Northern Ireland, the RAF men and women I spoke with were as individual as their heritage.

From afar, people view our uniformed services, such as the RAF, as a generic, homogenous group with a collective psyche. The truth is somewhat more prosaic: every member is different; the uniform and training are all that tie them together.

Britain's teenagers are often described as feckless, lazy and superficial, but today's airmen and women are all drawn from the same national pool and they are as professional, accomplished and capable as ever. Their kit is cutting edge, and the aircraft that they pilot include the Typhoon F2, the world's most advanced fighter jet. But the Royal Air Force is more than just aeroplanes; it is the men and women who operate, maintain and support them that give the Air Force its cutting edge and remain its most important asset.

Without a clear strategy, a robust command structure, world-class training, and the first-class people from all backgrounds who make up today's RAF, it could not undertake its diverse operations with the hallmark expertise, dedication and team spirit of which this nation is so rightly proud. The people I met highlight all these facets and portray an Air Force that, after more than 90 years of operations, still strives to be first; person to person, it is second to none.

For the most part, this book wrote itself; I asked the odd question, but my subjects did all the talking, my digital voice recorder noting everything silently. What follows on these pages are the results: the voices of British airmen and women who have travelled thousands of miles from home to face an enemy that fights dirty while they fight fair. They are a credit to our country.

Antony Loveless, March 2009

WING COMMANDER
ANDY LEWIS

OC 1(F) SQUADRON, HARRIER GR9 PILOT

The RAF's Harrier GR7s and GR9s have been a constant presence in Afghanistan since the first days of the conflict. Redolent of the Battle of Britain pilots waiting to scramble and run to their Spitfires at a moment's notice, the RAF's Harrier pilots do the same thing, dressed in their G-suits, their jets heavily laden with rockets, bombs, reconnaissance and targeting pods. Their primary role is simple: to provide Close Air Support to ISAF ground forces anywhere in the country.

Wing Commander Andy Lewis is the OC of 1(F) Squadron. He and his pilots juggled not only their aircraft, flying at 400mph and high level, but also a pair of binoculars in the cockpit, which they used to spot potential targets. Theirs was the personal liability of ensuring that their bombs went on to target, sometimes dropping them within metres of our own troops. Theirs was a different war, at once involved while being detached. They were there above the action, listening to the sound of bullets and RPGs whizzing past over the radio, as the Forward Air Controllers who direct their weapons relayed instructions. They saw first-hand the destructive effects of their ordnance on Taliban forces yet returned to the relative comfort of Kandahar Airfield.

I have the privilege of being Officer Commanding for No1 Fighter Squadron, which is a component of Joint Force Harrier (JFH). JFH comprises three front-line units – ourselves, No IV (AC) Squadron and the Naval Strike Wing – and between us, we've been deploying on rotational tours of duty in Afghanistan since 2004. We deploy to

Kandahar for between four and six months followed by eight months back in the UK where we are based at RAF Cottesmore.

I've had a fascinating career to date and so far, have loved every minute of it. My family have been supportive throughout, which helps, but I love what I do and am very much looking forward to the future. I've always enjoyed the pure flying but it's becoming increasingly complex as my ability to influence how both aircraft and air power are used increases. On that basis, I will inevitably find myself with my feet firmly on the ground as my career progresses.

I always wanted to fly but it took me three attempts to get into the RAF. I initially spent a year at Jesus College, Oxford. But having a distinctly mathematical brain, I didn't much take to the more general nature of the engineering degree course. After speaking to my tutor, I elected to move to Imperial College where I studied Aeronautical Engineering. As the RAF had already turned me down twice, I was determined to show them what I could do. Soon after arriving in London I was awarded a university cadetship on the University of London Air Squadron and went on to earn a first-class degree. After graduating in 1988, I completed basic flying training at RAF Church Fenton on the Jet Provost, followed by more advanced flying at RAF Valley and RAF Brawdy on the Hawk. I was streamed to single-seat fast jets and posted to my first and only choice, the Harrier, and got married during my operational conversion training, after which I was posted to No IV (AC) Squadron at RAF Gütersloh. We spent three fantastic years in Germany and I was thrilled to receive a posting to instruct at RAF Valley. That led to selection to fly the Hawk display in 1997 and subsequently the Red Arrows that same year. My tour in the Reds spanned the 1998, 1999 and 2000 seasons.

Selection for the Red Arrows was both unexpected and fantastic, and the realisation of a dream. Although even at the time I refused to say that it would be the best thing I ever did, because I think your life is over if you get to that stage; it was an awesome tour but three years was enough – I spent a lot of time away from home living out of a suitcase. My tour culminated with the role of the executive officer – or the Team Leader's 'right hand man'. Flying with the Reds is hugely challenging, an awesome experience and such fun. Without doubt it is the most difficult pure flying job there is; truly, it is the most difficult flying you will ever, ever do. Life in the Team is all-consuming. Three years flashed by. However, I can still vividly remember the catalyst for my wanting to leave. In early 1997, we were staging through Italy to Cyprus for seven weeks of intense training. I remember landing and seeing a Harrier mate running around with a pistol and survival waistcoat on. I said 'What's going on?' and he replied 'Can't tell you much at this stage but look at the news tonight, we're going in.' And that was it – the boys were on the first Kosovo strike mission. It just brought it home to me what I was doing – while it was an important job, it wasn't front line so I was determined at that stage to do my tour and come back to the front line and stay there.

My time with the Reds finished in 2000 and I returned to the Harrier Force. Barring a few Staff Tours, that's where I've stayed. I did a rusticated MoD appointment working with the Harrier Release Service, the Staff College at Shrivenham, and then I was Personal Staff Officer to Commander-in-Chief Strike Command Sir Brian Burridge and Sir Joe French. Finally I was appointed to my current role as the OC of 1(F) Squadron.

The squadron commander takes ultimate responsibility for operational output and the welfare of his people. The roles my officers carry out include the sixteen pilots, the Operations, Intelligence Officers. My four engineering officers head a fantastic team of over 140 engineers. Finally, the squadron is fortunate enough to have an Army Ground Liaison Officer on secondment. He is a captain in the British Army; as most of the work that the Harriers do in Afghanistan is in support of land forces, he's an essential asset. The success of Close Air Support in Afghanistan relies entirely on the very best air–land integration and my Ground Liaison Officer (GLO) is a fundamental and key part of this process. What he does is provide a link between us and whichever coalition ground forces unit that happens to be in theatre, providing us with detailed briefings of ground manoeuvres and tactics. Put simply, he gives a ground-centric perspective to a group of air-minded pilots.

Everything we do in theatre is about one of either two things. First, the Harrier is one of the fast-jet Close Air Support (CAS) platforms that allow coalition ground forces greater freedom of movement and protection from Taliban forces, and acts as a force multiplier, effectively and dramatically reducing the footprint of land units. Second, and importantly as today's air platforms are not one-dimensional, the Harrier provides a non-traditional intelligence-gathering capability by using both an advanced targeting pod and a joint recce pod, which together offer rapid and accurate battle-damage assessment and feed commanders the critical requirement of intelligence and situational awareness. Joint Force Harrier has been in Afghanistan for nearly five years now and we've acquired a wealth of experience and knowledge across the spectrum of combat-air operations. We can provide support to ground forces with a scalable and escalating choice of weaponry. There are two principal ways that we provide CAS: prior tasking, where we receive a briefing ahead of time about a specific operation or mission to support a ground unit, or through the provision of what's known as Emergency GCAS, which is redolent of the Battle of Britain Scramble. We'll get a call that CAS is urgently required and the duty crew will race to their jets, which will have been pre-checked and readied.

With prior tasking, what happens is we'll have been allocated a specific time window to provide support and we'll arrive overhead the ground call-sign at the appointed time with a frequency to contact the ground controller and provide support as required. The perspective from the third dimension is well received by ground forces unable sometimes to see a few feet away in a dense and hostile environment on the ground. Certainly since I took over command, I have seen positive progress whereby the ground units now see the benefits of providing more information for the aircrew and, as such, they now pass more details through – we'll get schemes of manoeuvre from the Company Commander, with mapping, phase lines, egress routes, etc and the pilot will fly with them to hand. The outcome is that before the aircraft is in the air the aircrew has an understanding of what he is likely to see when he arrives on scene. Ultimately, we would like to go a stage further on occasion – to plan, brief, execute, and debrief with specific ground units – but, nine times out of ten, that's not practical in Afghanistan.

In practice the aircraft arrives on station and when the ground call-sign states 'We are at Phase Line Blue' you know; you don't need to ask

'Where's Phase Line Blue?' Then, if the ground Commander says 'We're going to Contingency Plan Bravo' you'll know what that is, too. Ultimately it's all about reducing the time between a call for support and providing that support. The single most significant delay in delivering effect is the time taken to establish what's happening on the ground. A large part of the increase in our efficiency I have observed over time is due to our having that link with the ground forces through the Army's GLO that we have with us, and the clear understanding of a group of sharp young RAF pilots.

I believe that now is a great time to command a front-line fighter squadron. In many respects we haven't seen intense and prolonged service like this since the days of the Battle of Britain. The aircraft are infinitely more complex now so the aircrew, by the nature of the job and superior training required, are much older. Spitfire pilots arrived on squadron in 1940 with as little as 10 hours' solo flying in their log books and a few days later, they'd be up in the air fighting; it takes years to train Harrier pilots today. That said, the simple 'hours flown' metric isn't the important figure now; it's more the experiencing the different capabilities. You must have a basic level of experience and it's all down to qualifications in terms of, for instance, operational low flying; night low-level flying; carrier flying; flying on major exercises, etc.

What's interesting now is the sheer depth of experience that most of our squadron 'junior' pilots have. Although in many respects it's something of a misnomer to call them junior. Take one of my flight lieutenants; he's still in his first full year on a front-line squadron after leaving the Harrier Operational Conversion Unit (OCU). In terms of experience, he has flown more than 200 hours on operations and has 70 combat missions. Rewind just five or so years and 95per cent-plus of the RAF's pilots were retiring after full careers, not having got anywhere near those figures.

It's always the combat missions that stand out, and for me there are two of particular note from Afghanistan. The first one was in early 2007 and one of the junior pilots and me were on Emergency GCAS 30, which means we were on 30-minute alert to scramble. The adrenaline is always flowing when the GCAS bell goes; we have a proper old-fashioned bell for that purpose, just like those used in the Battle of Britain, and regardless of whatever alert time you're on – 30 minutes, 60 or whatever – when the GCAS bell rings, you drop everything and run because someone somewhere needs support and they need it *now*. Our *modus operandi* for GCAS is the same now as it was 80 years or so ago; ring the bell, run like hell.

When you're on GCAS, you wait around fully kitted up. All the usual admin is dealt with when you sign on for the shift – detail like your individual briefs, which include call-signs, areas of operation, weapon loads and tactics. You prepare all your essential flying kit beforehand so that you're wearing your G-suit, your personal weapon is to hand etc. Then you prep your aircraft before it is effectively 'quarantined' while you are on alert. You do your pre-flight inspection, set up the screens and switches in the cockpit and undertake preliminary start-up checks, check the weapons loads, basically pre-position all the switches so that when you jump into the aircraft, all you have to do is close the canopy and start the engines. Then, as the engine winds up to operating power, you're strapping yourself in and you're ready to go. Once the aircraft is set up, you hang your combat survival waistcoat by the cockpit ladder and leave your helmet on the seat and you're GCAS ready.

If we're away from the dispersal area, we'll have a secure radio with us at all times, and we'll be in a specially equipped 4 x 4 complete with '70s police drama red light. You occupy your time as best you can, always waiting for the sound of the bell to alert you to the fact that you need to get airborne as fast as possible. I'll take the time to catch up on paperwork and admin, which is a never-ending battle, some of the lads will try and relax, read a little – everyone has their own way of dealing with it. Once the alert is called, the reaction, while frenetic, is actually a well-oiled machine. Everyone stops what they're doing and runs to wherever they need to be – I think we're all aware that each second's delay on the ground translates to a second's delay in getting to the target area. By the time we get to the jets, the engineers will already be there waiting, with all of the Harriers' systems switched on. All we have to do is climb in, close the canopy and start our engines.

You can get airborne pretty quickly. As you get the scramble call there's a huge surge of adrenaline and you go through stages; the first is to get into the jet, start it up and get airborne, hoping that the aircraft doesn't go unserviceable on start-up. As yet, I haven't experienced that. Once you're taxiing out and are happy with the state of the aircraft, then you're really now into speaking to the pilot who's running the Operations Desk, to get as much information as possible; he'll be waiting for that call so he'll cascade some information down in priority order. He'll tell you to get airborne on a certain heading so, effectively, you're going in the right direction as fast as you can. You'll then give him a range and a bearing so you can work out how much fuel you've got, what you need, and then he'll give you the frequency. The rest of it then is over to you to establish a relationship with the Forward Air Controller (FAC).

When you turn up on frequency, and check in with the FAC, the adrenaline is pumping once again. At that stage, it can go either of two ways: you check in and very quickly you'll be aware that he needs weapons to help him out or, you'll check in and things will have calmed down a bit. In the latter case – let's say the context of the Contact has changed subtly – you throttle back a little and start conserving fuel because the longer you can loiter on-station, the more you can prolong your ability to provide overwatch to the troops on the ground in case something kicks off again. Almost invariably it does and then the adrenaline starts to reduce a bit, which is good.

So, that's GCAS. On the particular sortie I'm thinking of – it would have been February 2007 – we'd been scrambled in support of a 42 Commando operation called Operation Volcano. Their objective was to clear Barikju, a village of about 26 compounds just north of Kajaki that had been completely abandoned except for enemy forces. With the locals having fled, the Taliban were using it as a command and control node and the objective was to neutralise it. Just before we took off, the GLO handed us a Scheme of Manoeuvre for the operation and on it there was an image with the compounds numbered from 1 to 26. We got airborne as a pair in a matter of minutes and after completing our respective tactical departures, headed for Kajaki.

As soon as we were in radio range of the 42 Commando FAC, we checked in with him and he started to give us a full detailed talk on the layout of the ground, the position of friendly forces etc. Because of the information that we'd been given before the sortie, I interrupted him and said, 'Look, we've got this image, dated this, version this with this "gridded" numbered compound …' and as I talked I heard an audible sigh of relief from him. Once he'd established that we were singing off the same page, as it were, he immediately described the position of friendly forces who at that stage were 200 metres away from one of the compounds. He then said something like, 'We're taking heavy fire from that compound and we're unable to move, I need a 1,000lb bomb on that position.' The long and short of it was, the answer was 'Yes – in three minutes.' So we had a very quick exchange and three minutes later we'd done what was asked for – removed the threat.

To achieve that, a Paveway II laser-guided bomb was used, homed on to the compound using the Harrier's TIALD (Thermal Imaging Laser Designation) pod – we didn't have the more advanced Sniper pods then. No matter though; it was self-designated, and it did the job very effectively. Paveway II in its 1,000lb guise can be massively destructive – dropped on a building and set to detonate inside, the shockwave would blow out all the walls; there'd be a massive crater left but not much else. Using the TIALD to guide the bomb means we can illuminate the target with our laser without knowing its geographical co-ordinates. The TIALD pod was pointed at the target by the aircraft's navigation system, a live image repeated on the cockpit display. The aiming cross was positioned over the compound and pod switched to automatic tracking mode. That's basically it – at the appropriate moment during the attack, the TIALD laser is turned on, which provides the bomb's guidance system with the required information to complete the attack.

Things escalated pretty quickly from that point and in short order; we were asked to put some rockets down on to three compounds which were causing the lads on the ground some problems. My wingman, who was orbiting over the target area was listening in on this and immediately set up for the attack, which was nigh on instantaneous because he had the imagery there courtesy of the Scheme of Manoeuvre that we'd been given earlier. His Harrier was set up with two pods, each of which contained 19 CRV-7 rockets. They travel at Mach 3, so there's a massive amount of kinetic energy and very little dispersion, making them just the thing for situations such as this. They certainly did the job.

Immediately after that, we were asked to assist some Apache attack helicopters (AH) that were also providing CAS to the same Contact; a group of the advancing Royal Marines were taking heavy fire from a compound and wanted the AH to launch some Hellfire II laser-guided missiles at it but for some reason the Apaches were unable to identify the target. So I fired my Harrier's laser on to the compound and enabled the Apaches' sensors to pick it up. Once the target was illuminated for them, they were able to do their own targeting work and a few seconds later they hit the position with a Hellfire. We were fairly low on fuel by this point, but we were able to provide some further support before we returned to Kandahar Airfield. The Marines had identified another compound as the Taliban's centre of gravity for the village and the FAC requested another self-designated Paveway II. We were in a position to help; I set up on my attack run and so as soon as he told me 'You're clear hot', released the 1,000lb bomb into that compound.

With GCAS, you're on your way back as soon as you have released your weapons. Regardless of your fuel state, and if kinetic effect is required, your usefulness tails off pretty significantly once you've released all of your ordnance, especially back then when we didn't have the capabilities of the Sniper pod. Your focus at that point is to get both you and your aircraft back on the ground as quickly as possible so the engineers can do an operational turnaround and re-arm. The minute you land, you can then sign out another jet and declare yourself ready again, so the focus is very much in blocks in terms of the initial scramble, get yourself airborne, carry out the support to the Troops in Contact (TiC), and as soon as your usefulness goes, minimise the time between your decision to come home and being ready then to take on the next job. Effectively it's back to Ground Zero and starting again.

What made that sortie so satisfying was the efficacy of the CAS on the Royal Marines' objective. We didn't really get any feedback at the time as to the outcome or the effects of our mission – it was all over in a very, very short time and I had to fly back to London a week or so later. While back in the UK, I noticed a short piece about Operation Volcano on the MoD website authored by 3 Commando Brigade. On it, there was some video footage taken by some troops who were just 200 metres from a compound when the first of the 1,000lb Paveway IIs was dropped, and the noise and fallout from the explosion was incredible. But what really made me sit up and take notice was the narrative, which said that the Marines were able to clear the Taliban from all 26 compounds without any casualties and that the outcome was, in the main, as a result of the effects of the precision weapons released by RAF aircraft. That was somewhat satisfying.

We're quite remote when we're flying in support of ground troops and aiming to remain clear of the immediate threat envelope. We nominate a blanket height below which there is an awareness that the risk increases significantly so unless we're flying at low level as a show of force, we try and stay above that. The biggest threat to us at lower levels is from RPGs and small-arms fire although the big worry is surface-to-air missiles. The basic rule is that height is your friend – aside from being outside the threat envelope, the pace of life is slower, so you have more time; the higher you are, the longer the bomb flies for, so it's a more measured setup.

The other sortie that stands out for me was a mission that I flew with the flight lieutenant mentioned earlier, in June 2007 in support of some Canadian troops quite close to KAF. It was a pre-planned tasking, so we knew in advance what they were planning and when we were expected. He was a new pilot on the Squadron at that time; however, he had earned my respect and confidence quickly. He was extremely capable despite his inexperience. We were carrying out what we call 'Yo-yo Operations' – one of us would loiter on overwatch while the other would fly to the tanker and take on fuel. We'd been on station, flying overhead in support of them, monitoring the radio and talking to the Canadians. They were patrolling through a village and they described a normal pattern of life there, so nothing seemed out of the ordinary and certainly from my perspective sitting in the cockpit, there was nothing to indicate that they'd have any trade for us. I was fully expecting to return to KAF with a full weapons load, but things can unravel very quickly in Afghanistan and a situation will change literally in a moment.

Suddenly, we received a radio call from a very tense-sounding Forward Air Controller. He was embedded in a small patrol towards the eastern edge of the village and they'd come under intense fire – they couldn't move and he was requesting immediate support from us. We tried to pinpoint the position of the Taliban forces but it's not something that was immediately apparent – we'd been given a grid reference, but co-ordinates in an area with lots of compounds is only a stepping stone on the way to finding out where they are. The next stage is a balance between identifying a specific location, and having some initial effect. We decided upon the latter, so while my wingman remained on overwatch, I descended rapidly and flew at low level to provide a 'show of force'. At only 100ft above ground level and flying at 500mph, a fast jet flying overhead unannounced has an intimidating effect and certainly they could be useful in terms of shocking the Taliban into retreat. Basically, they'd see us and discretion would be the better part of valour – often, they'd shrink away once they saw we were on station and we wouldn't need to fire a shot.

On this occasion however, it was ineffectual. I tried twice but without effect; the second run was lower and on a completely different ingress heading just to be unpredictable but they continued pouring intense fire on the Canadians' position. So at that stage, I pulled back on the stick to gain some height and got on the radio to the FAC. We asked him for an estimate of the position of friendly forces in relation to the enemy and he came back with 100 metres, which is pretty close! Dropping any significant ordnance at that distance presents a much higher chance of fratricide. First, you can't limit the effects of a 1,000lb bomb to just enemy forces and second, it is sometimes challenging to identify who is where so we asked the ground commander to put down some smoke as a location aid. Almost immediately, he fired a smoke grenade, which instantly changed the picture; we were easily able to pinpoint the position of the Canadians relative to the Taliban so I felt much more confident about launching an attack. At that sort of distance, the effects of a 1,000lb bomb are too great and you can't guarantee you won't kill your own forces as well as those of the enemy so it had to be rockets; their effect at close quarters is deadly, but you don't get anything like the secondary effects.

With Danger Close weapon delivery, you always come in at 90 degrees to the position of friendly forces – that way, if you drop too early and the weapon lands short, or too late and the weapon lands long, you've less chance of it falling on to friendly forces. So we positioned for a rocket attack, which we started from the height which with the CRV-7 rockets, gives good visibility on to the target and it also gives you a nice steep angle for your attack dive, which minimises the spread of the rockets. You start the dive in the mid-teens looking for the optimum range to press the pickle button and fire the rockets, which travel at Mach 3 but take time to accelerate. That means you have a bracket of range to the target, which is the optimum position to fire from. So I tipped in to a nice steep dive and fired the rockets, which hit the tree line from where the Taliban were firing. Immediately the rockets were away, I pulled up again in a high G-manoeuvre in an aggressive recovery from the rocket attack.

That first strike put a lot of rockets down, which scored a direct hit on the tree line that was the Taliban's position. I spoke to the FAC and he said 'Direct hit, but we're still taking fire from one or two insurgents' and he called for an immediate repeat attack. So we came in and put some more rockets down, which did the trick. All the firing had stopped … fantastic. The whole thing happened very quickly and the adrenaline was pumping hard. One minute we were in the cruise, it's all quiet and suddenly, the man you're talking to on the ground is hiding behind a wall and he and his colleagues are taking intense and concentrated fire on their position. The Ground Commander at that stage was extremely worried, because it later transpired that he'd been of the view that had we not been there, he would have lost some of his men.

The interesting thing about this engagement – and I'm somewhat pleased I didn't know it at the time – is that after we returned and plotted the actual position where the smoke grenade was burning, it turned out to be 75 metres away from where the Taliban position was, not 100. When we spoke to the FAC later, he told us that he had actually thrown the smoke away from his position, so he was closer than we believed; having done that, he in fact repositioned even closer to the Taliban and took cover behind a bigger wall. When we plotted the final position of the Canadians in relation to the Taliban at the point the salvo of rockets was fired, it turned out that they were just 29 metres away from the tree line. The analogy I use is to compare this to standing with your back to a dartboard with your head at the double 16 and asking your right-handed grandmother to hit the bullseye, throwing using her left hand. Luckily, she hit the bullseye on this occasion but it won't have been a pleasant experience – the FAC said that they were completely numb for about 30 seconds after the attack. Bear in mind that CRV-7s are a low-collateral-damage weapon but they're still supersonic; so there's a salvo of rockets going past you at three times the speed of sound and they're going to create a massive shockwave and a huge noise when they impact and explode. That's complete sensory overload but they knew it was coming; can you imagine what it was like for the insurgents being on the end of it all?

Those two sorties aren't indicative of the norm, although it would also be fair to say that they're not that far off either; out here, there's no such thing as an 'average' sortie, so each time you're scrambled, it has the potential to develop into something similar. I can't say that they all stand out, but another sortie that I recall is notable because it was the first one that a Harrier had dropped a Retard 1,000lb since the Falklands War. This was again early in 2007 and I was flying with a young Navy pilot. It was a typical winter's day in Afghanistan, with cloud base stretching practically from the surface all the way up to 30,000ft. I was flying a jet with a weapons load that included the Enhanced Paveway II; these are fully autonomous when launched in cases where there is cloud cover over the target which may obstruct the laser and prevent weapon guidance. In these instances, it is steered to the target using GPS information.

Because of the bad weather, the Navy pilot's jet was carrying two 1,000lb Retards. These can be useful when the cloud cover reaches high altitude because they're dropped from low level. Retards are used because in low-altitude attacks, there is a danger of the attacking aircraft being caught in the blast of its own weapons. To address this problem, general-purpose bombs are often fitted with retarders that slow the bomb's descent to allow the aircraft time to escape the detonation.

We were originally sent airborne to one ground controller but, not unusually, we were quickly re-tasked airborne to a TiC elsewhere in Afghanistan. Very early on, we became aware that they needed weapons and it was another close one – not quite as close as with the Canadians but they wanted us to drop probably 500 metres from the FAC's position.

The interesting thing about this one for me was that, because of the thick, impenetrable cloud layer, I just couldn't see the target, so I was going to have to release based purely on the co-ordinates that the controller had given me. It was the first time that I had carried out this particular style of attack in anger and it was unnerving – there was total reliance on the accuracy of the co-ordinates being passed by a young controller under fire; the weapon would strike those coordinates. If they were wrong the consequences may have been significant. Two bombs were dropped in that mode, both attacks were successful, so that was a relief, but the ground forces were still taking fire from another position. At that point, we saw a gap in the clouds so we were able to offer the FAC Retard bombs, which he was happy to accept. The Navy pilot did extremely well – the weather was appalling but the troops were relying on us and it was very much a case of 'when needs must'. He went in and successfully dropped a 1,000-pounder at ultra-low level, which was fantastic – the firing stopped and the troops were able to continue to their objective.

When you release weapons at ultra-low level like that, the priority as soon as you've released is to egress as soon as possible to either position for another attack or route elsewhere and you can do that in one of two ways – duck down and accelerate into a clear area, or climb into cloud.

With the three squadrons that comprise JFH, maintaining the commitment to theatre 24 hours a day, 365 days a year, we effectively deploy to theatre for four months each year. I only took command of the squadron at the beginning of December 2006, and just five weeks later, we came out to KAF. That one was a five-and-a-half-month deployment, so pretty much all of the first half of 2007. At the moment, we are just coming to the end of another four-month deployment and my end of tour comes next spring. It's likely that the Harriers will have been replaced with Tornado GR4s by then as announced by the Secretary of State, so the chances are that 1(F) Squadron won't be doing another Afghanistan deployment. That said, you never know what might happen; you just never know.

I think the highlight of my time in Afghanistan has to be the reward of command; being the squadron boss is a real joy and it's a privilege to be able to watch everybody on the squadron develop. Watching their commitment to operations is inspirational; you'll get the young pilots, young engineers, old engineers – everybody is just so committed and it's very rewarding to be a part of that and, as squadron commander, to have an influence as their careers progress. That is without question the most rewarding aspect. It's not all sunny though and there are plenty of challenges, although they tended to be political rather than personnel-based, and none were 'show-stoppers'. The reality of coalition operations is that an element of inertia is introduced. There is a layered command organisation split by thousands of miles; the Air Tasking organisation is in Qatar; you've got an Air Support Operation Centre in Kabul; the Regional Commands closer to the front line and there are the task force HQs – the unique position we had as combat air on the front line was that we had dealings with all these at various stages.

Everybody, to a man (and woman), wherever they are, is doing his/ her utmost to achieve the same mission, and skilfully at that. I wouldn't describe it as 'too many cooks' – it's that there are Headquarters separated by thousands of miles with a distinct international flavour. It's the nature of coalition operations, though, and we get on with the mission. Having had the privilege of two distinct and significant deployments over 18 months, seeing how the lessons from 2007 have been taken on board and developed for this year, it's great. You do at times see a temporary (and short) regression when different units and personnel rotate in and out of theatre as they learn, but then it improves after that – in some ways it's like small perturbations as the campaign moves forward.

I know some people in theatre manage the way in which they report back to their partners on what's it like out here but it's the other way round with me; my wife manages me! She has lived with the Royal Air Force all the way through my career, so we've grown up with it if you like and it's familiar territory. I deployed very early on as a junior pilot to Turkey to fly missions over northern Iraq and I flew during the Iraq War and so, as every service wife does, she has effectively got used to the nature of the job and you have a way of dealing with it. We speak two or three times a week when I'm here – that's probably down to me as I prefer talking rather than writing or emailing. They're short calls, along the line of 'Anything changed?' 'No. Anything changed at home?' 'No. Okay, speak to you in a few days' time.' It's all very matter of fact, which is reassuring because it means business as usual – life is normal. My son is extremely mellow and laid back and he doesn't really get affected but I've noticed recently that my daughter is thinking about Afghanistan quite a lot and is very much aware of the threat to her Dad. I think she will be quite pleased when we go on holiday shortly after I get back, and that this stage of my career will be temporarily over.

I'm not defined by my job – I'm Andy Lewis, not Wing Commander Andy Lewis if I introduce myself to anyone. I'm a person first, a Royal Air Force officer, pilot and squadron boss second, and if people want to know about my job and what I do then I'll explain when and if they ask. That's probably a throwback to my three years in the Reds; you realise as you progress through the Tour that the red flying suit is the talking point not you as an individual. When off duty, I preferred to immediately change into civilian clothing and return to a semblance of normality. Naturally, I am interested in how my career will develop and I'm driven by challenging jobs which are at the forefront of what the RAF does. That's it – I just like to be at the cutting edge of what the RAF is all about and I'm fortunate enough to have been able to do that up to now. We'll just have to see where it goes and where my career will take me. I certainly don't see myself as a Chief of the Air Staff, and I don't imagine the RAF does either; a four-year degree and my time with the Red Arrows will have had an impact. However, there are plenty of good opportunities out there.

I am enormously privileged to be a Harrier pilot because it's a fantastic aircraft and, despite the banter I will receive for this, I enjoy the single-seat aspect of it. The Harrier is a real pilot's aircraft – there are aspects to flying it that are very challenging and I enjoy that. It's an utterly unique and idiosyncratic fixed-wing aircraft in that it hovers, so there's all that that entails; there's the Carrier Strike role, which is a completely different area again that the RAF plays a significant role in; there's low-level flying – it's just a phenomenal beast! I've flown every variant from the GR3 and I was one of the very first to fly a factory-new GR7; now, the squadron is flying a mix of GR7s and GR9s – we're not a complete GR9 fleet as yet. It's a shame in a way that people are starting to talk about it as an aged platform and when they talk in the same breath about the Joint Strike Fighter, it brings it home to you what stage of your career you're at. The JSF isn't a direct replacement for the Harrier – it's a completely different multi-role aircraft rather than a dedicated VSTOL platform. I suppose that when the Harrier is eventually retired from service, it – and those of us privileged to have flown it – will be part of a unique club.

As an aircraft, the Harrier is a very capable and proven platform whether in the air-to-air, ground attack or Close Air Support role, although air-to-air doesn't interest me *per se*; the requirement for control of the air as reflected by the aerial dogfighting in the Battle of Britain and over our soldiers during the Second World War in places such as North Africa, Italy and northern Europe is critical – an absolute requirement. What I am charged with at the moment is delivering support to the operational commander here in Afghanistan – supporting the boys on the ground – and we bring a hefty punch to the party. The Harrier's major selling point is its flexibility.

Without a shadow of a doubt, this tour has been the highlight of my career. It's the best thing I've done so far – it beats the Red Arrows hands down. It's being responsible for your people, their careers, and in some respects their lives. It's about having an influence in a significant part of what the Royal Air Force is doing on operations. All of that, and I get to fly the Harrier too! It's a huge responsibility but I just love it. And I relish it; it's much more rewarding that I ever thought it would be. Any job has to go some way to beat this one.

FLIGHT SERGEANT
ED COLLINS

AIR MOVEMENTS SPECIALIST

The six-strong unit of men and women that make up 1 Air Movements Wing at Camp Bastion are responsible for unloading cargo and passengers from C130 Hercules aircraft 24-hours-a-day, seven-days-a week. But, unlike other personnel in the same trade, they do it in desert conditions, against the clock, sometimes in almost total darkness with the aircraft's massive engines still running and often buffeted by high winds and debris.

It's a tough job in normal times but the extra challenges are imposed for very good operational reasons. Hercules C130s are high-value assets and the less time they spend on the ground, the less at risk they are from Taliban rockets and mortars. They might also be observed by enemy spotters gathering intelligence on aircraft movements. The process, known as Engine Running Offloads, nicknamed 'Hotlanding', requires an aircraft's freight to be unloaded and passengers processed in under ten minutes – a particular challenge for movers who often won't know the precise nature of the load until it lands. All soldiers inbound to Camp Bastion have to be combat ready, which means they are wearing full body armour and helmets, and carrying weapons when they deplane. This requirement, known as carrying 'Troops in Fighting Trim', poses an interesting but exciting challenge for the movers who are responsible for the safety of the aircraft and the people on it while it is on the ground.

Flight Sergeant Ed Collins is an experienced air movements specialist who has undertaken many deployments to Afghanistan since the beginning of the conflict. Unusually perhaps for a 'mover' he has also been involved in firefights with enemy forces.

My job here at Bastion means that I'm in charge of all air movements in and out. My home base is at RAF Lyneham where I'm with 1 Air Movements Wing (1AMW), which is part of 44 Squadron.

What movers do is wide and varied – we're in all theatres, home and overseas, benign and hostile – and wherever you find RAF aircraft of any description, you'll find us. You could summarise my role as being responsible for moving everybody and everything, basically all the kit and personnel on any aeroplane. It's specifically fixed wing while we're here in Bastion so it's essentially the logistics of moving people and things from point A to point B via aircraft, and that includes strategic and tactical aeroplanes.

I'm 34 now and the military is basically all I've ever known – I joined the RAF in 1997 and we were known as UKMAMS then – the UK Mobile Air Movements Squadron. We restructured to 1AMW not long before this deployment, although that's more for administrative reasons than anything, I think – our role is the same as it's always been. I knew of UKMAMS when I first joined up and the idea of it appealed to me, especially the travelling involved. I mean, some people join the military and they're lucky to travel overseas once or twice in their career and some never even leave the UK, but I've probably been everywhere in the world now, ten times over. For all that I knew about the job when I joined, I never imagined it would pan out as it has, but then, I never imagined Iraq would happen either – or Afghanistan, come to that. The world's a different place to what it was then.

When I first started on MAMS, it tended to be Vegas for a few weeks on fast-jet deployment, or Hawaii or San Diego – it was fantastic. I mean, I did a few tours in Australia, New Zealand and, really, all over the world, but it's changed now. Now the average bear comes to Afghanistan and that's about it – most of the young lads in my team have never known anything apart from this. Me, I've had a great career to date and I've seen things and been to places I could never have imagined at the beginning – I've had so many overseas deployments, I couldn't even hazard a guess at the number. My first proper operation would have been Kosovo in 1999. That was followed by Sierra Leone. Then there was East Timor, a couple of tours out here in Afghanistan early on in the conflict and many tours in Iraq – both Baghdad and

Basra. It's been interesting and while that's been great from a professional aspect, it does play havoc with your personal life.

Historically, we've always travelled wherever people need to get on or off aircraft, either operational or on exercise, but it's basically all operations now because that's 9/10ths of the MoD's work. I did quite a long time in Kabul and Kandahar and I was based with one of the front-line units for four years working on loan with the lads there – I've not long been back at MAMS. I have to say, working with the front-line unit was something that I enjoyed very much – it's probably been the highlight of my career in fact. I was responsible there for exactly the same thing – moving kit and personnel – but there I was a part of a very small team that deployed alongside the troops and the work was a lot more, er ... interesting! We did a lot of work establishing TLZs or Tactical Landing Zones, which can be a strip of ground anywhere long enough to take a Hercules. That basically meant marking out the strip for the C130s to land on, planning all the loads for infils and exfils and being responsible for loading.

That was interesting work – typically, we'd fly in by helicopter and then, generally, we'd call on the aircraft as we needed them. I'd come up with a plan or strategy to infill X amount of troops and X amount of kit into a TLZ, then break it down at the finish and extract all of the troops and equipment. It meant that I had to have a much higher level of fitness than the norm for this role because I was working on my own all the time. Out here, I have a team of lads who will build pallets or prepare things for me and we work as a team, but when I was based with the troops I had much more to do myself. I'd deploy as a one-man show for both exercises and operations, although I was able to call on extra people from MAMS if required.

The big thing for me was the planning of it – for instance, the boss would tell me exactly what he wanted to move, the timings, such as when we'd have to move it by, and finally, he'd tell me when a particular job was due to begin. I'd work it all back from there, figuring out how long it would take for an aeroplane to get from A to B, how long it would take for me to turn it around at both ends, how many lifts I'd need to move whatever kit was required from the base to the TLZ. Basically, I was the subject matter expert for the lads whom I was attached to and responsible to their QMS or CO for, depending on the job.

The logistics of setting up a TLZ for a Herc on an unprepared strip all are quite straightforward when you know what you're doing. Firstly, you have to pinpoint the landing zone. Basically, it entails going out with a penetrometer and firing down into the sand of a lake bed for instance – any big expansive area of land will do – and a penetrometer will tell you if it's feasible. You then mark it out lengthways, either north–south or south–north, whichever way using markers – blue bin bags if you have them or if it's at night, with IR cyalumes, dragon lights ... basically, anything that'll do the job. If a TLZ is going to be used more than once you'd have to move the whole thing sideways after three or four landings and take-offs on it, because the ground takes a hit and develops deep ruts. Obviously, the more ruts there are, the more dramas you have with wheels bursting etc, and the idea is to not get an asset stuck on the ground or you'd have to blow it up. That's happened before!

I'd be stood right by the runway when an aircraft was due in. I'd have a secure radio link with the aircraft – there'd be a signaller on board and I'd have one with me so we'd chat over the net as they made their approach, so they could advise me of their position and tell me exactly how long they had to run. Once they were on the ground, I'd be guiding the pilot to where I wanted the aircraft using red cyalume sticks ... you know, 'Right, to me, stop' sort of thing. We work very, very closely with the air crew – obviously aeroplanes are all to do with weight so there has to be a massive degree of trust between the air crew and me because if I tell them they have 10 tonnes on board but they really have 20, then they're all going to die. It's a big trust job and I've made lots of very good friends over the years.

I did a lot of work out here in Afghanistan and I've worked most of the TLZs in theatre, from Gereshk to Bamiyan – I've also worked in Kabul as their air mover. Bamiyan is a really amazing place and was famous for the Buddhas of Bamiyan statues that were carved out of a mountain in the 5th century – they stood for almost two millennia but they were dynamited by the Taliban in 2001 as they considered them to be 'un-Islamic'.

I'd be hard pushed to describe any particular operation as being particularly memorable because they were all bloody marvellous, to tell you the truth. With operational work you really feel that you've done something worthwhile. It's not like it is in Basra where you feel like you're a big sitting target and you spend most of your time taking IDF – I can honestly say that I feel I never achieved anything during my time at Basra, whereas out here I've achieved a phenomenal amount, so it's something that I'm happy to have done.

It hasn't all been plain sailing, though, and I've been involved in a number of incidents where I've taken fire, both in the air and on the ground. Several of them stand out – you don't like to think of them as being exciting, but when the adrenaline's flowing and you're working as part of a team returning fire, it's certainly memorable. Being shot at in the air is weird because you hear very little, if anything. I've been on several C130s or Chinooks where we've taken rounds – more on take-off than landing; rounds hitting the fuselage or inside the wing spar and inside helicopters. As I said, you hear very little, so the main thing you do is see it after the event, when you're on the ground – the average lad wouldn't even know it had happened. Quite often, we would land and we had no idea we'd taken rounds until the inspection – that's when you realise you've got holes in the airframe. You've seen tracer coming up but you haven't necessarily felt any impact on the aeroplane itself. During the course of my career I was in contacts more than a few times in Iraq, and I've been far too close to vehicle-borne IEDs etc going off on Route Irish driving up and down to town.

I guess it's not something that I ever envisaged doing when I first joined UKMAMs – being involved in a firefight, taking fire, dodging car bombs and IEDs, but if you're working in a hostile environment it's going to happen. People tend to forget that while not everyone in the military is in the infantry – in fact, the majority of personnel are in support or non-combat roles – all of us undergo basic training where we're taught to be soldiers first, if you like, and our trades second. You could be a chef, a driver or a mechanic, but if you're deployed to a combat zone in the military and you don't know basic military tactics or how to fire and strip a weapon, you're not going to be much use when the wheel comes off.

No particular incident where I've been under fire stands out but it's always the first one – the first time it happens – that you sit up and take notice because it's not 'normal'. It's a great thing 'normal' isn't it? What does it mean, anyway? I mean, normal is different for everyone so it's utterly meaningless. Taking and returning fire isn't normal for most people and it wasn't for me, but it became so. Normal is a constantly shifting state. I remember chatting about it with everyone after the first time and I soon realised that the rounds weren't that close, so I started to see it all from an objective perspective. You hear the sound when the fire is inaccurate, but when it's closer, within a few feet of you, you feel the disturbance in the air and you hear a 'zing' as the rounds pass by your head. It's funny, though, because as soon as you have a frame of reference for being under fire – something that you can refer back to because you've been there before – you find yourself responding without realising, and soon you're making decisions along with everyone else.

Take illegal checkpoints for instance. They were commonplace in Iraq and there are places here in Afghanistan where the Taliban set them up. Let's say you take a decision to drive through one without stopping, then you tell everyone that you've made the decision to drive through. You're almost expecting to get shot at and you know damn well it's going to be near but you've got a reference point because you've done it before. There's been many a time I've thought, 'Bloody hell, that was close!' but never have I thought that a situation was out of control or that I wasn't capable of dealing with it.

I remember one time that I took fire I was airborne in a helicopter over Baghdad city and the first thing in my head wasn't so much about the fire but more about the helicopter going down and it being torn to pieces. That was my first thought, 'Oh for God sake, not here – if we put down here, we don't stand a bloody chance.' That was the thing that weighed on me most heavily at the time. Certainly, with the lads that I was working with, I tended to feel comfortable with them all – you talk a lot to each other, everybody's mates and you all live in the middle of the desert together, so you tend to feel sort of naturally safer than you perhaps are. But the converse of that is that you are well equipped and able to deal with things. You have an awful lot of firepower; you have a lot of trust in the people who are there because they wouldn't deploy if they weren't capable.

You can have all the weapons and firepower in the world, but without a good team they're all worthless. So it would be fair to say that the team that you're with can be as effective a tool in doing your job as the weapon you have. A good team creates a feeling of security in what would, with a poor team, be an atmosphere of insecurity. And that applies too, to the aircrew; you know them, they are your friends and you know that there is no finer aircrew. If it is at all possible for an aircraft to get in somewhere to pick you up, you can rely on them absolutely – it's a given, they will do it regardless of how difficult it might be. I've been stuck in some places very much alone really; maybe a couple of us in places where you quite simply cannot survive if you're left on your own, and planes have broken in to get us out. It's an incredible feeling knowing that they'll land with two engines out to pick you up rather than leave you there. It's indescribable knowing that everybody will work for you to pull you back out. Generally, I'd tend to be the last bloke on to the aircraft because until the last person's in, I haven't finished my job. So, after the big secure feeling, gradually it draws down, the plane bugs out with everything and everyone bar you and one or two others. That's a really lonely time, but then to know they're coming back for you regardless is a good thing to have in the back of your mind.

Basically, when you're working with guys in the thick of it, or you find yourself in a difficult spot, you're all in it together, so it's in everyone's interest to make sure that we all speak the same language as it were. You're included in everything that happens because you depend on the guys and they depend on you – you're a part of that organisation and everyone in it will live and die for each other. It's a very, very professional mentality. It's a job where you gain respect from people over the years that you're there. People are more than aware of who you are and what you will achieve for them and everyone knows that you're after getting them there and back safely so that they can relax at the end of an operation knowing that they're not going to have dramas air side.

We also smooth things away. I've worked at civil airports in foreign countries, including down in South America and quite a lot in the US for all the exercises, smoothing in bits of kit that we need to get – you know things that we need to get in a hurry, customs, that kind of thing. We bid for the aeroplanes to take people on exercise and we're also responsible for the bidding of and the loading of ships on behalf of the service as well, which is something most people don't get involved with, because generally we're air movers whereas down there we're generic. Anything that needs moved by any means, we'll do it.

Of everything I've done on tour, of all the places that I've been fortunate enough to see, the one thing that stands head and shoulders above all is the friends that I've made. Without a shadow of a doubt, they are the most positive aspect of all. It's that feeling that someone's got your back and I've simply made some really, really good friends – what else could possibly compete with that? Even working here at Camp Bastion, there are so many people who come through here that stop in and say hello to me, it's a good atmosphere, certainly in the world that I've been privileged to work in. It's small and close-knit so you tend to know a hell of a lot of people really. That's the best part of all – I certainly haven't done any of it for the money!

There are a few negatives, although from my viewpoint, they're massive ones. I think without question, the biggest one for me is that I simply haven't been there for the people at home. I made the most of, and do make the most of, every second that I'm with them but it's simply not enough and that's my biggest regret in terms of my career – probably my only one actually. From a professional perspective and certainly in terms of experiences, it's been brilliant for me. The respect that I get for the jobs that I've done is fantastic and I've been promoted very quickly for my trade, so in those terms it's been very good.

I think the biggest challenge facing me now is simply the environment that I'm working in. I don't necessarily mean here – in Afghanistan the place – more here, at Bastion, managing people, and working with the young lads, having spent so much time working on my own. Obviously, I'm their senior and one of my biggest jobs is that I'm responsible for their welfare and I've never had to do that before, so I'm still finding my feet in that respect. I'm used to only having to think about myself, and I know I'm all right. The 'can I have a word in private, Flight?' sort of chat is without a doubt the most challenging aspect of my role now, which probably sounds bizarre after some of the situations that I've found myself in previously. Just goes to show, though, doesn't it – when you're within your comfort zone and it's something that you know, it's easy. This is all something that I'm just not used to dealing with. Put 18 aeroplanes in a line there and I'll take them all in my stride thanks and they'll all be finished for you in four hours flat. But you want to talk to me about something personal? Sorry, but I have to admit that I feel a little bit out of my depth, so that is without doubt for me the most challenging aspect of my job.

That said, it's an intrinsic part of my job so I do what I have to and I'm learning. I chat to the lads a lot and I think that helps. I don't think I'm necessarily your typical sergeant really because, having lived in a different environment for four years and seen how it can work, then I tend to give everybody the benefit of the doubt and treat everyone as an adult. I don't tell anyone to do anything because I don't believe I should have to, and so far it's worked well for me. I've got a really fantastic team here – incredibly junior – but in fairness they've come on a hell of a lot. I think I have a lot to teach people and it seems to be working. I have to say that that's an aspect that I enjoy hugely. It's probably the only bonus in terms of where I've come from before I was here and coming into this. I didn't want to – none of us ever have, because you find a niche in life and you want to stay in it, but unfortunately there is no such thing as a permanent role for Movers in what I was doing before. Also, the RAF isn't mad keen on anyone leaving for more than three years really, so I did quite well with four; they don't like the idea of people 'going native' as they call it – you can become too embedded in what you're doing so you lose touch with the RAF side of it all. So being here, now, bringing on the next generation if you like, is a big positive.

I love Afghanistan and I really want to see it all work out for the people here. I've seen more of this country than anyone else I know – probably more than 99 per cent of people – so I think I've probably got a decent handle on it. I love the Afghans as a people – they're fantastic generally. Obviously, it's a tiny minority of people with a distorted perspective who are engaging us and causing all the problems, and the sad irony is that for the most part, an awful lot of them aren't even

Afghans. The Afghans that I've met, those who I know and I know well are funny, humble, and generous – they're not bad traits to have, are they? They're interesting, kind, and intelligent people, really, really good people to know. I think this place – and my experiences to date – has had quite a profound effect on me. You know, you wonder sometimes, would the 'me' of ten years ago recognise the person that I've become?

I'm probably a lot mellower now because of the situations that I've been confronted with – they are going to have an effect on anyone and I've seen and done an awful lot. When everybody else is running around flapping about something, I can generally look back on another time where it's all been a hell of a lot worse, a matter of life and death perhaps, and use that as a reference – an anchor, if you like. It helps me to put things in perspective and ultimately, you think, 'Well, this is important, yes, but it's not worth getting in a state over.' So much simply doesn't matter in the great scheme of things, does it? I'm glad I've had the opportunity to interact so much with the Afghan military – the ANA and the ANP – because that has broadened my horizons massively. Travelling too, seeing sights like the Blue Mosque up at Mazār-e Sharīf, which is just fantastic. Certainly, because I've been here from early on, I've seen the whole thing progress; I've seen Kabul with nobody on the streets, with the Taliban still in control, so it's massively different now. I was in Kabul at the start of this deployment and it's beginning to become a proper metropolitan type of place – I mean people are opening shops and things and it's nice. There's music everywhere, and kids going to school – and girls going to school which, under the Taliban, was unheard of, so that's all fantastic. Everything I've done works towards positive.

I really miss my loved ones though. Nothing else – whenever I've been in some hellhole, or on the other side of the world in the middle of the night, you can keep your nights out, beer, a night with the lads. You can keep it all because wherever I've been, whatever I've been doing, the only people that I've ever thought about have been my family. I know that everybody handles their relationships differently, and we all manage our wives or partners differently. Most people I know here, though, don't share a great deal about what they do with their other halves because they don't want them to worry. I've never told my family about what I've done and where I've been, certainly none of the details. None of them really knows what I do and I deliberately keep things vague. One, it's very difficult trying to explain the sort of things we've seen and done to people because they have no terms of reference for any of it. And two, there's just no need for people to know – that's my personal feeling. When I tell them I'm going to the desert, they don't know which one. They know I go away a lot for work, they know I come back browner than they are, but I don't go into it at all or tell anyone anything about any of it.

I'm quite lucky I guess, because I still really enjoy what I do. If I didn't I wouldn't be here, so I think that's what I'm waiting for now – when that point comes, when I can say I don't like it anymore, then that's when I will leave. But this is what I do and I don't really know anything else, even in the RAF – I wouldn't know what to do if you put me in a pair of blues and put me in an office; I don't even have blues anymore. Just to turn up on a course I have to borrow them from other people, but I can't even remember the last time I wore a blue uniform; it's desert combats for me, working rig. Eventually, I'd like to go on to the training wing at 1AMW and share some of my experience, put it to good use. The stability would be good for my personal life too, what with a new baby on the way. I believe I have a lot to give, a lot to teach people about what is important and what isn't regarding aeroplanes, and I think that training is actually a little estranged at the moment. I've got some ideas anyway and that's what I'd like to do. I've still got another 11 years to do to get my 22 and when I think about what I've done in my 11 years up to now I don't want to do that again. My ceiling is Warrant Officer and I will reach that; I'm quite far ahead of my drag curve really, so if I want Warrant Officer, I'll make it if I stay. It's all down to whether I can face another 11 years really.

I've only another three weeks to go before the end of this tour and I'm really looking forward to going home this time. Every time I get home the first thing I do is jump in the car and drive straight to see the kids, just purely because I miss them. They choose a restaurant and we always go out. Without fail, we eat out a minimum of twice a day because I'm terrible at cooking and I have to make sure they eat properly.

So that's what I do to immerse myself in home. We always do exactly the same things after every tour and it's like a ritual every time I come back, so I'm really looking forward to that and the baby of course.

Everybody has their own way of re-engaging when they get home after a tour like this and I'm no different. You have to do something simply because the pace is so different and I don't think it was ever like this in earlier conflicts, but the jet age means you can go front line to front room in just over 48 hours; that's a massive change. I tend to keep incredibly busy to start off with but one thing I always find is that it takes me quite a while to switch off, so I can't lie in because I'm not used to it. I tend to wake up at 5 o'clock in the morning and do stuff, so I'll redecorate or I'll fix something or I'll go out for a run or whatever while my wife's still in bed. One thing is certain though – I think the time has come for me to slow down a little and I'm just looking forward to getting back. Funnily enough, being away simply doesn't hold the same appeal now.

SAC

SARAH JONES

CHEF

RAF chefs cover a far larger field of professional experience than their civilian counterparts: from cafeterias to five-star themed banquets, preparing in-flight meals, catering in the field under canvas and cooking for VIPs.

SAC Sarah Jones has seen both sides, having been a chef at a four-star hotel before joining the RAF. Sarah was based at Camp Bastion where she became the first female RAF chef to deploy to a Forward Operating Base, where she came under regular mortar and rocket fire while preparing dinner for the troops based there in austere conditions.

My home unit is at RAF Lossiemouth in northern Scotland and I'm a chef, although that's quite a recent thing. Until a year ago, I'd spent four-and-a-half-years as a catering accountant but that trade was disbanded so I retrained as a chef. I've kind of come full circle; I was a qualified chef in civvy street – I'd worked in four-star hotel kitchens before I joined up but I enlisted as a catering accountant because I wanted to leave the chef trade behind me; now here I am as a chef again.

I'm not entirely sure why but I'd always been interested in the RAF and I always wanted to join. My dad was in the Army and he wanted me to enlist in that, so I think I just rebelled and went for the Air Force instead. I've absolutely loved it, right from when I first joined, like the first week; I think it must have shown because my career has really taken off; I got Best Recruit at Recruit Training, then got Student of the Year at Trade Training and then last year I got an AOC's Commendation for an outstanding contribution to the RAF.

I've been in for six years now and this is my first Out of Area deployment – there wasn't much call for catering accountants on the front line! I wasn't in line for this deployment either but I really wanted to go to Afghanistan and do something, so I hassled the drafter; I was asking her all the time, making a right nuisance of myself and I was delighted when I found out I was actually going. It was quite hard at first because I came on my own – I think that's always the biggest worry for some of us in the RAF. In the Army, people tend to move together as a unit so they all know each other before they get to theatre. When I arrived at RAF Brize Norton for my flight out, I was sat there on my own while all the Army guys were in groups.

I had no preconceptions, absolutely no idea what to expect, but when I landed at Kandahar it was all a bit of a shock as it was under attack at the time. We were sat on the TriStar in body armour and helmets, we're in complete darkness because it's a tactical approach and landing, and we're just circling round and round because the runway had been hit. We had to wait until the debris had been cleared, so it was quite an introduction to my tour; I thought, 'What have you let yourself in for!' Mind you, I was only at KAF for a couple of hours – then it was straight on to a Herc and into Camp Bastion 1. That in itself was an interesting experience; I found myself in a room with what seemed like hundreds of bunk beds and a whole company of Paras and I was like, 'Oh no, it's just like Brize again and I'm the only girl – what do I do?' Actually, there was one other girl – Army – but I think it's different for Army girls; in the RAF, we're used to our single rooms and doing our own thing, whereas in the Army, it's multiple-occupancy dorms. I think you're treated more as an individual in the Air Force.

The next day we went out to the ranges and we had to tab all the way there, so there's me and all these Paras again, blistering heat and we're tabbing to the range to zero our weapons; two miles there and two miles back again. So it was a real wake-up call for me, a bit of a shock to the system, especially as my home unit is in the Highlands of Scotland – we don't get too much of this sort of weather up there! You know, I left that and 48 hours later I'm tabbing round here in 40-degree heat with my weapon, body armour, and helmet. Then as soon as I got back after zeroing my weapon, I was picked up at the gate of Bastion 1, taken to my accommodation tent, and it was straight into work in the mess tent – basically, 'Right, there you go – drop your kit and we'll see you in the mess in 20 minutes!' I remember it was a Sunday evening so we had all the roasts on and I was straight into it.

As you might expect, the kitchen facilities here are very basic but that in itself is nothing I'm not used to. The heat in the kitchen tent, though, is a nightmare – it can reach up to 75°C in there and it's truly awful. The main mess tents are air cooled, but there's nothing in the tents where the cookers are. We have air cooling in the tent where we prepare the food, but that's it. There's a little frying area in the main kitchen tent and that's worse than the main cooking one because it has four deep-fat fryers there and it's awful. From the minute you walk in the sweat is just pouring off you. It's so hot that when they walk into the kitchen, it feels like cool fresh air when you walk out again, even though the temperature outside might be 50 or 55°C. I guess you sort of acclimatise to it but it's still a shock to the system.

There are eight of us on each shift and we'll prepare six main choices for dinner each night. We're catering for around 1,500–2,000 people, but the standard of food is actually pretty good, in spite of the limitations. I get a lot of comments from the Army guys who say that the food here is actually better than what they get back on their home units. We work on a cyclic menu and it rotates on a monthly basis, so there's plenty of choice; most of the troops at Bastion are only passing through on their way to or from the FOBs (Forward Operating Bases), so to them, there's always something different. The rations that we have to cook with all come in on ice in trucks and because it gets so hot here, we've taken delivery of mushrooms, say, that have cooked on the journey. That said, the conditions are infinitely preferable to what you get up at the FOBs.

I ended up cooking at a FOB because I pushed for it – I wanted to get out and experience what the guys had to live with, work in the real Afghanistan rather than within the wire back here at Bastion. We look after two FOBs from here – FOB Edinburgh and Now Zad, and I was really chuffed to get Now Zad because they get a lot more action there. I was doubly pleased because, historically, it's always been Army chefs at the FOBs and I was one of the very first RAF chefs to go; certainly, I was the first female. There's no pressure on you as a chef to go to the front line; if anyone's nervous about it, the bosses are really good, they won't force you. But like I say, I wanted to go, so the next thing I knew I was on the roster; I had my R&R – I went home for a week mid-tour – and then I was back here. It was a little bizarre on R&R; I ended up watching the first series of Ross Kemp in Afghanistan and he was at Now Zad. I got a bit of a shock when I saw just how intense the fighting was there and I thought, 'Oh no, what have I done?' But I think the reality is always a little different to your preconceptions – you have no frame of reference for something like that before it happens, but when you're living it, it becomes 'normal' for you so it didn't seem so bad.

Getting in to Now Zad for the start of my deployment there was great; I love Chinooks, so it was really cool being transported in on one and I loved getting an escort from an Apache gunship; the flight was truly amazing because I hadn't really seen Afghanistan properly prior to that point and it's just such a breathtaking landscape. Flying through the mountains was incredible but when we landed, it was right into full-on tactical mode; you have a very short window to get everyone off, get whoever is bugging out onboard, and then it's up and gone again. So I'm stood there, with my Bergen, helmet and rifle, and I'm wearing Osprey combat body armour which weighs 15 kilos; I felt almost immobile; I only weigh about 50 kilos, so it's not like I'd have been able to run for cover if needed. All I could see around me were mountains and then out of nowhere, an Armoured Personnel Carrier rocked up, I piled in the back, and I was driven off to the FOB where I got my brief.

It was fairly quiet when I arrived because there was a company of Estonian troops manning the FOB and they were ripping out. Obviously, there was a clear and constant threat from the Taliban; we had a small degree of protection from the topography, which gave us some cover in the DC from Now Zad itself. But the Green Zone was only 200 metres away and that was Taliban controlled, so they could launch attacks when they felt like it. That gave me a week or so to feel my way around and generally make myself at home. I'd deployed with one other person, an Army lance corporal, so we were the new complement of chefs – just the two of us – but I was the only female. Being a FOB, accommodation was really basic – it's not like they were going to have female-only ablutions or rooms! So I shared with the other guy, my fellow chef; we set up a little room next to the kitchen, which was like an outdoor oven because it had concrete walls and no air-conditioning. So once again, the heat – it truly was something else!

It's funny but for all the privation there, I wasn't really conscious of it at the time. The only thing I really missed was a proper hot shower and a toilet that flushed – I think that was the worst of it! We didn't even have chemical toilets at the FOB – just a plank with a hole over an oil drum that had to be burned off every day to dispose of all the waste. It's really not very pleasant, so that took me a while to get used to – it's funny what you do get used to when you have to though, isn't it?

The other chef and I were cooking for the whole camp. There were the Estonians and then about 18 British – 7RHA and 9 Squadron Para engineers. The facilities were really basic there, quite shocking really – our basic building block for feeding them all was Compo Rations, the 10-man ration packs that the military uses on operations. They're a little bit different from the one-man ration packs but it's mostly just tins really – you get things like five tins of meat. There are different menus: you have diced beef, diced lamb, or chicken, or minced beef; you have the four choices and that's it. Then you'll have dried mashed potato and there will be a dessert in there like tinned fruit cocktail, that sort of stuff. We'd do what we could to make the menus more imaginative and tasty. We'd get air drops every now and again and we were quite lucky. We had a couple of drops in the time I was there where I managed to get things like fresh onions, tinned mushrooms, tinned potatoes. A few bits and pieces, and you can drop cereal in as well, like cornflakes, muesli. It's always a massive morale boost for the guys when the RAF come and drop it in, it lands and then the Para engineers would drive out in four-tonne trucks with hydraulic lifts to pick it all up. It's hit and miss, though; sometimes the chutes don't open properly so the pallets come straight down and stuff will be all over the place. The guys could be out for four or five hours picking everything up.

I was quite lucky because the guy that I went out with had been out before, so he'd briefed me beforehand on what we'd be doing. I was planning on taking spices, all sorts of things, but he said we wouldn't need anything because everything necessary was already there; all we had to add was imagination. We cooked all sorts, really – we made a lot of curries, because they're always really popular with the lads, but we even did good old-fashioned nursery food like cottage pies and stuff – we'd whip up the mash potato for the top, make it a bit special. And we did fresh stuff for them whenever we could – we gave them a pizza night once a week, which was a massive amount of work for us because it would take ten hours to do chips as we'd have to wash and chop all the potatoes, and then blanche and refry them. That kitchen was a nightmare – concrete walls, no air con, two fat fryers going and the oven – you'd just be sweating non-stop from the minute you started. Thing is, the lads would come back in after a patrol and you'd see their faces when they saw we'd done homemade chips and it was all worthwhile. They would be so happy and when we saw that, it didn't really matter how long it had taken us, it was seeing how made up they were and it kind of made all the hassle worthwhile.

You can probably imagine, but they'd get so fed up with the same old stuff – like 'Oh God, not rice and pasta again!' The Army ration packs are big on things like spaghetti bolognese, chilli con carne, and stuff like that, and the lads really grew tired of it on a long-term basis. Decent food made such a difference to morale. Even breakfast came in a tin – sausages, bacon grill, beans, tomatoes, all tinned. We had powdered eggs and porridge but we always did our best with what we had and we never had any complaints.

I remember the first time I walked into the showers – I just saw all these naked guys and I thought 'Oh well, no room for modesty here.' The showers were really simple affairs and the water came from Jerry cans. It wasn't hot obviously and it was really basic – there were just these two little shower tents, like little things you zip yourself into – not unlike some little phone box. The zips didn't work and I think I just got to a point where I lost all my inhibitions; you literally don't care, you lose it all and don't bother giving it a second thought. It all goes out the window because at the end of the day, everyone is there to crack on and do what they have to do – you can't get too precious about washing and showering. And when we're all living in such close proximity, it's just not practical. Any sense of decorum or personal modesty, well I think everyone leaves it behind at Brize Norton when they board the plane into theatre.

I don't think I had a proper sleep in the whole four weeks I was there. I'd start at 05:00 every day and we'd rarely be finished much before 20:00 when dinner was all squared away and that was every single day of the deployment. The work was quite arduous, too, because if I wasn't cooking, I was carrying Jerry cans or the big ten-man boxes of Compo, so I was physically tired. It was just the conditions really; all the heat in the rooms, no air, it's impossible to sleep when it's like that. Plus there were all the contacts.

There was a hell of a lot going on just outside and we'd sit and watch it from the FOB – just your basic combat tourist kind-of-thing. There'd be tracer going up and it was all kicking off. I remember too that one of the soldiers got his leg blown off about two minutes from camp. I think that was the first time it all came home to me, you know, 'Shit, this is for real.' You know, up until that point, you're fairly remote from it, even with it going on a few metres away and rounds being fired at us inside. You're kind of detached in a way, but someone who you know being blown up tends to hit home. When the Estonians extracted, we had a company of US Marines take over from them. They undertook some really big ops, they were really going for it and there was an awful lot happening. Once they did that, the Taliban really started trying to smash the place up and we started to draw a lot more fire.

The first rocket I experienced was bizarre. I remember I was in my room alone and I heard a '*whoosh*' and the mad thing was that I was reading a book and it was describing the noise that a rocket makes as it comes in when you're being shot at and how you never forget it kind-of-thing. It was just totally bizarre that I was reading it one minute and the next, I heard the sound as one flew over, followed by a '*Boom*' – there was a massive explosion. I looked out and saw all the guys, like, pinned to the wall and I thought 'Oh shit, I don't know what's going on here.' It's funny, because you're not aware of it but with all the training we get, everything just becomes instinctive. We tend not to realise just how well trained we are, but I had my body armour and helmet on and I didn't remember actually putting them on. In the event, I think the Taliban fired four rockets into the camp that day and it went on in a similar fashion for four days in a row; it seems like we spent the whole time stood to with our helmets and Osprey on.

I recall one night that I was sitting there with the British lads, drinking a cup of coffee; these were the boys that went out on the ground, had all the contacts with the Taliban and we were sitting around watching their videos of what they'd done during that day and the next minute – *'Bang!'* Same again, another rocket had come in and the air horn had gone off so we went running for cover, but morale was still so high – it was unbelievable. I was so annoyed – I remember running with my coffee and I was more pissed off that I might spill it than any threat from the rockets. I was running and thinking 'Sod you; I'm not going to miss my coffee just because you're firing at us!'

I always wanted to make an effort, especially when they had the big ops because, sometimes you knew the boys would be out on the ground for, like, 12 hours, and for them to come back to Now Zad and have something decent for their dinner – the boost it gave them was huge. Food was really important to them and I just wanted to make it count, do the best I could. I used to worry about them because you get quite close you know, there's a real bond between everyone and every time they went out, I'd be thinking 'I so hope everyone gets back OK.' You get so close to people within a matter of days because of the circumstances you are in and the shared experiences.

I remember one time we were under attack and the warning had gone off; we were taking fire, there were rockets and rounds coming in like 50 metres from the Sanger and some of the guys still turned up for dinner. We'd normally have dinner prepared for 18:00, so these boys came to the mess facility with their weapons, still dressed in their Ospreys and helmets. Obviously, with us being under fire we hadn't put dinner out as normal – we'd held it back in the kitchen so they were all looking around as if to say 'Where's my dinner?' So there we were in the kitchen, cooking in our Ospreys and Helmets – and the heat was just beyond words! Even putting the meals out was hard work because we were so bulky in all our gear; it was an effort to carry them. Looking back, I think that was probably one of my highlights of Now Zad – putting dinner out while under fire and dressed in Osprey and helmet. It's one of those moments I'll never forget; one minute it was complete pandemonium and then everyone's just sat there eating their dinner like it's the most normal thing in the world.

It's weird really but morale at Now Zad was sky-high then, the guys all seemed so happy despite what was going on. At Bastion on the other hand, you live in a kind of bubble where inside the wire, nothing really happens, nothing changes from one week to the next. Consequently, people are always going on about they want to go home, they miss this and they miss that, this is going on, that's going on and it brings you down a bit. I've never experienced morale like I found at Now Zad – it was the highest I've ever known anywhere. The boys would have a campfire going of a night-time and everyone would sit around singing stupid songs or telling stories of what they did.

We were able to keep in touch with home from the FOB because there was a satellite phone that we could use. It was not brilliant but we had a text link there that was really good – it was like a computer but you could text mobile phones from it and get them back. My nan and my dad would both text me every day so it was really cool, a way to stay in touch. We'd get something like 200 credits a week, which bought a lot of texts – that was a really big boost; you felt a lot closer to people. I got a lot of support from my unit back home too, so I wasn't tied to texting home every day. My flight sergeant at Lossiemouth was brilliant – he'd ring my Nan up to let her know that I was okay whenever something happened and we were locked down on comms, so they became like best friends! It's always harder for your friends and family back home than it is for those of us out here – I hadn't been at Now Zad long when Sarah Bryant was killed. When it was first announced on the news, they just said the first female to be killed in Helmand Province, there was no name given. It was all over the news so I think a few of those close to me got a bit of a fright from that really. All said and done, though, we have a great support structure and I've felt really well looked after.

I don't make a big song and dance about the fact that I'm a girl, but I think we all do what we can to be ourselves; I brought my hair straighteners out to Now Zad with me so I was all right! I must be the only person to have ever taken a pair to the front line but it was great fun. I know it was a big wind-up while I was there – on the last night I straightened all the boys' hair so I know they appreciated it.

I remember when I was finally extracted from Now Zad; we'd been hammered for something like the whole of my last ten days. The Taliban were constantly hitting the HLS with rockets and mortars, although they were usually off target, but just before I was due to bug out, they had one that landed just 50 metres from the Chinook. I got down there and even the Army guys that I was with felt edgy; I'd never felt so exposed in all my life and everyone was taking up firing positions, but the boys were really good to me – they said 'Just do as we do, we'll look after you' and suddenly – I've never felt so happy – over the horizon I saw an Apache gunship and a Chinook next to it. They put down about 200 metres from us and we had to make the run across open ground – I don't think I've ever run so fast in all my life. Running with all my kit on – all 50kg of me, with a month's worth of kit in my Bergen, my helmet, rifle, 120 rounds of ammo, my med kit – I ran on to the Chinook and then we lifted off and that was it; the next thing I knew we were landing in Bastion and that chapter of my life was all over. I think it was the adrenaline buzz more than anything – it takes over and you're just a passenger really.

That whole experience at the FOB was the undoubted highlight of my deployment for me, something I thought I would never get to do. I was on such a high for most of it and people couldn't believe that I was RAF – never ever – they all thought I was Army! There was one day, and the boys were having a knock about and I was wearing an RAF baseball cap. A couple of the boys went, 'Oh, what have you got that on for?' and I said 'Because I'm RAF.' They laughed and said, 'Shut up, you're not RAF you're Army, aren't you?' and I said 'No, I'm RAF.' They couldn't believe it! I guess it's natural really – Army are the dominant force outside the wire and it's not like I went round telling them all as soon as I got there, so I guess it was a bit of a shock to them. They never expected to see an RAF female out there at the front line. I never thought I would see myself in this position because I'm not real big on the whole 'girls in the forces' thing; I don't like people making a big deal of the fact that I'm a girl because at the end of the day I get paid the same as the guys do, so what difference does my sex make? I think it is brilliant that the RAF is out here and I'm doing the same job as a lance corporal Army chef. It's about time that we started going forward instead of backward and saying that I can't lift a rifle. People can get rid of that and say 'Right, now we're there.'

I really enjoy my job, being in the RAF, and I've decided that when I get back I'm going to go for my commission. The Air Force is changing as a result of what we're doing out here and I want to do my bit, pass that positive experience on, just to say to the lads coming out here that they will have a good time, that there's nothing to worry about – it's all in your mind isn't it, it's just attitude. My tour here is for four months but I'd love to extend it to six. I tried to but I was told that I probably wouldn't be allowed, but you never really know what's going to happen and things can change at a moment's notice. It's my 30th birthday in August, which will coincide with the end of my tour, so I'm kind of hoping I'll be home in time for that now.

I live on unit up at Lossiemouth now but I'm from Cumbria – so when I go back and take some leave, that's where I'll go. It's a beautiful part of the world and I'm actually looking forward to going home and seeing everyone. When I go back I think we'll go up on the hills and we'll go to the Lake District, have ice creams, drink – just do stuff like that. It's funny, alcohol plays such a major part in people's lives back home and you come out here and think you're really going to miss it – being dry for four to six months, you think 'How's that work?' Thing is, though, you really don't miss it – you exist in the bubble that life here is and it doesn't figure, so you just find other things to do instead. You certainly don't miss the hangovers!

If I'm looking forward to anything at all – aside from the obvious, like seeing my friends and family again – it's just relaxing and having a bit of privacy, just having my own space again. We're five to a tent here, so privacy is a relative concept, although they're a great bunch – they're all Army girls and really good fun. In our down time, we usually stick together so we'll play cards, go to the coffee shop and watch a bit of football, that sort of stuff. Everyone works different shifts in my team, but the Army girls are great.

I found it quite hard when I went home on R&R. I think a couple of my friends thought I seemed a bit more highly strung. I think the whole experience will change me when I go back. I'll never complain about stupid little things any more like I used to. I think that what happens here gives you a whole different perspective on life. When I was at Now Zad, a teenage Afghan boy was brought in with his legs blown off, and something like that really changes your perspective. I get so fed up with people watching the news and saying 'Why are we in Afghanistan. Why are we doing this?' They see the headlines and don't bother to read up on what's behind them – if they can't make sense of it all in a two-minute soundbite, they don't want to know. I know there is a lot of fighting going on in-theatre, but so much of what we're doing is hearts and minds. You look at what we're doing at Kajaki, the medical care we're providing to Afghani civilians and surely, if we can give them power – if we can make a difference, then surely it's worth it. I think a lot of the time, the media is quick to jump on stories of the lives lost, but not always so willing to promote the good that we're doing out here. And we are, we're doing a lot of good.

SQUADRON LEADER MATT CARTER MC

FORWARD AIR CONTROLLER

For the troops on the ground in Afghanistan, air power can mean the difference between life and death. Close Air Support might be delivered by the Apache gunships, bombers and fast jets in theatre but it is co-ordinated and controlled by Forward Air Controllers who bear the onerous responsibility of ensuring that rockets, bombs, and cannon fired from the air hit their intended targets and not friendly forces, who may be just metres away.

Flight Lieutenant Matt Carter was employed as the Tactical Air Control Party (TACP) officer with 3 Para Battlegroup HQ and was awarded the Military Cross for his actions as an FAC in a number of major contacts. His citation reads that Carter 'directed close and accurate Attack Helicopter fire immediately, without prompting and with devastating results'. The citation adds that 'he exposed himself to significant risk as he forced his way forward into the front of the heavy fire-fight'. In respect of one of his actions, the citation adds that 'Flt Lt Carter repeatedly exposed himself to a significant chance of being killed and, because of this gallant behaviour he made a decisive contribution to allowing the platoon to regain the initiative.'

In one of the many actions singled out, Carter found himself just metres away from Taliban forces, with himself and his colleagues in grave danger. In another, he was aboard a Chinook helicopter which drew heavy Taliban and RPG fire while on the ground. It lifted off after just 20 seconds on the ground and, fearing being left behind on the aircraft, 'Flt Lt Carter jumped 15 feet from the tail ramp into the darkness, realizing the vital role he had to play in calling in air support to suppress the Taliban gunfire.'

'Flight Lieutenant Carter gallantly and repeatedly exposed himself during all contacts with the enemy at a very high risk of being killed. This, coupled with his ruthlessly efficient prosecution of air-delivered fire in the closest proximity of a determined enemy, single out this brave and courageous officer for very high public recognition.'

I'm 35 and I'm currently SO2 RAF Regiment Recruiting, but when I was deployed to Afghanistan with 3 Para on Op Herrick 4, I was a flight lieutenant and OC of 613 TACP (FAC) (Tactical Air Control Party – Forward Air Control).

A TACP has four people – the officer, a senior NCO who acts as his 2i/c and two SACs who act as signallers. In April 2006 we deployed as a single battlegroup commanded by Lieutenant Colonel Stuart Tootal; we were the first conventional British troops in Afghanistan and were deployed following the then Defence Secretary John Reid's quote, 'We hope we will leave Afghanistan without firing a single shot.'

I'm married, and three months before my deployment in April 2006 my wife gave birth to twin boys; they're now three. I deployed when they were just three months old, and when I got back in the October, they were sitting up eating sandwiches, wondering who I was when I walked through the door. That was hard.

It did place extra pressure on me at the time, though. I mean, for the whole of the pregnancy it was quite difficult because I was away training to become an FAC and learning my job as OC of the TACP, and then we had pre-deployment training, which was probably nine months' work before we went, so that covered most of the pregnancy. Thankfully the boys were born over Christmas, so I was definitely going to be home for it. It must have been really tough for my wife when I deployed – although she was proud of what I was doing, she certainly didn't want me to go, but she knew I had to. She tried to hide her feelings because she didn't want me to worry, but it was very difficult for her. And it got worse as the tour went on, with certain things that came out in the Press.

A TACP's job is really quite complex; if you imagine a 3D battlefield, there will be friendly and enemy forces on the ground, with numerous air assets inside and outside of that area – they'll be at different heights and locations. The TACP ensures that those air assets don't come into conflict with each other or with friendly mortar or artillery fire and that they don't fire on friendly forces or civilians. It's vital that bombs, shells, or missiles fired from the air hit their intended targets, as the potential for tragic errors is obvious. The pilots can be anything from several hundred feet to 25,000ft up, travelling at high speed and with just metres separating the British or other ISAF troops from the Taliban forces they want taken out. Boiled down to its basic elements, the job of an FAC is to speak to the pilots and 'talk them on' to the enemy positions. We make the decisions – essentially, an FAC delivers an attack from the air himself and the aircraft and their pilots are basically extensions of his weapon systems. Obviously, to achieve what is required, we'll be with the front-line troops at all times.

We can bring a disproportionate weight of firepower to bear on any target, so it's imperative that we do so with meticulous accuracy. We'll frequently direct the employment of weapons of up to 2000lb weight in varying quantities, and given that some of the engagements in Afghanistan take place at 50 metres, the margin for error is tight. Avoiding fratricide and reducing collateral damage are always at the front of your mind, but you must maintain proportionality. You have to be conscious, too, of the different rules of engagement that exist for each of the nations that might be providing CAS (Close Air Support). I might be directing RAF Harrier GR9s or French Mirages to drop bombs on Taliban positions or to fly low for a show of force. Another time I might be talking a USAF AC130 Spectre or some Apaches on to targets.

The very nature of our role means that while we're doing it, we'll be under fire in the middle of a battle, so it's very challenging. Friendly forces might be in six or seven separate positions, so we'll be talking to them and co-ordinating their requests for assistance, directing the air assets and talking to Chinook pilots inserting troops or ammunition or evacuating casualties. The topography in Afghanistan provides a lot of cover but many houses and compounds look the same. There will also often be civilians living in the area so you have to be extremely careful.

My first patrol was an overnighter with A Company, 3 Para. I was attached to Patrols Platoon when the company deployed to Gereshk in the very early days of the tour. I was the FAC for that party; there were no others on the ground at that time. The idea was to establish a few initial patrols and get a feel for what the ground was like. We struck out about four klicks, but almost immediately we started to experience real problems with our radios. The Bowman radio didn't work properly, so we went to ground in a poppy field overnight while we tried to sort the problem out. It couldn't be sorted, so at around 08:00 the decision was taken to tab back to base.

When we got back, Colonel Tootal was going to conduct a *shura* with the Gereshk Chief of Police for the first time so we mounted a big security operation to protect him. I got up on top of the police station while this key engagement was going on, controlling a pair of Harriers on top cover. To tell the truth, it was all quiet at this point and I thought that's how my whole tour would be ... it's a gorgeous sunny day, the jets are circling overhead, the guys are patrolling out on the ground below me, and there are no enemy. The meeting seemed to go well; when we left we headed towards the north of Gereshk and the pose relaxed a little as we approached the edge of town; people were chilling out a bit because we were on the outskirts of town and the immediate danger was over. We were still in helmets rather than soft headgear, and the heat was really oppressive. It was amazingly hot; about 45°C I reckon, and I'm carrying about 90lb of kit. When you're wearing a helmet and Osprey, all your kit, water, weapons, your radio ... well, you have to be fit to do the job, just to walk.

Suddenly, we got shot at. We were in a kind of open area, about 300 metres long by 200 metres wide, surrounded by compounds and we were ambushed. There were no warning signs; there was no eerie quietness, and there were loads of children around us but they still shot; they didn't seem to care if they hit the kids. It was probably only three or so enemy firing AK47s at us, but that was the first time I'd been shot at and it's not something I'm ever going to forget; I was terrified. There were a lot of rounds fired and I don't think I was in any immediate danger but my heart was racing. A few rounds hit one of the Land Rovers but we were fairly spread out so we dispersed ourselves and made sure we had cover. The Land Rover was about 20 metres away from me and I heard the rounds hit it, heard a few ricochets. We were in contact but we didn't know where the enemy was and were worried that we might be outmanoeuvred.

I was on my radio immediately, talking to the Harriers; I called in the contact and asked for a show of force as we extracted from the contact area. I couldn't call ordnance down on the Taliban because I didn't know where they were. The Harrier was over us in less than 5 minutes and it was incredible; he was so low, probably around 50ft and it took my breath away, but it worked; this was the early days so it had an effect. The contact stopped and we were able to extract. That was a real turning point, I think – that was when Lieutenant Colonel Tootal and the troops of A Company suddenly realised that air power was going to play a major part in this deployment, it was that dawning moment. It was a defining moment for me, too, because aside from the first-hand example of how effective the fast air could be, I realised that whatever was above us would be much better able to locate the enemy than we would – so I thought of ISTAR and its capabilities. There's no doubt I was nervous and scared at the time but I just went into my drills. It was very early days and I remember thinking, 'God, am I going to be shot at on every patrol?' We really had no idea what it was going to be like then.

There were a few lighter moments before it turned really bad, like a helicopter patrol into Gereshk where we landed into the DC and as we landed on, it took the roofs off people's houses – they were tin roofs – and I was thinking, 'Christ, we are not going to get a friendly reception here!' But that was a real lesson. It could have turned really nasty but the people living there were fantastic. They were smiling and laughing; seeing the helicopter was a novelty then. I'd a young boy come up on that patrol and he kissed my hand. They were really happy to have us there. In fact, that was the initial reaction we had in most of the places we went into. It was only when the real contact started and the villages starting emptying and we started fighting the Taliban regularly, but we didn't want to go in and start a fight. It was the fact that we were contacted and we had to beat them every time we'd a scrap with them.

We were engaged in quite a bit of hearts-and-minds stuff then. For example, on one patrol through Gereshk, we went into the hospital and saw that the beds had a lot of blood and pus on them. The sheets were disgusting, totally unhygienic. There was a washing machine that had been donated by USAID, the American Development Agency and it was just sat there, still wrapped in plastic in the same state as it had left the factory; it hadn't been plumbed in. So we said we'd come back and sort it all out, thinking it would be a great initial hearts-and-minds thing. You have to remember, at this point, not a round had been fired.

I don't know why, but DfID told us it was out of the question for us to undertake the job; that came as a real shock. It was a relatively simple task that would have had massively disproportionate benefits and we were blocked from making it happen. There were other small initiatives that we wanted to get going that would have made an immediate difference and we weren't allowed to do those either; that was really frustrating. We were being told about a pan-agency approach but it was at that time very early days and it wasn't tied up together like it became later. Despite that, we did have some successes, though, and I think the Taliban then realised that a lot of what we were doing was helping the communities to favour us. All the Taliban had over the communities was fear really; they'd offer the sons and fathers a choice – fight for us or we'll kill you – so they really started to make life hard for us.

The next major event for us was the first major battlegroup operation, Op Mutay. Intelligence had highlighted a key Taliban compound just outside Now Zad and we were tasked with securing it, breaking in, and searching for Taliban fighters or weapons. So it was an air assault operation; A Company would air assault in from two Chinooks and co-ordinate the search, and there were to be two cut-offs – the Gurkhas establishing one in the north and Patrols Platoon doing the same in the south. We drove from Bastion to Now Zad – the journey is about 70km, and we didn't have any ballistic matting back then so it was all a bit, 'Christ, I hope we don't hit any mines!', or that kind of thing. We were in WMIKs and I was in the back of a Pinzgauer with my signaller, Rusty; his role was to provide protection with his rifle because I couldn't listen in on the Battle Group Net and do my job and fire at the same time. We arrived the evening before the op and holed up in the police station.

ABOVE: *Andy Lewis, OC 1 (F) Squadron runs through his flight plan seconds before scrambling his Harrier GR9 on a Close Air Support mission.*

(All photographs © author unless credited otherwise)

BELOW LEFT: *Ed Collins of 1 Air Movements Wing. Ed deals with the movement of all passengers and freight to and from Camp Bastion. His face has been obscured in this photograph for security reasons.*

BELOW RIGHT: *Sarah Jones, the first female chef to deploy to a Forward Operating Base.*

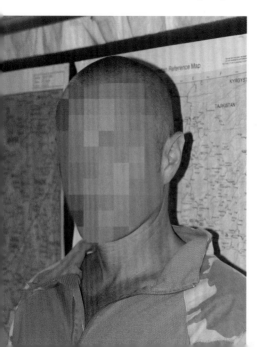

ABOVE LEFT: *Matt Carter, pictured at Buckingham Palace with his Military Cross. Matt was the first RAF officer in 50 years to receive the award.*

(© Sgt Graham Spark/Crown Copyright)

ABOVE RIGHT: *Roly Smith, the OC of 591 Signals Unit, pictured inside the operations room at Kandahar.*

BELOW: *Matt Bartlett stands alongside a C130J Hercules after completing his pre-flight inspection, shortly before a sortie from Kandahar Airfield in November 2008. His face has been obscured in this photograph for security reasons.*

ABOVE LEFT: *Chinook pilot Eleanor Lodge on her bunk in the IRT tent. Chinooks are in high demand in theatre. Their pilots regularly have to land while under fire from Taliban forces.*

ABOVE RIGHT: *Chalkie White, who worked alongside frontline troops providing fuel for Hercules and Chinooks from a desert landing strip.*

BELOW LEFT: *Bob Judson, COMKAF. Air Commodore Judson took over as the Commander, Kandahar Airfield (KAF), in July 2007.*

BELOW RIGHT: *Wilf Pugsley sits on one of the operating tables at Camp Bastion's Medical Treatment Facility where he worked as the consultant general surgeon.*

ABOVE: *Neil 'Ebbo' Ebberson, Nimrod navigator, at work.*

BELOW LEFT: *James Taylor, Chinook engineer. James had a lucky escape when a Taliban rocket landed next to the Chinook he was working on and ricocheted through the passenger compartment. It failed to explode.*

BELOW RIGHT: *Seth Setterington of the RAF Fire and Rescue team at Camp Bastion. Seth was on IRT duty when they were scrambled to deal with a crashed Reaper MQ-9 UAV.*

ABOVE: *Remote control war: the control console for a Predator MQ-1 UAV, predecessor to the Reaper MQ-9. The pilot sits at left, with his sensor operator on the right. This is almost identical to the control console that Flt Lt Garrick Hill uses when launching the RAF's Reaper in Afghanistan.*
(© US Dept of Defense)

BELOW LEFT: *Eileen Buchan, who was attached to the British Embassy in Kabul where she worked on the FCO counter-narcotics team.*

BELOW RIGHT: *Si Scholes of the RAF Regiment stands on the cardboard sheet that served as his 'bed' for the three months he spent at Sangin in 2006. Si served as the FAC for 'A' Platoon, 3 Para, in a deployment that saw them engaged in contacts with Taliban forces on a daily basis.*

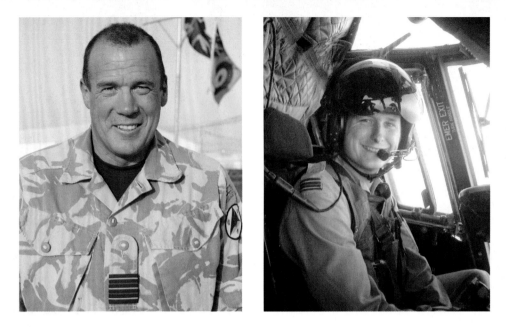

ABOVE LEFT: *Andy Gray, the Chief of Staff of 904 EAW.*

ABOVE RIGHT: *'Frenchie' Duncan, the Chinook pilot who was awarded the DFC for a number of actions, including a sortie in which he saved the life of Mohammad Golab Mangal, Governor of Helmand Province.*

BELOW: *Members of 51 Squadron, RAF Regiment, conduct a routine patrol outside Kandahar Airfield.* (© Cpl Scott Robertson/Crown Copyright)

RIGHT: *Close air support: a soldier from 16 Air Assault Brigade watches as a 540lb bomb explodes on an enemy position at Musa Qala in August 2006.*
(© Cpl Mike Fletcher/ Crown Copyright)

BELOW: *Hellfire: a British Army Apache AH-1 providing close air support to ground forces launches its Hellfire missiles to take out Taliban fighters in Helmand Province.*
(© Staff Sgt Mike Harvey/ Crown Copyright)

ABOVE LEFT: *Brown-out: a graphic demonstration of the difficulties faced by the RAF's Chinook pilots when landing in the dusty landscape that delineates so much of Helmand Province.* (© PO Sean Clee/Crown Copyright)

ABOVE RIGHT: *Dust cloud: brown-outs don't just affect Chinook pilots. Here, a member of the British Task Force shields his face from the downdraught caused by a Chinook from 18 Squadron, after dropping off supplies.* (© SAC Andrew Morris/Crown Copyright)

BELOW: *Over-watch: an Apache AH-1 approaches Camp Bastion after providing over-watch on a mission involving the Chinooks just visible behind. RAF Chinooks in Helmand Province always fly with a wingman for protection, and an Apache AH-1 to provide heavier firepower in over-watch.* (© Crown Copyright)

We left early the following morning and went to establish the cut-off. The suburb was on the western side of the town and, as we left, we drove over a big ditch, went around a corner and all hell broke loose – we started taking heavy fire from four or five Taliban in a compound about 40 metres away who immediately opened up on us with AK47s and RPGs. The Paras tried to fire back with .50 cals but the ammunition was faulty and their guns jammed; it transpired that there wasn't enough propellant in the rounds so they didn't produce enough gas to recock the weapons. Eventually the whole batch was trashed and a new supply brought in. Because of the stoppages, we were all firing back at this stage. How nobody was hit I'll never know – there were so many rounds flying. An RPG hit a tree right above me, showering me with branches and crap before detonating in an airburst on the other side of a wall. That was really close!

There were eight WMIKS or so and Rusty and I were in the back of the Pinzgauer – it's just a small open truck, literally an open vehicle. As soon as we came into contact, we both dived for cover among all these water bottles in the front but there was truly nowhere to hide. It was at that moment that we realised we had to get on with the bloody job so I said to Rusty 'Get up, get up and start firing!' and I got on the net to the Apaches. At the same time the Gurkhas were ambushed – they were about a klick north of us with an FAC of their own who was trying to talk to the Apaches, so there was confusion initially with a lot of people dropping call-signs; we learned a lot of lessons that day in how to manage that.

Anyway I made contact with one of the Apaches; I think the Taliban were trying to outflank us as they'd moved off slightly from the original ambush site, so I talked the Apache pilot on to them; I'd done a battlespace management map beforehand, which was absolutely key – I'd numbered houses and things and made sure the pilots had all of those maps so we were all reading from the same page as it were. Once the Apache crew had identified the enemy, I called for 30mm cannon on to them and they let them have it; the AH's 30mm cannon fires 10 armour-piercing HEDP rounds a second and they fragment on impact like a grenade, so the guys who were firing at us were completely destroyed. Being near to it was bad enough – really loud, devastating firepower – but I have never lost any sleep over their deaths. They were trying to kill us and it was my job to save *our* lives. That was the first time that a British Apache had been used on operations.

Once the firing stopped, we got on the move again. We were driving along a narrow track and had only moved a short distance before we found ourselves in another, more intense ambush. It seemed like every single compound started opening up on us as we passed – I mean there were grenades being thrown over walls and stuff, loads of RPGs, AKs being fired at us. I can remember an RPG flying over the top of our vehicle – we heard the *whoosh* and we just looked up and saw it – the first generation ones seem to move really slowly and you can see them coming. Luckily it missed a tree that was near us and hit a compound beyond us.

With all of the .50 cals out of action we were firing personal rifles, pistols – it was really close country. Rusty is firing back, the Paras are dismounting and returning fire and even I'm firing back – it was all hands to the pump – while trying to keep a clear picture in my head of where everyone is and what's happening. As we moved along, there were RPGs hitting the ground in front of us – there was an entire cornfield ablaze. It seemed like we'd entered a village populated exclusively by Taliban gunmen and we were taking small-arms fire from every angle, although luckily they were pretty bad shots. They were pretty well organised, though – I could see small groups of men to my left who were firing and manoeuvring.

You never really get used to being shot at, but you do learn to deal with it – you have to. Your training takes over and you just act. I had to manage the air space for the battlegroup because by this time the helicopters were coming in and I had to talk to them and make sure they knew there were contacts going on. Rusty was really good – he gave me covering fire while I was doing all of this and at the same time he liaised with Mark Swann, the captain in charge of Patrols Platoon, so that he knew what was going on and I knew what he was doing. That way I was able to keep control of it all.

I'll never forget, but the vehicle is kind of rocking with the weight of fire and Rusty is firing with the barrel right next to my left ear and I'm talking to him, rolling around on this really rough terrain. I shouted at him: 'Do you know where to point that bloody rifle?' and he said: 'Yes I fucking do!' and he started firing at the enemy. I thought he was going to shoot my head off – it was that close! It was quite an amusing thing and provided a bit of light relief; it's a moment that we've talked about a lot since because he could've easily shot me in our first major contact!

Eventually, we got out of that second ambush but it was bloody hard work; the vehicles would stop, the Paras would jump out and engage the enemy in one compound, then mount up, roll a bit further, stop and do it all again. They killed a lot of Taliban in that contact and after a while we found some cover and stopped in a more sheltered location. It provided us with a defensive position so we halted while Captain Swann came up with new orders and then tried to establish the cordon.

We were still trying to do this when A Company arrived and came straight into their own ambush; we were trying to get to them to provide some support and then we came under another heavy contact from a number of enemy based in and around a farmhouse and a tree line. We got to within a few metres of the house but then we effectively became pinned down in two groups behind two walls, separated by a gap of about 50 metres. We had to find a way to break the deadlock because every minute wasted was an opportunity for the Taliban to get some reinforcements and surround us – we had no idea how many we were fighting, but it felt like the whole of Now Zad. I knew I needed to get some air support in to deal with the guys in the tree line and the farmhouse, but I couldn't call fire in at that stage because I wasn't certain exactly where all the Paras were. Also, the walls we were taking cover behind were only 30 metres away from the house I wanted to call fire on to, so we were Danger Close and I had to be absolutely spot on with my instructions to the Apache pilots. The only way I could be sure was to run through the gap to see for myself.

I'd watched Paras running across it as they were moving blokes forward and I'd seen rounds impacting the ground at their feet as they ran, kicking up dust. There was nothing for it, though; if I didn't go, there would be no air support. One of the sergeants tried to stop me, but when I told him, he obviously realised our position and waved me on. It was bloody terrifying, but it's amazing what adrenaline does for you. I was completely focused – I knew that the only way out was to call down some fire from the Apaches and that was a much greater motivator than the fear was an anchor. That's how it felt at the time; with hindsight, I haven't got a clue what drove me – I just knew I had to do it.

Obviously, the Taliban started firing at me as soon as I started running, but I made it across in one piece and slumped down behind the wall absolutely gasping for breath and drenched in sweat. From my new position, the guys next to me were all firing into the house and taking a huge weight of fire back. Bear in mind that although I could see the house clearly from where I was, the Apaches are a lot higher up and further away – probably 2km or so from our position. The imagery they can see on their screens from their Target Acquisition and Designation Sight system is quite incredible though – its array of lenses includes a 127-times magnification day TV camera that can read a car number plate from over 4km away. The problem is that to them one house looks just like another unless it's identified specifically. Also, they can see people running around, but it's absolutely imperative that they identify the Taliban position and not ours. Given how close we were to the target, the choice of ordnance is vital too; there's a real chance of fratricide with rockets at that distance and it's even close for 30mm too – although the Apache's M230 cannon is accurate to within 3 metres, our position relative to the target was still outside of what's considered safe distance back in the UK. So I had to get it right – and make sure the AH was in the right position to fire. You always want them firing at 90 degrees relative to your position so that if the ordnance falls short or lands long, it's not going to take out friendly forces.

I told Mark Swann that I needed to mark the building for the Apache and the guy next to me – a Para called 'Bash' picked up a Light Anti-tank Weapon (LAW). As he did so, he was shot; a tracer round hit him in the chest but his body armour took the impact and it ricocheted off his spare magazine; talk about lucky! The impact knocked him over, but he simply dusted himself off, got back up and picked up the LAW again. So I got on the net to the Apache and said, 'Right, we're going to mark the building with a LAW.' The pilot thought he'd misheard and came back with 'Confirm … with a LAW?' So I confirmed it. Bash fired and *bang*, the rocket went into the house and exploded. 'Yep, I've got the building,' the pilot came back.

I said, 'Look south from that building and you'll see a wall with a load of Paras behind it. You're clear hot, initials MC.' Whenever a Widow calls in anything that's Danger Close, you have to give the pilot your initials to indicate that you're taking responsibility for it if it goes wrong. He said, 'Roger, commander's initials are MC. Engaging now with 30mm, keep your bloody heads down,' and then this hail of fire rained down on the house, which made the whole world around us feel like it was erupting. The power and the noise of the 30mm is truly awesome and it completely devastated the Taliban in the house, killing or injuring every one of them, because we stopped taking fire from that location immediately and the people who were firing from within the woods extracted out. It just shows you what a brilliant weapon it was. I then went through and cleared the house with the Paras – there were splashes and pools of blood, some flip flops and other stuff in there, but no enemy; I think that was when we learned that the Taliban take their dead and wounded with them. We did a clearance patrol in the garden to make sure there was no other enemy there, which was bloody scary because it's such a close country – trees and walls are really close and visibility is terrible, there are just so many places for the enemy to hide.

So we withdrew and moved out of the area into the open a bit and I was now in a position to start thinking of the bigger picture and managing the airspace for the whole battlegroup. I got on the net to another soldier attached to 3 Para as an FAC. We had A10s in our airspace and I teed one up for him to drop a bomb on an enemy location; I told him where our guys were and then talked aircraft on to where he was. I could also turn my thoughts towards helping A Company out with some CAS. I was controlling a B1B, which although it was at 5,000ft, was unbelievably loud, so I called in a show of force. It wasn't wholly effective by then, but the Taliban had started withdrawing anyway, which gave A Company some room to breathe. Eventually, A Company was able to conduct the search and they found a major weapons cache, so the operation was a great success. We'd been involved in three big contacts as a battlegroup, spread over six hours. How nobody was hit, I'll never know; we confirmed 21 Taliban killed. But it's hard to believe we were under fire for the best part of six hours; you're so busy all the time, I thought it had only lasted two hours. And

I think the fact that we didn't drop any bombs that day is a perfect indicator of just how close the fighting was.

The next real big engagement for me was Operation Augustus on 14 July, which was a deliberate battlegroup operation to capture or kill a key Taliban leader in the north of Sangin. It was planned as a night air assault operation – land as close as possible – say 100 metres away, use the element of surprise and take out the target. A lot of planning had gone into it; five Chinooks would deploy us and there was also a land element involving Canadian forces and Patrols Platoon who were driving in to provide cut-offs. So there were lots of different aspects to it. We knew the area but we didn't know what sort of opposition we were going to get.

I had everything teed up – Global Hawk, U2, a load of CAS stacked up, an AC130, Apaches … we knew we had a lot of support with us but we weren't expecting what happened. Basically, we were deploying in two sticks – three helicopters in the first wave, two in the second – and each contained about 40 Paras and one quad bike. But as we made our approach, all hell broke loose: they were waiting for us. Conditions were far from perfect – it was pitch black, 40 blokes on each chopper, all carrying heavy loads, gear, and ammo. And the ground was really bumpy with loads of ditches. All that, and under fire too. The pilots did – and are doing – a brilliant, brilliant job under massively exacting conditions, flying into firefights, taking a lot of punishment. They're exceptionally brave people and they're doing an outstanding job.

I was on the first Chinook lift along with the battery commander's TAC Group; we had to be on the first lift so I could control the air space and he could control the artillery fire. So we get close and a Dushka heavy machine gun starts firing at us. The door and tail gunners are returning fire like there's no tomorrow, there are RPGs being fired at us and here we are in an airborne petrol tank; your life is in the hands of the pilots and the rear gunners and you're completely reliant on the guys on the ground missing you. The most scary part of any mission for me was always the insert and exfil; it was terrifying, to be honest with you. Remember, this was early days and one of the lads got hit inside. A couple of Paras in one of the other Chinooks got shot –Private Steven Jones took a round in the shoulder and he was *still* desperate to get out and join the fight! We landed on and he was, 'Right, I can still go!' and his boss was 'No, come back!' They were superficial wounds thankfully … well, as superficial as it can get when you're shot.

So we land on and it's taking an age to get everything and everyone off. We should have only been on the ground for 20 seconds but we were there for over a minute. I was the last one to get off with my signaller, Sausage, and there were two guys in front of me, Colour Sergeant Stuart Bell and Sergeant Webb. We're taking fire from 360 degrees now so the pilot was desperate to lift; before we'd set off, the Paras had told the crews that if they found themselves on the ground for more than 30 seconds they were to lift off, even if there were troops aboard. I think there must have been a bit of a misunderstanding between the pilot and the loadmaster, though, because as Bell and Webb stepped off the ramp, the pilot started to lift. Well, they just fell off the ramp in mid-step; Bell fractured one of his legs and Webb broke his hand.

So we're just sitting there thinking, 'Shit!' We couldn't see the ground; Sausage and I just looked at each other and had the same thought. I don't think it was a conscious decision for either of us but there was no way we could have been left on the helicopter – can you imagine the ribbing we'd have got if we had? Also, I could only do my job on the ground – we were in the middle of a contact and I had to start controlling the assets to deal with it. I knew we couldn't have been that high because it was a quick decision; we knew we had to go bloody quickly because the aircraft was lifting so we just looked at each other and went, 'Right, go!'

We must have been about 15ft off the ground and as we jumped, the helicopter took our feet from under us, so we sort of somersaulted and landed on our backs, on to our gear. I was carrying about 90lb or so, what with the radio and the FAC kit, so although I was winded, we landed in a ploughed field so we were both absolutely fine. If we'd been another second or two slower in jumping, we would have been 30 or 40ft above ground, so the outcome would have been entirely different. But then you can go on forever like that; what if there'd been rocks instead of a ploughed field? What if we'd been shot as we stepped out? None of that happened; it's just the way it was. As for the other guys – they didn't jump, they fell, and that's probably why they got their injuries.

It was absolute carnage on the ground, complete chaos; it's pitch black, although we've got infrared cyalumes on the back and sides of our helmets, but we can't see a thing. It took us a second or two to orient ourselves but there's intense fire coming in from all sides, rounds, and RPGs flying and everyone is spread out taking cover in ditches and wherever they can. It was total confusion; people are shouting, trying to link up with whoever they're supposed to be with, the noise of the gunfire is deafening, and there's tracer fire overhead. The enemy fire was pretty ineffective but it was impossible for us to return accurate fire because we were keeping our heads down and we couldn't be sure that our own guys weren't in the way as everyone was so hard to identify – literally all you could see was enemy fire coming at you. The mission was in danger of being bogged down before it had even got under way and there's no way that the other Chinooks could put down while this was all going on.

We weren't sure what compound our target was in – there were three or four for us to choose from – but I could see a line of green tracer fire from one of them following the Chinook we'd flown in on. Close Air Support is perfect for a situation like this, although again, we were Danger Close so I got straight on the net and spoke to the AH and had him pour some fire into the compound. Seconds later, the AC130 spoke to me, so I cleared away the AH to give him clear fields of fire.

The AC130 Spectre is an absolutely awesome piece of kit. It's basically a converted Hercules C130 with one of the most complex aircraft weapon systems available, so it's able to fly at low speeds and can loiter for some time without refuelling. It uses high-definition low-light TV, infrared and radar sensors to locate ground targets, and has massive firepower – 40mm cannon, a 25mm Gatling gun and 40mm and 105mm howitzers. The crew were great because they said, 'We can see exactly where you've all deplaned, the Chinooks have gone, I can see the enemy around you, I can see four around a machine gun. ...' That was just brilliant, fantastic. You can see why they're used so much in high-intensity ops.

I talked them on to the compound and called for 105mm shells from the AC130 to destroy that position and it was incredible to see. It moved around the different positions, 360 degrees around where we were and just took them all out. We were taking fire while this was going on, from different locations, but most of it was going over our heads because the enemy couldn't see us. I fired a load of 40mm grenades and 16 105mm shells at different targets around our position and it completely annihilated them all. It proved to be completely decisive in that mission and allowed us to regain the initiative; all firing stopped so we were able to search the compounds. Our target had escaped but he was tracked by ISTAR and later killed as a time-sensitive target. That mission was a great success – we found loads of drugs, weapons, money and evidence.

Another Op that stands out was Operation *Mar Chichel* ('Snakebite' in Pashtu) on 6 August. The Pathfinders had held Musa Qala for almost two months but were taking a real hammering from the Taliban, and *Mar Chichel* was a huge battlegroup operation to get them out and a relief force in. A week or so earlier, a patrol from D Squadron of the Household Cavalry had attempted to help relieve some of the pressure but was ambushed at a nearby village. They'd gone in through a fairly narrow area and two Spartans were blown up by roadside bombs in an action that saw Lance Corporal of Horse Andrew Radford win his Conspicuous Gallantry Cross. We went in to recover the bodies and destroy the vehicles afterwards and it was hell – the temperature was 55°C, real punishment in itself and nearly everyone went down with heatstroke. We just couldn't operate in the kit we had, it was unbelievable. So for Operation *Mar Chichel*, the CO made a bold decision; no one needs to wear body armour.

That was a gutsy call but that's the kind of CO that he was. I think he'd realised that the weeks of fighting and living off composite rations in temperatures of up to 50 degrees was having a debilitating effect; wearing body armour, we felt fatigued, which affects your situational awareness. Allowing us to undertake operations without having to wear it ... I guess he thought that any physical protection that we lost as a result would be more than made up for by our ability to move faster and remain alert longer. We'd also use less water, reduce the risk of heat casualties ... and that in turn meant there'd be no subsequent risk to helicopters that might have to extract people due to heat exhaustion. That decision went down really well with the guys.

We had to get through several compounds to secure either side of the road that led through the Green Zone to Musa Qala. To achieve the initial break-in, air power was essential because we identified a massive IED among lots of blue containers that were lined up against a wall – that was our only way into town. I called in some fast air and dropped a 500lb bomb on to it and there was a massive secondary explosion. That enabled us to make progress on the initial phase of our attack. We fixed bayonets and started breaking into the compounds and working through each building to achieve the objective.

A large group of Taliban – eight or so – were just north of us and they opened up from the cover of some long grass. Sadly, Private Barrie Cutts, a 19-year-old gunner from the Royal Logistics Corps was killed. I tasked an Apache to have a look. The pilot saw the eight Taliban as they attempted to extract. There's nothing like the Apache's Flechette rockets for multiple personnel out in the open; once in flight, each rocket releases 85 inch-long Tungsten darts travelling at 2,460mph. They'll shred anything within a 50m spread and if they hit a human target their supersonic speed creates a vacuum that will suck up everything in its path. Once we'd agreed on the target, I took them all out.

Those incidents pretty much sum up the tour that we had; basically, every time we were on the ground, we were shot at. The weight of fire in a lot of places was unprecedented; it was non-stop and every FAC in theatre was busy. It would have been completely untenable for the Paras on the ground to achieve their objectives without Close Air Support. Every single patrol that went out had to have an FAC with it – that's the importance of it. Afghanistan is a land-centric war that couldn't be fought without air power. And often the ground troops couldn't destroy the enemy with small arms or .50 cals, so we'd call in air power to do the actual striking. It's a symbiotic relationship really; they both need each other. As it turned out, almost everything that we did was Danger Close; I think the Taliban knew that and they didn't want to fight too far away from us because they knew that we could drop bombs on them with impunity; the closer they got, the more difficult it was for us. There's a grudging respect for the Taliban; they may not be very well equipped and they may not be professional but they are certainly courageous. A few are Tier 1, die-hard fundamentalists. But a lot of them are local, forced to fight, and there are a lot of imported fighters, especially from Pakistan. We fought Chechnyans, Iranians, Pakistanis – they're the professionals.

We lost 15 people on that deployment, with 46 wounded; that's 61 people who to a lot of people back home are just names, but you get to know some of them very well indeed; you live with them, fight alongside them, laugh with them. Those of our friends who were killed made the papers back home and you'd often read about their deaths, but there's almost no coverage of the wounded and the really seriously injured – people who lost limbs, were burned and maimed, and whose lives were irrevocably changed. Why the lack of coverage for them?

There's no question, but going home was the definite high point for me. We handed over to the Royal Marines when we left and we were under contact during the handover! We were due to board one of the Chinooks that had brought some of the Royal Marines in but there was a massive contact going on and I was talking to an F16 pilot even as we waited. So I'm now saying to this guy, 'Hey, we're taking really heavy fire here and I need you to drop now!' We've got the helicopters coming in to get us so I need to stop the contact and people are being wounded. Anyway, he dropped the bomb and it all went quiet, enabling the helicopters to land. I can remember as my Chinook lifted off, though, I'm looking out the back and enemy mortars started hitting the HLS and I said to myself, 'Get me out of here, I've had enough!' It was quite unbelievable; no one expected it to be like that.

I suppose my experiences in Afghanistan have changed me on both a professional and a personal level. From a professional perspective, I've never known more about air power and its capabilities – we really forged the way forward for air/land integration, basically writing the book as we went along on how to do it. It represented a sea-change from what we had done previously. I trained the next group to deploy in how we'd done things and they've just come back from Afghanistan having replicated our MO successfully so, from that aspect, it's fantastic.

On a personal level, my wife says she's noticed changes in me. She says that I have a much shorter temper than before and far less time for things that annoy me – and trivial things that other people find important, I just don't get; I can see that they're futile but they're really important to other people. I found the most difficult thing was the lack of interest – it's not their fault, the intensity doesn't exist in normal life, but people just don't understand what it's like out there. It was difficult to reconcile – you know, just going in to Sainsbury's and seeing everyone getting on with their normal lives. Some woman would complain that there's something she wants not on the shelf. That is not important – these are minor, pathetic things – but yet they are important; in their life it's the biggest thing that's worrying them at the time. I've lost a bit of my empathy too, I suppose. I'm working on it, but I think what happened out there will always be with me. I think it just makes you a harder person. And if there are any long-term effects, I'm not entirely sure you can stop them from occurring; I know a lot of guys who have been deeply affected by the tour. It's not your everyday experience.

You exist in a bubble in theatre; life moves at such a different pace and you have no frame of reference – it's like a parallel world. I had to completely stop myself from thinking of home most of the time. And when I'd phone my wife it was just for the weekly 20 minutes; I wouldn't do any more than that. It was hard, but it was the only way I could deal with it; I had to be separated from it because the thought of never going home, or going home injured, or the thought of having twin boys who are three months old … if I'd allowed my 'real' life to intrude on the one out there, if I'd thought about that – I'd never have been able to do my job.

Obviously, what with the kids, I had a lot to divert my attention when I came back. They were only nine months old. That really changed our sense of priorities – things like that take over so I can't just sit down and dwell on what I've just been through. My whole focus has shifted on to the boys and I have no time to wallow and reflect. Of course, I did, but I tried to do it away from the family. I went through decompression when I came back, and at the time I thought it was a waste of bloody time. With hindsight though, I think it was a really good idea. It was definitely a good idea that the Paras didn't go straight home to Colchester – two days in Cyprus between end of tour and their return meant they had the chance to settle any frustrations or resentments that might have built up while they were away and they had ample time to build up their tolerance for alcohol again!

A while after I got back, my boss called me in and said, 'Right, you're going to London for drinks with the Chief of the Defence Staff at Christmas. We've chosen you as a sort of slap on the back, a "well done", for what you did on Herrick. You can take your wife and you'll have dinner with the CDS and a night at a hotel.' I thought, 'Blimey!' You know, brilliant, fantastic – a real honour. Sir Jock Stirrup was CDS at the time, so I was really chuffed. We went up to London and I saw a couple of people who I get on very well with and knew from Afghanistan – Major Hugo Farmer and Major Mark Hammond. We got together, and we were saying to each other, 'This is a bit weird – what's going on?'

So they sat us all down and someone came to the front of the room and said, 'I'm here to tell you that a number of you have been given awards.' And he read through them all – Navy first as the senior service, then the Army and then me at the end as the lone RAF guy. And he said, 'You've been given a Military Cross' and read out the citation. That was a complete shock to me, the first I knew of it.

I still hadn't really told my wife what had gone on. She knew I'd been in contacts because she'd heard a radio interview while I was in theatre; there was a journalist with us who'd recorded me calling in the AC130 during Operation Augustus with the sound of all the gunfire in the background. She knew it was me straight away. But we're at this hotel in London and the guy's reading the citation, and my wife heard the whole story. She couldn't believe it – she kept saying 'You did what?!' Actually, she was gobsmacked! But then so was I – I didn't even know what a Military Cross was then. It was the last thing on my mind, that people would be getting awards. It was really amazing.

We had a fantastic meal and quite a few drinks that night and the next day we had a press conference where Sir Jock Stirrup introduced each of us to the Press and read out our citations. I felt very guilty by then because I'd had a chance to think and while it's fantastic to be given an award, I don't think I did anything more than the rest of the troops over there; we were all in contact. we were all doing our jobs, and all doing the business. My second-in-command or signallers were no less brave than I was and they didn't get an award. You don't find bravery, it finds you. It was just the fact that I was written up by Lieutenant Colonel Stuart Tootal and the battery commander. I still feel like I don't deserve it, though. Everyone was very brave in the things they were doing over there, but saying that, I'm still immensely proud of having been given a Military Cross – it was the first MC for 50 years awarded to someone serving in the RAF Regiment so I was really pleased about that.

When I went up to Buckingham Palace for the investiture I brought my mum, dad and my wife along. Prince Charles pinned it on to my chest and he was fantastic. They're very good at what they do; I mean he knew a bit of the background behind what had happened and for the 40 seconds I was talking to him he asked me what it was like to be an FAC. But, yeah, unbelievable – a brilliant day.

I honestly think that there should be some way of recognising the wives and families; to me, it's my wife who deserved the medal. Like all those left behind, she had to try and get on with some semblance of life on her own without ever knowing where I was or what I was doing. Coupled with that, she had the twins to cope with. To me, that's far harder than anything I did.

SQUADRON LEADER
ROLY SMITH

OC 591 SIGNALS UNIT

No 591 SU is responsible for monitoring RAF communications security. Its remit incorporates Limited Electronic Sweeps for Clandestine Eavesdropping Devices, a role that it now conducts worldwide. The unit has the capability to conduct a wide range of computer security tasks on all computer systems throughout the RAF, establishing a range of defensive measures to protect the information on individual systems and major network systems.

In the current era of expeditionary air operations, 591 SU personnel have increasingly been deployed to Out-of-Area locations to perform a range of tasks in support of air operations. Squadron Leader Roly Smith is the OC of 591 Signals Unit and is based at Kandahar.

I'm based in Lincolnshire and when I'm not in Afghanistan my role is as the OC of 591 Signals Unit. Our remit is simple in theory – basically, it's to prevent our secrets being given away to the enemy. My role out here is as the lead for information assurance in Op Herrick, so it's same meat, different gravy – I'm out here to ensure that we don't give our secrets away to the Taliban. To put that in practical terms, the things that I'm interested in potentially are based around internet usage. A lot of open source material is published on the internet, so professionally I have an interest in how the internet is being used.

My job here is specifically concerned with all British forces in theatre – basically for all of Op Herrick within the whole of Afghanistan. My role as the OC of the unit back at home is right across the RAF but the job is broadly similar. So it's internet, it's welfare, phone usage, the protection of our computer systems, telephone networks … basically any ways in which we can be unintentionally leaking information to the enemy.

I don't do any monitoring here, as such. Most of my day-to-day work is reported to me as incidents, which either the police have come across or system administrators have reported to me. I act as the central focus for all computer-related incidents, so if somebody loses a USB stick then that would come through me; if somebody reported a virus on a system that would come through me; malicious phone calls made to families in the UK, they get reported to me; then I report them back to the UK, so I act as the central focus within Herrick for all of that. I'll touch on blogs – basically, if it's published openly and easily accessible then I need to know about it. Facebook can be a concern, although usually you need to be a friend of somebody to view what is on their profile; however, there are networks where anyone who is a member of that network can view any other member's profile.

Our ultimate objective is to stop the bad guys getting hold of useful information and really there are three things you can do to achieve that. The first is education; a lot of people aren't aware that they're actually giving away information – I call it unconscious incompetence. A good example of that would be a British soldier taking a photo of his friend with all his kit laid out and posting it up on a blog, which we've seen in Op Telic and no doubt we will continue to see. That type of information when published gives a lot of intelligence to the enemy which could potentially be very useful. It might sound innocuous enough, but information can also be intelligence – it depends who is looking at it, but the bottom line is we don't want to give it away. As I said, something like that – a photo on a blog – that's not done consciously, it's done without thinking, so education is really the key here.

The second thing is monitoring, and that is really about ensuring that awareness and education is up to date. Finally, there's the technical compliance side, which is kind of a safety net, to make sure that our systems are as secure as they can be. To a degree, it feels like we are always reacting, playing catch-up with technological advances, but it's not just technological – it's also cultural. The youngsters, the next generation coming through, are a digital generation. They've grown up in a world where the technology that those of us over thirty have had to assimilate is second nature to them. They have integrated digital culture seamlessly into their lives so that for many, the internet, videogames, downloading music on to an iPod, or multitasking with a cell phone is what they do. They're the kids who, when they were working on a homework assignment, had several other tabs open on the PC where they would chat with friends, browse the web and listen to music, while absent-mindedly channel surfing on that old technology, the TV. They've never known a world without technology, and social networking sites like Bebo, MySpace, and Facebook are part of their lives.

There is a wi-fi system on trial down at Camp Bastion, which I think could be hugely beneficial if it's taken up. I think that the majority of younger people actually use the internet as much for communication as they do the telephone – in many cases they use it more frequently because Skype, AIM, or MSN are all useful tools and they're probably more familiar for most of the younger people in theatre as a method of communication.

The key to effecting change, shifting people's perceptions, lies in education. It's all about making people aware – making them aware about what they're putting on their blogs, Facebook pages etc. On 591 SU, the unit that I command back home, we go out and talk to those on the courses, the pre-deployment courses etc, to try and drive that message home. We're there to raise people's awareness of what information can be used for by the enemy and to just make them think twice before they do something which they might think of as perfectly normal.

There are countless illustrations of other compromise or potential problems, but in terms of completely unclassified examples, mobile phone usage is of particular concern to us in this theatre, and here I'm talking about the threat from British soldiers even switching on their personal UK mobiles while they're deployed here. If a UK-registered phone is used in this theatre it has the very strong potential to be flagged and monitored by 'unfriendly organisations', be they state or otherwise. It's not just the contents of any conversation between UK forces and their friends or family back home that are of concern to us, it's the numbers that they dial or text outside of Afghanistan which could then lead to malicious calls to that soldier's family. That plays into the hands of enemy psy-ops against us – it is something that has been well documented in the press.

Then there's the triangulation aspect; a UK soldier out on patrol who has his phone switched on could, under certain circumstances, give the position of his whole platoon away, so it's certainly a concern. You can actually go on to websites now like www.traceamobile.com to track your wife, your kids etc, so it would be child's play to the Taliban here in theatre. That's a more abstract worry, though; in the main it's more a psy-ops issue. It puts a load on theatre every time a family member is called up and told that their loved ones are in danger. So there's an operational impact and obviously a psychological impact on the people out here and those back home.

Here in theatre I don't have a specific team assigned to me. What I do is I reach back to the UK to provide specialist advice and teams into theatre, so some of the work that they will conduct for me is Tempest checks; they will come out and do computer network defence testing, compliance testing and monitoring. In fact, on the Air Force side, 591 is the largest and has the widest portfolio of capabilities within defence, so the Royal Air Force really has got the lead in this area, which is why the posting here has been exclusively filled by the RAF. The other services can't provide any of that; they don't have that skill set.

The reason why the RAF has that capability and the other services don't is, I think, down to several factors. Certainly the Army has reduced its monitoring capabilities in light of the introduction of Bowman, which in itself is secure; they've therefore been able to let a lot of that go on to the back burner. My sister Army unit is called the LIAG – the Land Information Army Group – and they're Territorial Army civilians who work in industry on computer network defence, so they're very specialised and quite focused just on computer network defence. Of course, being TA, they are mostly part-time, so to get them into theatre isn't straightforward – it requires them to leave work for an extended period of time, and so on. The Navy has a team but it is quite small and they tend to focus on defensive monitoring of HF nets mainly, whereas 591 SU has got a much wider portfolio of capabilities such as Tempest – defensive monitoring and an education team. It also monitors the internet, so it's got a much wider set of skills.

If we identify a breach the process varies. We have no control over what goes over the internet but, for instance, if someone posts something to a site such as PPRuNe (Professional Pilots' Rumour Network) or ARRSE, which is the Army Rumours network, which we spot, we do have contacts within those websites – the moderators – and they are very good in terms of removing things voluntarily when we point them out.

One of the things that's particularly important, and that we take all possible steps to prevent, is the premature leaking of information regarding deaths of British servicemen and women here in theatre. As soon as word gets back to the Ops room of any fatality among British personnel, we implement something called Op Minimise whereby we shut down all our welfare networks. That means that the internet, email, the Paradigm phone system – it's all closed down until the fatality has been correctly identified and the next of kin notified via official channels. Only then will the details be released to the media and the welfare networks opened up again to all, rather than just operational traffic.

While I don't have a direct team within theatre, I can draw on the team and resources of the JFCIS (Joint Force Communications Information Systems), which is the organisation responsible for all British comms within theatre. It's headed by a Royal Air Force group captain, but the majority of the manpower is actually provided by an Army unit – 16 Signals Regiment. Nonetheless, it's very much a joint team. Here at Kandahar, we have also got TCW, the Tactical Communications Wing, and they provide all of our first-line support. At many of the other locations, we have probably a majority 16 Signals Regiment but we've also got TCW forward to provide specialist support. While it would be fair to say that the Army make up the majority of personnel here, we more than make up for it in augmentation.

It's interesting how the perceptions of our friends and family back home have changed recently, so it's only fair to assume that there has also been a change of thinking among the wider population. I don't think that anyone I know regards what I do out here as a safe, desk-bound job. I've been in the RAF for over 15 years now so I've seen a lot of changes, but one of the most major is that so many people in the service have deployed on operations, whether in Kosovo, Op Telic, Op Herrick, or elsewhere. Plus my teams at 591 SU are constantly out on ops – again, in Iraq, Afghanistan, and all over the world. Their friends and family know only too well what it's all about.

Obviously, doing what we do based at KAF, or Bastion or wherever, is never going to expose us to anything like the level of risk that the guys in the FOBs live with, but there's still the threat of IDF from rockets and mortars, which tends to interrupt play throughout the week. But for me personally, I think that the largest challenges working out here, both from my own and from a communications perspective, are actually the environmental issues – the heat, the dust and all of those things which affect our systems. You also need to have as good an understanding as you can of the pressures that are on the infantry and the people deployed forward. The rules and regulations which were put in place at the main operating base don't quite apply down at FOBs, so you have to be permanently mindful of the balance between security and operational necessity and the conditions in which they are working.

I have to say, from a personal perspective, this has been a fascinating tour for me. I've been in theatre for ten weeks now and have just got back from R&R so I'm midway through, but it's been interesting and I've garnered some useful experience. From a personal viewpoint, I think one of the highlights for me was getting down on to the ranges with the Americans and getting to fire a few of their weapons. We're all on the same side and they're quite open and amenable in letting us go down to the ranges – they use our weapons, we use theirs but it's all under careful control and it's good to blat off 200 rounds from their light support weapons. For me, as an RAF guy, I enjoy that, and they've got a good simulator down there, so you can try a little bit of urban clearance on their computer ranges etc. I thoroughly enjoy any time I can get down on the ranges so that would definitely be a highlight. That said, it's all thrown into sharp relief in coming back from R&R – that's always a bit of a low point for everyone. You get the R&R blues for a few days but you soon shake it off.

It takes some adjustment getting used to living in theatre because however safe and established it is here at KAF, it's still an operational deployment and life is a world away from what you're used to. You miss the colour – KAF can be a very monochromatic environment, what with the sand and the dust that coats everything in a fine talc-like powder. You find yourself missing colour – some nice green grass, trees, even a bit of rain sometimes! Obviously, you tend to miss your family and friends but it's also the more mundane elements of life, or the minutiae that you find yourself thinking about in quiet moments. I have a passion for flying model aircraft – I build and fly them, both aircraft and helicopters, and I use them to do a little bit of aerial photography, which I find interesting. They're all electric aircraft, so they run on specialist batteries and motors which allow them to fly upside down and pull stupid stunts or hover; even the helicopters can all fly upside down and bounce around the sky because they're not fossil-fuel based, so they can't be starved of juice. It's a relatively new technology that allows them to be more powerful than their fuel-based equivalents. I love it!

My family is back in Lincolnshire in married quarters, and having children means I'm all too familiar with the frustration affecting everyone else in terms of communications, although I think that we're very well served here at KAF from a communications perspective. We have plenty of welfare internet facilities so there are plenty of PC terminals in air-conditioned cabins that people can use when they're off duty, to browse the web or email home. Then there are the Paradigm phones – every person deployed to theatre gets 30 minutes of calls home each week, which is all paid for and you can top that up by buying credit if you wish. I think it goes without saying that everyone would love wi-fi here – that would make a huge difference to everyone at KAF, but that's something that needs to be addressed in the future. We're exceptionally well-off here compared to a lot of other places where the comms aren't so good. A lot of people further out have to use Meridian phones etc, so I think at Kandahar we're extremely well served and I think that's probably true at Bastion, Lashkar Gāh, and Kabul as well. The FOBs are where it's really needed.

Aside from the security aspect, I think that there are three things that affect and consequently inform the issues that define my role in theatre, but I'm not sure that I could put them in any particular order. One is the availability and control of stand-alone IT; one of the problems

FLIGHT LIEUTENANT
MATT BARTLETT

HERCULES PILOT

The RAF's Hercules C130 aircraft move everything from ammunition and ground-support equipment to passengers and their luggage; in fact more or less anything required for the ongoing operations in Afghanistan, which can fit inside the aircraft's hold. The detachment prides itself on the adage, 'if it fits in the back of a Herc, it will go in a Herc'.

The crews and support personnel are working at a high tempo, with between two and three sorties being flown every day. Add to the equation the environmental factors such as the heat, dust and wind and it's easy to see how well the personnel and aircraft are performing in difficult conditions.

With most of the flying done at night, the engineers do their work during the day in temperatures as high as 55°C.

Flight Lieutenant Matt Bartlett is a Hercules captain based at Kandahar Airfield and has done two deployments to Afghanistan.

I'm with XXIV Squadron based at RAF Lyneham, which is the home of all the RAF's Hercules C130 aircraft. I joined the RAF in 2000 having completed four years at university, during which I received a bursary from the RAF for my final year.

I've always, always, from my earliest memory, wanted to fly, and the Air Force was the only way that I was going to do it. I grew up in the North East of England and although I was certainly never deprived as a child, there was not a lot of money knocking around, so I knew I'd never manage to finance flying training myself. I knew I wanted to fly from the time I was knee-high and for me, the route to doing it was always going to be through the RAF, so that was what I set my sights on. I think that everybody dreams of flying fast jets when they join, but I learned quite early on that it wasn't going to be for me. I did my elementary flight training while I was at university, where I flew around 96 hours on Bulldogs, and at the end of that, I was streamed on to multi-engines, which for me meant the Hercules. I completed my first tour as a co-pilot flying the C130K before transferring onto the J model as a captain. I've got around 3,000 hours logged now and I love it.

I knew Lyneham and the Herc world was for me because I'd spent some time there before I did my conversion training; it's a great job, a fantastic aircraft and what particularly appealed to me was the crew atmosphere at Lyneham; I'd spent a month up at RAF Kinloss beforehand, looking at the Nimrod, but the combination of the crew and the prospect of flying the Herc really sold it for me. The RAF operates two types of Hercules. The original C130K model, which came into service in the late '60s, flies with a basic crew of five: a captain, co-pilot, navigator, flight engineer and loadmaster, and if you're going away from home base you'll also fly with a ground engineer (GE), so 5 + 1 is the minimum you'll take.

The 'J' model is more modern, with a smaller crew: a captain, co-pilot and loadmaster plus a GE if you're flying away from home base. It's a tactical air transporter and we use it to carry anything from troops to vehicles – if it fits inside, it'll be carried on a Hercules. A decent load would be up to around 13 tonnes of freight and/or passengers – that would enable us to have sufficient fuel to undertake a meaningful sortie and not be overweight on landing, because a lot of the operating limits depend on landing weight rather than at take-off. Basically, the forces and stresses involved at landing are far greater than those for getting airborne. We're quite fortunate in that all the Hercs involved in normal ops in Afghanistan are 'J' models, and with it being such a modern aircraft, it isn't subject to the same restrictions that the harsh operating environment there places on some of our other airframes. The 'J' flies on four modern free turbine, turboprop engines and they are hugely capable when operating at the altitudes and temperatures in theatre that are so restrictive to older engines.

I've done two deployments to Afghanistan so far and I should have another two or three to do in the next year. My first det came in June

2008 and I was flying as a captain. When we deploy, we do so as a full crew for however long the deployment lasts – in our case, a month at a time – you work with the same guys. Back in the UK it's a bun fight; that gives us a lot more flexibility back home, as obviously some guys will be on leave or on different courses so the ability exists to pluck people from different places. It's my responsibility as captain to ensure that my crew are fit to deploy – there are certain hoops that everyone has to jump through, common core skills such as weapon handling tests, zeroing of weapons, CBRN drills, annual fitness test and such like.

I was really happy when I found out I was being deployed to Afghanistan, although I felt mild apprehension; not because of where I was headed or what I might have to do but because it was my first operational deployment as a captain. I think it's natural to feel slightly apprehensive at that; it would be cavalier not to and I think that a little uncertainty raises your senses and awareness. That said, I was really excited about going and I couldn't wait to get out there and do the job. I'd deployed on Op Telic as a captain on a number of occasions previously but Herrick felt different – it would be my first deployment in the TACAT (Tactical Air Transport) role where we would be flying airdrop sorties and landing on short, unprepared strips.

We were based at Kandahar when we deployed – the airfield is very firmly established now. We flew out as a formed crew from RAF Brize Norton and, on arrival, went straight to the Passenger Handling Facility with everyone else from our TriStar. We collected our bags, weapons and the like, and were then 'processed' as it were, so that there was official confirmation we were in theatre. After that, we were met by our Chief of Staff who took us down to the C130 det which is held within 904 EAW and that's where we had our proper arrival brief – we picked up ammunition for our personal weapons, morphine, tourniquets, field dressings and all those bits and pieces that you need while you're out there – and hope you'll never have to use. Then you start the process of reading and signing for all the local orders, flying order books, secret folders and the like, just so you are up to speed with all the procedures and protocols that are current at that moment in theatre. Fourteen hours after that, we were flying our first mission.

Most of the mission profiles that we flew in theatre were quite straightforward really – air transport between Bastion, Kabul and Kandahar, airdrops to resupply the FOBs, that sort of thing. A typical day would probably see us flying Kandahar to Bastion and back four times a day, so that's eight sectors. We'd crew in 90 minutes before departure. Before we walk out to the aircraft, we'll get an Intel brief, file the flight plan and check the weather for all the destinations we're due to go to, look at NOTAMs etc – they tell us which runways might be closed, or that a certain bit of airspace will be active or whatever – then we'll pick up our rifles, ammunition and the secret folders that we fly with detailing all the relevant COMMS procedures, frequencies, arrival and departure procedures for all the airfields that we'll visit.

We fly by day and by night in theatre. I think in the last four weeks of my detachment in June, I flew more than twice the number of hours by night compared to what I did in the day. We'll fly all sorts during the day if it's safe to do so and the mission demands it – it's just sometimes it's safer at night and we can undertake whatever suits the objective. We carry freight and passengers from point A to point B or sometimes we'll airdrop stuff for resupply. I've done a few daylight sorties to Farah, which is out to the west of Kandahar – it's literally a little dirt strip in the middle of nowhere. Kabul is one of the places where we won't normally go by day because the perceived threat there is so much greater – it's a huge city and the airfield is quite confined. You're restricted as there's less opportunity to fly random or offset approaches so that you're not lined up on the runway centreline at ten miles out much like everyone else would be, going to a normal airfield. We try and keep things as random as possible and Kabul Airfield doesn't lend itself to that very well, so we tend to go there only in the darkness unless there's a very good reason such as aeromeds, which is another big thing we do.

With aeromeds, we tend to move casualties who have already been brought into Bastion or Kandahar – they'll have been stabilised and will need moving on. It varies greatly from walking wounded who can help themselves, to really critical cases that will have what's called a CCAST (Critical Care Air Support Team) along – CCAST literally tend to everything, short of doing actual airborne surgery, although I think they'd do that too if they actually had to. They, like the MERTs (Medical Emergency Response Teams) on the helicopters, do a phenomenal job – they must see and endure some terrible sights but it's a peculiarity of the Hercules that we (the captain and the co-pilot) are completely detached from it all as the cockpit is only accessible via a staircase. Invariably, we're sat at the front with the engines running, while loading or unloading, and the loadmaster is at the back seeing everything and having to deal with the aftermath. It's a weird disconnect for us – we're so close but so far removed at the same time. It's peculiar because we work in such a tight environment as a crew – we live together, work together, and yet we're on the same aircraft and the loadmaster is being exposed to so much more than we are at the front.

Of all the mission profiles that we undertake, I think that airborne resupplies – airdrops – are by far the most challenging. About a week or so before the actual drop, the planning is usually done by the FOB or location requesting the resupply; they'll detail exactly what they require and where they want it dropped, which could literally be anything: rations, water, and ammunition – we dropped toilet seats on one sortie, which was one of the more peculiar things I've seen go out the back. With the 'K' model Hercs we can even drop Land Rovers, which is great to watch. We also drop a lot of HESCO – you know, the blocks that they fill with earth to build the walls with – so they'll bid for what they want and tell us when they want it.

The FOBs rely heavily on airdrops for resupply because everything else has to be moved by land or helicopter, which is time-consuming and risky – anything moved by land is very manpower-intensive and prone to IED attack, so it's hit and miss as to whether stores will get through that way. If a Chinook is used, its payload is significantly lower than what we can push out the back of a Herc. There are plus points to the other methods; if it's coming in by road, it arrives at the camp gates and goes straight into where it's required, and if it comes in by helicopter they will invariably land in the camp itself. For an airdrop, the DZ is going to be away from the FOB, so they'll need to recce the area, secure it, and then spend a finite amount of time on the ground collecting all the pallets that we've pushed out. Like most things in life, it's a matter of compromise.

We work out the height we are going to drop from, depending on the
weather and the load, and we'll plan the drop four to five hours before
we are due to get airborne. A lot of the accuracy relies on predicting the
wind and knowing the exact weight of the containers. The CDS
(Container Delivery System) in the 'J' model C130 consists of two
banks of containers in the back of the aircraft, and depending on
whether it's a Mark 4 aircraft (which is longer) or a Mark 5 (the shorter
one), will determine how many containers we can actually get on.
Obviously, the mass is an important figure, too, but realistically we'll
push out about 13 tonnes on each drop; each container is good for
anything up to about 1 ton, really. The navigation kit is very clever;
basically you program in the surface wind and it will take a feed of the
actual wind at altitude; it then calculates a ballistic wind, which is
effectively the average wind that the load will experience for the
duration of its fall. It then says, 'Right, you need to fly over this point,
on this heading and at this speed' and the container will land on
the DZ.

It's all done automatically, that's the beauty of the system, although
there are certain things that have to be actioned as we're running in;
we open the back of the aircraft manually, and at 15 seconds the call is
'Action Stations' and the loadmaster moves a switch at the back to
de-isolate the system. With five seconds to run, we call 'Red on' and he
moves another switch to finally arm the system. At zero or 'Green on',
the system automatically releases the containers. It's up to me to be in
the right place – the kit tells me where to be but I have to put the
aircraft in the exact location. As they go out, the loads are retarded by
parachutes, which are extracted and deployed automatically. However,
not every parachute will work perfectly every time, leading to another
problem we have when we are doing a lot of containers at once –
multiple drops suffer from something called 'air stealing' where a
parachute will inflate below another parachute and steal the air from
it, meaning the uppermost won't inflate properly; it's something we
call 'candling' where the load falls to earth without the proper
retardation of its parachute. It's quite rare – I would say one canopy in
every two drops or so, which doesn't sound fantastic but actually we're
getting 90 per cent of the load on to the ground. So long as it's not their

fresh rations it's not such an issue – the guys depend on them and they get really upset if the load breaks up, for obvious reasons. If it's bottled water, it's not such an issue.

Our drop speed is quite slow, so it's clearly when we are at our most vulnerable. With two banks of eight containers going out the back, it takes a finite time for them to leave the aircraft so the spread of that departure means that the first container will land within say 50yd of the PI (Point of Impact), but the others are going to be some distance away. It's getting better over time but there's still a huge perception gap between what the guys on the ground expect and what we're actually capable of. I think a lot of the Army lads expect pinpoint accuracy because they've seen the RAF launching precision-guided missiles that can strike a specific target, even one inside a building 30 miles from launch! On that basis, many of them think that they're going to get 12 tonnes of stores delivered to them and it's all going to land on an area the size of a piece of A4 paper just 10yd from the camp gates, which would be brilliant if we could actually deliver that. Unfortunately, you have the time it takes for everything to leave the aircraft and then the time that each load sits under the canopy when they're going to be affected by ballistic winds, so the first load will land close to the intended point of impact but the last container out could be 1,500 metres away. Fortunately, once the guys have seen what happens, they learn the mechanics of how it actually works PDQ!

There are plans afoot to try and reduce the spread but there are other planning factors involved in that and other considerations; what happens if by trying to reduce the spread the loads land on top of each other and end up having to be written off? There's so much that goes into it, so many variables and so many factors, it's almost impossible to change one thing so that everything becomes better. What would be a major help to us at the moment would be more feedback from the guys on the ground – the status quo tends to be a policy of 'no news is good news' so we presume that everything is okay unless we hear anything from the DZ. Ideally, we'd get a strike report telling us where the nearest container to the planned point of impact was and the survivability of the load, because not every load will hit the ground and survive.

For me, flying airdrops is when I feel most vulnerable, flying so slow.

We vary the times that we fly over the DZs (Drop Zones) and we'll change the run-ins that we use over them too, although it's highly unlikely that anyone who doesn't 'need to know' will be aware of where we're going or when we'll be there. By necessity, FOBs are situated in or near built-up areas so depending on wind direction, we might have to over-fly some very urban areas. Small arms are prolific in Helmand and there might be a day when somebody is disgruntled and in their back yard, waving his AK47 and having a go. We wouldn't know anything about it unless they scored a 'lucky' hit or until we landed and did a walk around to check the airframe, though. It's weird at night; we fly without lights and the only illumination within the cockpit comes from the faint ethereal glow of the instruments. Even they're barely lit because we fly on NVGs, which detach you from everything still further; unless there are tracer rounds arcing into the sky at night, you won't see it and you won't hear it.

I guess the threat to us as individuals is pretty remote; we're at the extreme limit of capability for small-arms fire, so it's not like it is for the guys on the ground. And the threat to the airframe is pretty limited; the Hercules is pretty robust and it's got a lot of redundancy built in; there are a lot of systems but it's engineered to be that way so that it can suffer damage and continue. The cockpit itself is armoured and we all fly with body armour so I wouldn't say that I feel hugely vulnerable. I think that the biggest threat to the aircraft wouldn't be them shooting at it and its systems failing – it would be a lucky shot indeed that got into the cockpit and took out both pilots! The only other real threat to us would be a SAM [Surface-to-Air Missile] that took us down; even if we got the airframe down in one piece, we'd be far behind enemy lines. That is a real possibility and not something I like to dwell on, although we've all been trained for it; hopefully, we'd get picked up pretty quickly. Our best defence is our tactics, which basically dictate that we stay as high as possible for as long as possible and remain out of the threat band. All the aircraft we fly in theatre are fitted with defensive aids and they can defeat any threat currently known.

If I've got any frustrations, and this is probably going to sound really petty, it's not being able to get a hot meal. KAF is very well established and maintained, but they feed at regular daytime hours. When we work the night shift, we don't get up until the evening, and by then we've missed lunch and we're too early for dinner. We go to work and fly sorties until the early hours and by the time we've shut down the aircraft and booked off, nobody wants to wait around until breakfast as we need to get our mandated crew rest so that we're legal to fly the next day. There are ways and means of getting food if you like, but it's really frustrating that there isn't a feeder where you can get a proper meal. It's not only us – we're in a war zone, so by necessity a lot of flying takes place at night. It's being addressed but it's one of those things that shouldn't even be an issue; it sounds so pathetic. An Army marches on its stomach and the Air Force flies on theirs. Food is a huge morale thing in theatre; on the odd days that you hit the feeder and the times just work for you, you think, 'Right, we're going into work a little bit later, if we get up half an hour earlier we can get dinner and go straight on to work' and everyone says 'Oh wow, brilliant.'

I think we're really lucky being based at KAF, especially compared to what the guys on the ground have to hack. I miss my girlfriend hugely, but that goes with the turf and I suppose in that regard, I'm luckier than most as she is in the RAF too and has a better understanding than most of how these things work. I can tell her, 'I'm going away and I might not be able to speak to you for a month' and she just gets on with it. It's always harder for the ones we leave behind, having to get on with life as normal. I miss her dearly though – and I miss the rest of the family. Outside of people, I think I probably most miss having a beer after work; Kandahar is completely dry but it's not the idea of going and getting completely hammered – I miss just being able to sit with the crew and talk over the mission over a can or two of ice cold lager. Yeah, I think that would be it – especially in June or July when it's really hot! And real tea as well – the tea bags out there are atrocious, so most of us have started taking our own!

There are some great pluses to our job in theatre. I mean for me, the first thing is the flying; I just love flying, it's all I ever wanted to do and I'm still doing it – I still get a buzz from it. The flying in Afghanistan really is something special; it's beautiful, one of the most spectacular countries I've ever seen and its scenery is second to none. It sounds ridiculous but it's the sort of country I'd love to go to on holiday and climb mountains in, just not at the moment! It's stunning: you talk to people, try and describe it but they don't get it – it's just incredible. I love the transition as you leave the desert behind and travel across the Green Zone, and then you've got the mountain ranges around Sangin, which give way to Kajaki and the emerald waters at the dam. It's quite breathtaking.

More practically, though, I think all of us draw immense satisfaction from the airdrop missions that we fly; it's particularly rewarding knowing that you've resupplied a FOB with enough ammunition, water, or food and rations to keep them going; it's hugely satisfying knowing that those guys on the ground are getting what they need. I'm under no illusions that we have a very nice existence in Afghanistan and there are some people out there who are working very, very hard in some horribly austere conditions and who are getting attacked by the Taliban every single day of the week. I take my hat off to those guys – they're the ones who are really earning their money. It's a weird existence up there in the cockpit at night, looking at the world down below though a set of NVGs. You can see tracer, explosions, flares going up, so you know that our guys are in a contact but we're several thousand feet up and completely detached from what's going on. In some respects, it's like watching a movie with the sound turned down, except you know that it's our guys down there and the bullets are real. I've never had to shoulder my rifle in anger and I've never had to fire a shot or had somebody shooting directly at me.

Sure, I've been at Kandahar and been on the receiving end of rocket attacks a few times a week and yes, that can be a little unnerving, but actually it's not a direct attack against me, it's not somebody looking directly at me and saying, 'I'm going to kill you.' The rocket attacks become more of an annoyance sometimes but it's the law of averages really – if they throw enough rockets at camp, they'll hit something important eventually. It's like that old IRA saying – 'you have to be lucky every single day, but we need only be lucky once'. In some respects, it's not just the awful loss of life that would entail if a rocket landed on the Mess during dinner or took out a Herc waiting to take off; I think the backlash at home from something like that would be difficult to bear. So for me, I'm quite happy with our tactics and the way we go and do business.

Although I haven't actually flown any in theatre, one of the more solemn jobs that we can undertake is that of repatriations. The Hercules fleet used to undertake them all from Camp Bastion but things changed back in June 2008 when the C17s took over the role. I've spoken to some of the guys who have done it and while it's not a particularly nice job, it's a vital one. Everyone does it with the utmost dignity and there's a right way of doing it. I guess people are proud to do it in a way, but it's not the sort of job you want to do. Repatriations used to go into Brize Norton but there's long-term work going on there now so they're all going into RAF Lyneham. I did one in the UK a couple of years ago, flying a fallen soldier and six of his family and members of his platoon to RAF Aldergrove.

The whole station stops when an aircraft arrives carrying our dead – rightly so, I think. Everyone there pays their respects and there's a formal ceremony of repatriation, so the coffin is marched off the aircraft into a hearse and all the family are there to receive it. The local town closest to Lyneham is Wootton Bassett and every time a funeral cortège goes through, the whole town stops – never less than 150 people, sometimes as many as 500 every single repatriation. [Wootton Bassett had not received the media attention it has at the original time of writing, now the high street is full with mourners paying their respects every repatriation.] They've turned out over 100 times now and everyone lines the streets. By way of a thank you, we put on a parade for them in 2008 – it was a tri-service affair, not just Lyneham personnel, with a couple of fly-pasts. Just a really big thank you to the people of the town for the way they've honoured our dead servicemen and women. It's really quite moving.

It's really quite a bizarre war, what's happening in Afghanistan. There are so many of us out there and even from an RAF perspective, we all experience a different war that depends on what we fly or the job we do. You've got the RAF Regiment guys living rough on 48-hour patrols where they're talking with local Afghanis, rebuilding communities and dodging IEDs and mines, while looking for the Taliban. Then there are the support helicopter guys who land in hot LZs, taking fire as they transition in and out. The fast-jet crews engage Taliban on the ground and there's us flying the Hercules at altitude and living in the relative luxury of KAF (Kandahar Airfield), away from most of the trouble. All the personnel at Kandahar do a great job in supporting the operational output, but might not know too much of the war except for the occasional rocket attack. The medics have one of the toughest jobs, dealing with the horrific injuries our troops sustain. We all see a different war.

So many of my peers talk about how their experiences have changed them, how what they've seen and done has shaped their personalities and I guess that might even be true for some of my own crew, where the loadmaster has had to deal with severely wounded soldiers in the back. I wonder sometimes if I should feel a certain amount of guilt because I haven't been exposed to it; I don't know if that's right or not. I would like to think that if I had to deal with what some of the others have, I would be able to cope with it and still be able to get on and do my job. Perhaps the fact that there is that disconnection and distance from everything allows me to focus on my job and not be distracted, though. We all have a job to do and we all do it to the best of our abilities.

FLIGHT LIEUTENANT
ELEANOR JAYNE LODGE

CHINOOK PILOT

RAF Chinook helicopters form part of the Joint Helicopter Force in Afghanistan and are the backbone for the provision of tactical mobility for land forces. They transport supplies and troops across country, and also fulfil the role of Combat Air Ambulance. Crews on the Incident Response Team live, eat and sleep in a single tent, waiting for the call that will see them airborne as quickly as possible, flying a surgical team to the aid of wounded troops, civilians – and even Taliban fighters.

The flying skill of the pilots is legendary; often landing under fire, they've been known to touch down on one wheel to allow casualties to be loaded, while holding the rotor disk to one side so as to avoid striking a nearby building. The RAF's Chinooks are in high demand in theatre; this means that their crews are stretched to the limit, working long hours under punishing conditions that stretch the helicopters' capacity to the limit.

Flight Lieutenant Eleanor Lodge is a relatively junior Chinook pilot with just a few years' service, but she has acquired considerable flying hours in a relatively short time span, due to the intensity of flight operations in theatre.

I'm known as Elle and I'm a Chinook pilot with 'A' Flight, 27 Squadron based at RAF Odiham. There's no service connection in my family – just me, but I hadn't initially planned on a military career. I'd always wanted to fly; I originally wanted to be an airline pilot so I started looking at the RAF as a way into that, although I soon changed my mind when I saw what the RAF could offer. I put my application in before I did my A levels, left school in August 2002, aged 18, and started training with the RAF that October. I joined as a direct entry pilot, got my wings in 2005 and my first det [detachment] to Afghanistan came in December 2006.

I was made an operational captain for the first time in October 2007 and I'm approaching 800 hours total flying time on type now; enough to be able to operate the aircraft to a relatively competent degree, although not quite enough to deal with everything it's going to throw at me. That'll come with time, though.

This is my third tour in Afghanistan; we did two within two years but Chinooks are in such high demand here so the pace is relentless. This det is slightly different to the others I've done in that it's May to July so the conditions really take their toll on the aircraft; it's hot, so they perform less capably than they do in the winter. It's also silly season with regard to the Taliban; the locals have finished harvesting the poppies and the Taliban are resupplied with money to enable them to come out and fight – it's been very noticeable since we arrived at the end of the harvest; this time of year is always the worst.

We deploy as individual flights from Odiham – we have five flights split between the two squadrons, 18 and 27, so every ten weeks a new flight will come into theatre. Mostly we come out as a formed unit so we know the guys we're flying with fairly well. I look forward to coming out here so I'd even say I was excited about this one. It's a cliché the military often come out with, but it's my job to do it – it's what I joined to do and I feel like I've done something productive in my career with this.

I'm single so I just have my family back home – my mum and my sister. It's not as hard for me on deployment as it is for some of the others; I don't have a young family or children to leave behind. I don't think my mum worried too much on my first det but it's got harder for her with subsequent tours; I think it's because my last two tours have been in summer; the Taliban are much more active then, so there are more British casualties and that means Op Minimise is in force more frequently. On my last det, five Paras were killed in the same week, so we had almost no contact with the outside world until their next of kin had been informed. The boss has been really good, though – when we're out of touch he's phoned home for me a few times and I think my mum found that reassuring – you know, 'How are you? How are you getting on? Are there any issues with Eleanor out in theatre?'

I think it's a lot harder for those left behind than it is for us out here in theatre; if they don't hear from us for more than a couple of days, they start to worry. They'll tell themselves over and over, 'Well, I'd have heard if something had happened,' but they still worry. I know if mum rationalises it she'll be ok so I don't stress about it – it's much worse for the guys who have wives or children back home, though.

Our role here varies depending on where we are – KAF or Bastion. We do a certain amount of Roulement – we rotate through on a cyclical basis, spending a number of days on taskings at KAF and a number of days at Bastion on QRF or MERT (the Medical Emergency Response Team – also known as IRT). Routine taskings include flying resupply runs to the FOBs, inserting and extracting troops at District Centres, etc. When we're flying from the forward base here at Bastion, IRT basically means we're Helmand's Combat Air Ambulance and we're on permanent notice to move within 30 minutes. The aircraft has a full medical and surgical response team in the back that are able to perform surgical interventions on guys in the air, together with a Force Protection team of infantry troops; their role is to fan out when we land and protect the surgical team as they load the casualty on board. We also never fly alone; whenever we're in the air we're supported by an Apache gunship providing overwatch. The IRT is there 24/7.

Everything we do with the aircraft here is vital to the guys on the ground but, certainly for me, I really feel we're making a difference when we're on IRT; that's the element I prefer working on. When we're on IRT, we'll spend 48 hours on call, living and sleeping in the Incident Response Team tent; this is our home for the entire shift and whenever we leave it – for meals, say – we take the radio with us and go as a team. We'll work as a crew for the whole time, so when we first come on shift, I'll give the brief so the guys in the back know who's manning which gun etc. Then we'll go to the ops tent and check what's happened overnight. The aircraft is ready to go – I'll do my walk around and inspection when I come on so that if we get a shout, we can get in the aircraft and after a quick look around to make sure everything is as it was, I can just start her up and lift. Once that's all done, it's back here to wait.

It's not perfect in here, but it's more than adequate for a combat zone. There's a crew area as you come in, with sofas, a DVD player, TV, magazines, etc; there's filter coffee on tap. It's air-conditioned but that's about it. The frame cots aren't the height of luxury – there are eight in here, four on either side of the tent. All of us would be perfectly happy to just sit here and wait for the two days that we're on; if we get a shout, it means somebody's been hurt. We have a phone in here so we can be told where we need to go and how serious the casualty is. So basically we're tied to this tent, rather than wandering off around the camp, or we might go and see the medics. It's just a matter of waiting for that call to come in, so in many respects it's redolent of the old scramble during the Battle of Britain – 'Wait for the bell, then run like hell!'

On average, we lift within 9 and 11 minutes of a call; it's two long rings for an IRT shout and two short rings for admin. The crew will be picking their stuff up, strapping their sidearms on, grabbing their kit even before the second ring has finished – we're ready to go within seconds.

Our primary concern is for ISAF troops but we'll also be scrambled for locals and even Taliban fighters wounded in contacts. When we were out here last time, we learned that the Taliban were deliberately targeting civilians to try to tempt the helicopter in. One shout I went on was a member of the ANF who had a gunshot wound to his arm but he'd also been shot in the face with a pistol. We didn't know this at the time because all we saw on him was a square dressing over his chin and he was holding a little sick bowl. Every now and again he would lean forward and spit blood into the bowl. As it turned out, the bullet had gone in left of his chin, tracked his jaw line, and popped out the back. When the medics checked over the rest of his body, they discovered one of his legs was amputated from the knee down.

We get called out for a whole range of injuries – you just never know what you're going to get. It can be anything from heatstroke to blast injuries or bullet wounds. A lot of people have D&V – that's a real risk here and some people really get very ill. A guy from one of the Scots groups the other day had taken a round through the inside of his thigh and it travelled down and smashed his femur up completely before exiting. Then there are hornet stings – and a guy the other day had been pricked with a hypodermic needle. You have the legacy from the Russians – children finding and playing with mines etc. One of the crews brought children in with bad burns because they'd been messing around in an electricity station. We picked up a guy from a FOB who'd been doing press-ups in his tent and a dog had run in and headbutted him in the temple really hard. Another guy we picked up had been electrocuted. Mad stuff; you couldn't make it up.

Often, the very nature of what we're called out to puts us in the firing line, but it's a tough call for whoever has to make it; obviously, every time you send a helicopter to an event like that, you're risking the aircraft and the lives of the people on board. That has to be balanced with the fact that we want to get people out and save their lives if at all possible.

You get times when it can be very risky and it's not just from incoming fire; if you speak to any of the pilots who've been out here a few times, they'll be able to tell you of a time where they couldn't see very much, that they were swapping control between the front crew every few seconds – of having a close call with a brown-out or dust landing. We had a close call the other day whereby I had to overshoot and abort a landing because of a sudden brown-out; if my crew hadn't operated in the way that they did, it could have been very nasty.

Having said that, it's never fun drawing fire – we're a big target and the Taliban would just love to bring one down. They've even sent suicide bombers into local markets before, specifically to draw us in because they know we'll deal with injured civilians and there are numerous examples of us responding to calls like this and taking fire when we land or take off. The Chinook is well armoured. One really memorable incident occurred just yesterday morning when we flew in to recover the body of WO2 Michael Williams, one of the two Para guys who were killed. The HLS was hot for a long time; I believe the Paras were involved in a six- or seven-hour rolling contact. He was killed fairly early on but they couldn't get us in to recover him. By about 10:00 yesterday morning, though, it was a bit quieter so we were dispatched. We ended up going in and I put us down in a compound where we were partially shielded on three sides by 25ft-high walls; one of them had been destroyed.

We got a call from the Apache that was on overwatch that our HLS was taking fire so we knew someone would probably have a go when we came out and sure enough, as we lifted and transitioned into forward flight, I heard the 'ting ting' of incoming rounds striking the aircraft so I knew we'd taken at least two rounds. So I flew away, very fast and low until we'd cleared the area. Aiden, my co-pilot, checked over the aircraft and made sure we hadn't lost anything major – luckily we hadn't. It was quite noticeable, the change in the crew, once we got to height; Aiden was the first one to crack a joke, as usual, but at that point it was like, 'Ok, we're all fine – bullet didn't hit us.' We get back, take a look – I noticed we'd taken a round, halfway between where Tiff, one of my rear crewmen, stands and where Aiden sits, right into the avionics cabinet. And you think, 'Oh, that's quite close really. Right, what's next?' And we were back up there flying again within three hours I think.

I took incoming fire on my first det, too. It was on a routine tasking and we were taking an underslung load into Sangin. We'd been told at the brief that it was fairly quiet – this was when the Marines were in there – but it turned out not to be as quiet as we'd hoped. We were taking a load in so we were quite slow and suddenly we started taking fire; we lost various aircraft systems that time, one of the rounds had taken out the flight computer. We started flying away and had to get rid of the load we had on – as we released it, it took down a wall in some woman's garden! The irony was that the load was five tonnes of food – we didn't feel so bad when we realised that it was pork casserole, though, so it was no use whatsoever to the Taliban!

The rear crew returned fire from the M-60 on that occasion; again, we got back, realised we'd lost quite a lot of systems at that point, like electrical stuff. We lost a lot of our flight instruments and there was a strange feeling on the controls from the autopilot – the aircraft was bouncing around, which obviously it shouldn't do, dials were spinning, and stuff like that. My only thoughts at the time were, 'We just have to keep moving, get away from here.' There were wires – telegraph poles, I believe – so I'm thinking, 'There's the wires, we're going over the wires' and once you're clear of that and flying low, your next thought is the ground; you need to stay close to it and those buzzwords come back from training – get low, get fast.

Your training does kick in. Back in the UK you're told that if you get shot you need to check your crew and your aircraft, and all that becomes automatic when you get out here. I heard all the voices talking – my captain, the rear crew, the Apache pilot – not over each other though; it was all very calm. We cleared the area, and then we heard the Apache pilot relaying his intentions to us and you could hear his gun going off in the background.

We landed at the nearest FOB, which turned out to be Gereshk, and when we looked the aircraft over, I realised one of the rounds had gone past my bum and through the wall just behind my seat where it had taken out a load of electrical wiring; that was a long fix-up. Just a couple of millimetres either way, though, and that would have been my lot! It transpired we'd come under contact from four separate firing points and the guys on the ground told us that four RPGs had been fired at us too.

I think when your time is up, your time is up, but if the rounds are flying and there's enough lead in the air something will hit you – the Chinook is a big, lumbering helicopter so it's not a difficult target to hit. Our best defence is the Apache – that can put down a lot of withering fire. Otherwise, all we can do is fly very low and very fast – and the guys in the back can put down fire from the Miniguns on either side of the fuselage, or the M-60 on the ramp.

There are some lighter moments in what we do and they're not always where you expect to find them. On my first deployment – I hadn't been here long, it was just after Christmas Day, 2006 – we were called in to extract some British troops who had come under heavy fire at Sangin. So there was an HLS prepared for us with three walls around the outside; it looked relatively benign. We had contact with the troops on the ground but we flew in at night so visibility was poor and there was some chat going on between the loadmaster at the rear of the Chinook and the troops we were supposed to be extracting. The normal drill is that once the ramp's there, the troops who are waiting run on as quickly as possible and we lift them the minute the last man is on.

On this particular occasion, the troops seemed completely unwilling to get on to the aircraft, which is very unusual to say the least; it also puts us in mortal danger – the Taliban aren't daft, they'll have a go at us whenever they can and if we spend any more than 60 seconds on the ground, we're likely to get mortared. So the loadmaster was screaming at the troops to get on but the platoon commander appeared to be shouting at the loadie to go away.

While this is all going on at the back of the aircraft, I noticed that directly ahead there was a well-known hotel and at the top I saw what I can only describe as being like fireworks; it looked like a Roman candle had been lit, and I remember thinking, 'What a very nice thing to do on Christmas Day – it's not even a Christian country!' There seemed to be some kind of electrical discharge around it, though, some kind of static activity as well. It was quite bizarre, but your brain tries to make sense of what your eyes are seeing and all I could think of at the time was 'Christmas festivities'. Like I say, it was all rather incongruous.

It took a bit of toing and froing and lots of shouting between the loadmaster and the platoon commander but eventually my loadie realised that the troops were all lying on the ground … and then it dawned on him that the only reason that troops lie on the ground behind a Chinook that's come to pick them up is that they are taking fire. When he looked carefully he could actually see rounds exploding at the rear of the aircraft, which explained everything to him – and what the platoon commander was actually saying was, 'Fuck off!' because the only reason they were taking fire was because we were drawing it. We were like a bullet magnet to them! So, he relayed the message to me and I put power on, lifted the collective, and got us out of there.

It was only after the event – when the various reports had been submitted – that we pieced it all together and actually worked out what happened. Basically, the Taliban had set up an ambush for a Chinook and we were their prey – we landed straight into their trap and they immediately started pouring rather inaccurate fire into our HLS. The thing that I'd seen on top of the hotel – the thing that I'd thought was like a Roman candle – turned out to be seven rockets, all lying flat and aimed right at our aircraft.

The rockets were on a command wire and there were two Taliban on the roof waiting for us to put down right in their sights – which we did. When we landed on at the HLS, their plan was to initiate the command wire and fire all seven rockets off simultaneously; their strategy was that out of the seven, at least one would hit us and they'd have the biggest coup and PR victory of the war to date – a British Chinook and all its crew, with a few troops waiting for extraction thrown in to boot.

Rather than everything going to plan, it transpired that whoever had laid the command wire for the rockets and set the whole thing up wasn't too hot on the vagaries of electrical theory and had wired the command line directly into the industrial electricity supply at the hotel. The guys on the roof were vaporised immediately that they pressed the tit, the ultimate architects of their own misfortune. Not only did the rockets fire, but they took out the Taliban that had fired them, too, because the electrical charge had gone straight through the pair of them.

So basically what we'd seen was the Taliban smoking – properly! The rockets caused a back blast as opposed to the forward blast that the Taliban were expecting, and as they were poorly aimed, they blew out the whole top floor of the hotel. As it turns out, the top floor of the hotel was the perfect vantage point for multiple Taliban gunmen to ambush the troops on the ground – so that's exactly what they used it for. The resulting explosion killed all the gunmen, and the troops on the ground stopped taking fire. All this was taking place as we transitioned and got the hell out of Dodge – we flew right over the resulting carnage but, obviously, as soon as this happened, the contact stopped. A short time later, we went back and extracted the troops as originally planned!

One of the things about a deployment here is the flying; every landing in Afghanistan is 'interesting'! We did an op last October where the last phase of it was to put a fire support group in; it was behind a ridge line where we'd just dropped off about 300 Gurkhas and it was in the middle of the desert and we thought it was going to be a nightmare. We had an underslung load, a five-tonne gun underneath us, so it had to be very carefully put down. We knew it was going to be a hard one, being in the middle of the desert – very dusty. In actual fact, the dust cloud was over a kilometre long from one of the aircraft trying to get in; the pilots were swapping hands every two or three seconds. When we were flying in, there was no margin for error – if you don't get it dead on, you overshoot. If you don't, you risk being dragged down and over by a five-tonne gun.

Back wheels on ridges, too – that's always very interesting. We practised that for another op last October. We went out into the mountains between the Green Zone and Kandahar and put down with the back wheels on a ridge, but keeping the front in the hover over a drop with the troops coming off the back. The first day we did a practice run and then the second day we took a cabinful of troops. It's a tough manoeuvre because you have one rotor head that's on the ground and the other rotor head is still trying to fly – we're completely reliant on the rear crew to keep us informed. Bear in mind, we're 30ft or so forward of the ramp and below us, through the clear glass under our feet, all we can see is a 2,000 or 3,000ft drop. The back wheels are on the ridgeline, so the loadmaster is in the back hanging off the ramp and screaming in our ear to keep the wheels down, 'Nag, nag, nag!' It's the longest 30-second unload of troops I have ever experienced. My God, the time goes so slowly.

One of my greatest frustrations is nothing to do with flying, the conditions, or anything like that, though. It concerns how we're treated as female aircrew by the higher ups – there seem to be two sets of rules in force between Kandahar and Bastion. When I'm here, I live, eat and sleep in the same tent as my crew; at work, it's not about male/female – we're all part of the same crew and I'm sharing a living and sleeping space with the guys who I depend on in the aircraft and who depend on me, the same people I'm taking risks with. You don't worry about somebody seeing you in your underwear, it's just not important; nobody gets precious, we're all in the same boat doing the same job.

Unfortunately, Kandahar has a 'no mixed accommodation policy'; on my first two dets, at KAF, I lived in the same block as the boys from my Flight; that's how I believe it should be because these are the guys that, yesterday, I relied on when we were taking rounds, and who were talking about the stuff to help me get the aircraft away. However, a few rotations ago, one of the girls on the Flight was told she had to move into an all-girls block. It ended up with the girl who was here before me being in a room with three females, all non-aircrew, all working different shifts, and she didn't sleep because they didn't understand the concept of aircrew rest, that need for us to have eight hours minimum sleep, and that's vital. She wasn't getting any uninterrupted sleep so she was an ineffectual operator because she was constantly tired. Eventually, they had to come to an arrangement where she was allowed to live in a room in an aircrew block on her own, but she had to use another all-female block for showering.

So that's what I came into; I was living in a block with the Sea King crews – all boys; I had a room to myself but I had to go to the block next door to use the sinks, toilets and showers, and my block was about 200 metres from the one where my boys lived. Certainly, the impression I get from the lads is that they don't object to my living with them; it creates more of a hassle for me to live separately – and from the point of view of talking through stuff, like yesterday, the last thing you want is to have to go back to a block on your own and be in a room on your own; we share the risks, we share the work, and we share the aftermath; we're supposed to be a crew, not four blokes and a girl.

For us, it's all about the lads – those who are living in basic conditions in the FOBS, taking fire, advancing to contact on a daily basis; every single one of them is precious to us so we might bitch among ourselves but we don't really care about how many hours we have to work. There are real people out there – boys, really. Half of them, before they joined the Army, probably couldn't even find Afghanistan on a map, and here they are spending six months of their lives up to their eyeballs in it. Everybody has a little bit of a sacrifice to make. We certainly don't begrudge them what we do.

Also, we had a big issue with regard to our clothing; what we wear now is called non-fast-jet flying clothing and it's almost identical to what the troops have – desert DPM shirts and trousers; ours is fire-retardant, but it rips too easily. It was pushed through for us as quickly as possible because, originally, we were wearing standard desert clothing which isn't fire-retardant. There are a couple of subsequent evolutions going on, but it was all driven by the fact that we don't want to look like aircrew, so we want something made out of the same material as our flying suits but that makes us look like everyone else; we want to blend in. If we go down outside the wire, it'd be bad enough being caught by the Taliban, but if we stood out as aircrew things may not be good for us.

It's not all bad, though; our survival jacket now incorporates integrated body armour, which is not perfect but it's streets ahead of anything else we had and there's an updated version of it in the post as we speak. We have several options when it comes to boots; these ones I'm wearing are American and are fire-retardant. But there's not a specific RAF desert flying boot yet.

The MoD are looking more and more now at buying off the shelf where possible, but obviously still not as much as we'd like. There are some processes that are taking time to adjust but in general it *is* getting better – as long as we continue to make some noise about it.

Things are changing within the RAF. Over the five years I've been in it, there's been a massive swing pro-helicopters. We used to be the poor man's people of the RAF here on the Chinook fleet; it seemed the RAF expected JHC to look after us but JHC said, 'Well, you're RAF so they'll look after you' and ultimately, we felt no one was looking after us. It's a lot better now and we have support helicopter-specific equipment coming through that would have potentially have taken a lot longer previously – the CCHS are a good example; they're the new rollers we have at the back of the ramp that make it massively quicker to get kit on and off.

There's still a Heath Robinson approach to some things, though: the crewmen's seat in the back is just an ammo box with a cushion on top; they haven't procured a bespoke one. Then you look at the ballistic protection fit – that wasn't thought necessary at the outset but then we all thought, we really do need it and we got it within a month.

The Chinook is a hugely capable aircraft, which is one of the reasons that they are in such high demand in theatre but they lose some capability in this environment. For instance, in the UK we can lift about 11 tonnes if we strip the aircraft and make it light, but here it's high, it's hot and the air's thinner so the blades don't work as well, so we lift less. The main issue, though, is the dust clouds when you land in the desert; trying to land when you've lost your reference points due to a brown-out and you can't see the ground ... that's not funny.

Generally, we only fill our tanks two-thirds full out here, to give us lift. Usually the helicopter is so forgiving that in other environments we can brim the tanks, but out here we are more limited. The thing that takes up the most room is mail and it's the one thing we never turn down because we know how important it is. So much of it is coming through now – the welfare shoe boxes etc – and guys are going mental on Amazon or play.com and so we're getting it by the four-tonne load! The guys really appreciate the welfare boxes. We get quite a few that come to us here at Bastion or in KAF but we just take them all to the troops at the FOBs and hand them out there because it lifts their morale so much. We've been known to literally stack the aircraft floor to ceiling. The guys are used to it now and prioritise handwritten mail and then squeeze in whatever else they can. It really hit in 2007 with the postal strike – everything dried up and the knock-on effect lasted a couple of weeks. But when it started again, I've never seen anything like it!

I think the SH fleet is pretty well regarded now by the Army; I think the troops appreciate us. We do what we can but ultimately the buck stops with us; we do our best and I really believe a lot of them do appreciate that. One of the frustrating things is that when you're on an IRT shout, there are a few channels of authority that it has to go through before they'll say, 'yes, we've got a guy that's bleeding to death'; however, are we going to risk this £20 million helicopter and the lives of the people on board to go and get him? So we find ourselves just turning and burning; we always want to go but we have to wait and that's very frustrating. As soon as the phone rings the blinkers are on: someone's in trouble and we want to go get them.

It doesn't happen so much now but certainly on my last det, we'd normally take the QRF with us, which was eight guys down the back, but on one occasion, they hadn't turned up. Thankfully we were going to a fairly well-established FOB so I just said, 'Sod it, we'll go without them.' This guy couldn't wait, so as long as we had the medics on board and the full crew, I thought we'd be ok; it was a judgement call. Apparently the QRF hadn't got the call. The control room has a cascade list with regard to who to phone next; when an IRT shout comes in, the ops room will be an absolute zoo. Generally, we're the first guys on the aircraft so we can just ring through asking for whatever we need. But we understand that they have to be sure that it's safe for us to go in and that it's going to be worthwhile.

I have to say, there are so many positive aspects to our deployment here, but for me, it's great when you bring somebody back all trashed, and you know that it's you – the whole crew and the medics in the back – that are the difference between someone living and dying. Knowing you've lifted somebody from harm's way and got them back here, to the hospital, is great. Like the guy we casevaced, one of the Scots Guards, I think; he could have potentially lost his leg but it's great, knowing he's now back in the UK and he's still got it.

On my last deployment, they said, in a two-week period there were 11 British troops that statistically shouldn't have made it, but they did, and they put that down to the reaction time of the IRT. Everybody hates statistics but that's one you can't ignore; that's people making a difference. Thanks to what we're doing, there are kids out there getting read stories at bedtime because they've still got their dads. You can't put a price on that.

Resupplying the troops is great, too; when we extract them from a FOB and take them home and you can hear the cheer over the sound of the engine and blades … you just think, 'Great!' When we were here last time, we pulled the Royal Anglians out, and four weeks earlier they'd lost three guys to a 'blue on blue' incident with the US. We got a crate of Coke for them because we knew they were coming home, and we'd done something similar lifting some troops the day before and it went down well. As we lifted off from Kajaki, you could hear the cheer over the engines. We flew over the base, got up to 3,000ft and I was like, right, we're safe, so I said to my crewmen, 'Give them all a Coke'. They couldn't believe it! Looking down to the back of the aircraft I've never seen such happy faces over a can of Coke! That's always very good.

I think my deployments here have changed me a bit and not necessarily in positive ways. For example, I find myself feeling very uncomfortable around groups of Asian people now. I know it sounds awful but I do; here, a group of men like that could be just the local elders or a group of Taliban intent on trying to shoot us out of the sky. So for the first few days back, it makes me feel a bit uncomfortable and it's not something I can do anything about – it's not a conscious thought. It's the same for the guys out on the ground to a greater extent; when they finish their deployment, they go to Cyprus and have their post-traumatic stress stuff done – the Army calls it 'decompression'; allowing the guys to let off steam before they get home. We just go straight on leave.

Also, my perspective on life is a little different now – I go back and go off on holiday and do what I want to do instead of, say, saving the money. If I want to do something, I'll go and do it. Life's too short.

Some people have trouble re-engaging when they get home after a tour but I think I'm quite lucky really. I usually go to a friend who lives at RAF Benson; she looks after my car so she'll usually pick me up and I'll go and stay there for a few days just to chill out. It's quite a nice arrangement because she is married to a Merlin pilot so she's fairly used to having him come back. So I can talk to him about work stuff and I can talk to her about other stuff – she has to get up and walk out when we talk about work, though! Then normally I'll go on holiday with a friend because, like I said, life's too short to wait for things.

This time I plan to do a lot of water sports – I have no desire to see sand or desert or anything like that, or sun even!

FLIGHT LIEUTENANT
JAMIE 'CHALKIE' WHITE

TACTICAL SUPPLY WING

Formed in 1971 to provide deployed support to RAF aircraft operating away from their home bases, Tactical Supply Wing (TSW) personnel have seen operational service in 15 different countries. Since 1999, the Wing has been Joint Helicopter Command's specialist aviation fuels support unit.

Flight Lieutenant Jamie 'Chalkie' White has undertaken a number of deployments to Afghanistan and has worked alongside front-line forces providing fuel to RAF aircraft on desert landing strips.

I'm Jamie, although nobody calls me that anymore – I'm known as 'Chalkie' to almost everyone I know. I'm a team leader with the Tactical Supply Wing, or 'TSW', and our primary role involves supporting deployed helicopter operations. What that means is providing and storing aviation fuel on the battlefield, and we specialise in providing rotors-turning refuelling to all deployed NATO helicopters in theatre.

This is not my first tour – I've done a number of tours in theatre, although I'm currently driving a desk here at Camp Bastion. I guess that we have quite a low-profile, and play an understated role in TSW – no in-theatre deployed helicopter ops could take place without us. People back home know that the Army and the Royal Marines are engaged in front-line ops, but I don't suppose too many people think about support arms of the Royal Air Force being up there with them – in many cases, though, that's where we operate.

I was involved in quite a memorable mission back in September 2006. We deployed as a squad of four guys: me and three other lads from Camp Bastion out to a place in the middle of nowhere – basically, an empty, soulless patch of desert somewhere in the middle of nowhere. With us were a Force Protection team to provide an outer cordon for the whole of the airfield part of it; there were also a few Afghans who came in and out.

In total, there were about 30 of us there to set up a temporary 'airfield' in the middle of the desert, so that we could support Chinook and Hercules ops in and out of our deployed location. Myself and my team of three were to set up and run the 'airfield' with the FP guys providing Force Protection. We set ourselves up in a dried-up wadi about 6km by 4km, in which we established a refuelling site for a pair of helicopters and the sole point to the rest of the protection was to give us that refuelling site, which they needed for the missions they were carrying out. We were down there for about two weeks in total.

If you can imagine a completely flat and featureless piece of desert, that's what we set up our airfield in – it was a huge basin surrounded by high ground. Off to one side we established our domestic area, so built ourselves shell scrapes there, kept our kit there – it was literally just a cam net with some holes in the ground. A way off from us we placed the fuel tank, which has got a receipt line, and then on the back of our Land Rover we had a pump and filter. There were two issue points from which two Chinooks were able to refuel and the whole frontage of the refuelling area would have been around 100 metres.

There are a number of ways of doing something like that – setting up in the middle of nowhere I mean – and the way that we did it for this particular mission was by deploying from the back of a Hercules. Hercs are great for these sorts of ops as they're tactical transporters, suited for short take-off and landing from unprepared landing strips, or empty desert in this case. So we had a Land Rover and trailer, with our kit, weapons and everything strapped to it. There were four of us, so obviously two in the vehicle and two on foot. The trailer had the fuel tank on top of it and, as for most of the technical kit we needed, we had to fit it all as best we could into the back of the Herc or pile it or strap it on to any available space on the Snatch; you certainly wouldn't have been able to drive it down a UK road, given how overloaded it was!

It was a completely Heath Robinson approach, but so much of military operations follows that philosophy. People talk about 'military precision' but the reality is that so much of what we do is based on personal experience and ingenuity – that's one of the things that I think really sets the British forces apart. We won't necessarily have all the kit we need to achieve an objective but, somehow, everyone manages to make it all work and it all comes together. The job needs doing so by hook or by crook, you make it happen.

The thing about the task force is that they're very quick – you're on 24-hours' notice to go, to plan it and to execute it. We were down there for about 14 days, like I said. The way the system worked was that we would drop the kit, and we were up and running ready to receive fuel within an hour of hitting the ground – we land on and away we go.

It's a front-line military op, and obviously in wartime a lot of the usual stuff goes out the window – it has to. We land on top of the ground and need to be operational asap, so all the normal environmental stuff that we'd consider in a training exercise, or back in the UK – we just don't have the option to do that. It's fly in, drive out the back and away you go. The way we fitted the tank on top of the trailer in the back of the vehicle was that we could kick one end of it and it would roll off and roll out. It's something, as with any of these, the more rehearsals you do and the more you prep it beforehand, the better it goes. The fuel is taken straight out of the Herc and put into it.

The tanks are collapsible and rubber-backed with a 45,000-litre capacity – a Chinook, if it's flying on vapour, can drink about 2,500 gallons, so there's a fair bit there. When they're full, they stand about 4 or 5ft high. You literally clip everything together, lay it out, cam net over the top and it's ready to go. It took five separate Hercules flights to fill up but they were coming back in every 24 hours, so that wasn't a problem. When you're ready to bug out, it just rolls up.

When we deployed, the Herc just dropped us off and then left – it was on the ground for just long enough for us to get our stuff off and draw fuel and that was it, it was gone. There we were on the ground with our FP troops ready to live off what we could carry.

To be honest, it wasn't so bad. By far the worst aspect of day-to-day living was the flies – they were like nothing I've ever seen or experienced since; it was a like a plague of biblical proportions and they were just in your face all the time – it's so frustrating, really annoying! We had limited water, too, just what we could carry, so we were only washing at a fairly basic level but even then, it doesn't take the flies long to find you! We ended up putting up mozzie nets and living in them.

And the food was a real nightmare. Obviously out there, on a mission like that, it's rations, and sadly for us, we had the American MREs rather than our own. I mean everyone moans about the British ones but at least they taste of something! These had all the taste of ceiling tiles.

One of my team, he's a Coke addict. He doesn't drink tea or coffee, he just drinks Coke all the time. The Herc crew were very good to him because they kept bringing us little goodie parcels every couple of days and they brought him a crate of Coke and he was absolutely made up with it until he noticed it was the Coke classic stuff with the vanilla flavouring in – he was nearly suicidal!

For this op, he was the first bloke on the ground with the recce team to set out the Tactical Landing Zone. So he was setting out the refuel point such that we could taxi the Herc up to it and still have clearance for two helicopters in there, and it fitted in with the Force Protection plan and the mortars and all the other bits and pieces. So he literally was third guy out of the Herc and he had a great time, going around on a quad bike armed to the teeth – he really loved it. Once we'd set that out, the first priority was to get the fuel farm in, get the vehicle set up so that we had the pump and filter ready to use, the idea being that as soon as we'd taken in some fuel, we could issue it straight out again.

Once we'd done that, we then had to wait for another couple of hours as it was a turnaround for the aircraft to go and fill up, get back and give us more, so we started on the domestic stuff, which was digging the shell scrapes, setting up the cam net, getting ourselves comfortable, basically. So the first day was really just establishing things. The Force Protection team were out patrolling, clearing the area, and setting up their cordons, and they were round about 100–150 metres away at nearest.

We were in a basin so there was high ground all the way around us, so they'd set snipers up all around there. They had the mortar team located so they could fire out into the various wadis if there were any Taliban incursions within our area of operation – actually that happened on a couple of nights. In the basin where we were, the team set up four machine-gun posts and the guys were doing roving patrols out and about. And also they were flying out up into the hills and patrolling back in, so we were well defended. With all that, we were bound to have the odd contact with Taliban forces over the two weeks and, as I said earlier, that happened on a couple of occasions.

On one night – I think it would have been about 02:00 – we heard the mortar teams firing out. So they'd kicked off and obviously you wake up pretty quickly, grab your rifle from the sleeping bag as you climb out and stand to. The guys in each of the fixed posts had their own arcs to cover and we had two guys protecting our rear; we were given the middle bit to cover – we were told, 'If you need to fight guys, that's where you're going to be going!' They were fairly blunt about it; obviously they had to be – it was, 'If it kicks off, shoot back!' The mortars started to fire again, so there were quite a few rounds going out and then it all quietened down again as quickly as it all kicked off. I went over to the lads to find out what was going on and it transpired that they'd had a couple of trucks loaded with Taliban that the snipers had spotted coming down one of the wadis, and during the contact the mortar teams just opened up and flattened them. While it was reassuring, it was still an experience.

At the time, you don't have the chance to feel scared – you're so hyped up, scanning your arcs, listening and watching, waiting for the rounds to start flying. It's confusing, dynamic, so information is king and you just want to know what's going on. Another night, a Harrier came along, bombing things not too far away, and that was quite a reassuring experience because you're thinking, great, that's our guys fighting back.

About ten days in, one of the lads and I were out doing the QA checks, to see if the fuels were quality stuff, a lab-testing type thing. We did everything in pairs, because of the separation thing and because the other guys were so far away, you just didn't want to wander off on your own. I was looking at the hydrometer thinking, 'I haven't read one of these in a while.' Then I heard, 'Right Boss, get your weapon ...' and I thought 'Oh, here we go again' and I was instantly switched on.

There was a Toyota Hilux – they're popular with Terry Taliban, those

– parked a short way off with five guys in it. They'd just stopped, and were staring and shouting at us. Both of us thought, 'Fuck!', so we made ready. My oppo took a covering position, angled off so he could shoot at them and I started walking towards the vehicle, making it obvious to them that we didn't want them anywhere near us, and they're just looking at us. I literally got up to the door and was thinking, 'Right, now what do I do?' So how do I escalate this now and make it look like I'm more serious? I put my weapon through the door window and I went to put my hand on the door handle and they drove off. Things like that, you think over them after the event and you wonder – what were they planning, what were they doing there? At the time, you just react to it. Things do go through your head; it's kind of like a car accident where things go really slowly.

Time becomes elastic when you're under stress like that, so it feels like everything is happening in slow motion when you look back over it. At the time, we were just thinking, 'We're all right but we'd better get across there and let people know it's happened.' We went back and finished off what we were doing and two or three hours later, we sat down laughing and crying; it was that moment later when you suddenly think, 'Fucking hell, that was close!'

After that, we were on a heightened state of alert and it was constant, just constant. The difficulty with this one was that we were literally out in the middle of nowhere, and not far off from our location was like a link between two roads, one going north, and one going south. They would cross from one to the other by driving across the wadi, so we had all sorts of stuff coming along. Mostly, it was just farmers, who weren't really interested in what we were doing. It was quite odd because you can see it from their point of view – 'Who the hell are they, what are they doing in this wadi?' It must have been just as surreal for them as it was for us. That was day 10, and then on day 12 we received news that there were something like 200 or 300 Taliban making their way towards us and they were about 20 klicks away, so we had a bit of a shocker there. It was a case of get your sketch maps out, you're going to Kandahar, and you've got an hour to sort yourselves out. But they never materialised, so we stood down.

It was a bit of an emotional roller coaster, that mission. For a few days it was just us, there were no contacts; then there were the outgoing mortars and you could hear the snipers; then we had the situation that I've just described; then we heard there were 200 Taliban inbound so we were getting ready to bug out at an hour's notice; then it was down again.

Funnily enough, you don't feel like you're living on your nerves all the time, though – it's not like that. You're trained, you have a job to do, and things happen so quickly, so you just sort of prepare yourself for it and then deal with whatever you have to. You know what you're going to do and you get good briefings. Also the FP guys are really good at looking after everybody – because they do it all the time, it doesn't affect them in the same way as the rest of us. But they really do put their arm around you, metaphorically speaking – they're always asking, 'How's it going, do you need anything – is there anything we can do?' They were really good guys and a pleasure to work with.

It was very much five days of boredom, 20 minutes of panic. It's not like it is at Bastion. If there's nothing to do here, we can go sunbathe or go down the gym but, out there, there is just nothing to do. That's harder than dealing with the stressful bits – you've already geared yourself up to cope with the stress in some ways. There's also an element, certainly for me, that this is what we've trained for and this is the aspiration we have so let's go and do the job, so you want to be there.

Looking back, I think it was a very valuable experience, although there were a couple of things that were a bit of a dilemma. One was that, having filled the tank, it had about 30 tons of fuel in it towards the end of the mission, and the Herc could only take so much of it back, so when we came to leave, we ended up having to get rid of it. The question was do we leave it or do we burn it? We had all sorts of arguments and radioed back saying we should burn it. Eventually the decision not to burn it was for tactical reasons; I guess it was the lesser of two evils. It's an interesting confluence of the normal moral arguments and decisions you have to make in a war environment. I guess it is one thing dropping big bits of steel on people and shooting back at those who are shooting at you, but that fuel thing is just a different class of problem. I mean my day job, the one I do now – it's all about sustaining fuels and everything I do is about trying to limit the amount of damage we cause. Seems kind of ironic against the backdrop of what we did there.

With that particular unit, we were quite lucky – it was what's called a formed unit so we didn't deploy as individuals; you're with the same guys that you work with back in the UK and they were all my team anyway. So when we got back to the UK we were all together. It's a little bit like a small family. My dad was in the Air Force, and I remember as a kid it was more social and everybody did things in little groups; the squadron would have a night out, and it's still like that at TSW in some ways. That family atmosphere is still there; we'd all sit down and have a beer together. It's quite close-knit so there's an element of support there straight away because you're with your mates. And the banter's vicious most of the time; you really don't get away with much! So that immediately helps things because the people you've shared the experience with are with you when you get home.

The Air Force support network is getting better, I think, and as I said, particularly with TSW – because you're working with the same guys time and again, with only about 210 guys on the wing anyway – it's such a small family, that everybody knows everybody pretty intimately anyway, so we do keep an eye on each other really well. That's the beauty of it and that's why the guys can do the sort of jobs that they carry out.

The tour last time was quite different to this one. Bastion's quite built up and is pretty well founded now, but when we got here in 2006 there was next to nothing here – in fact when we first arrived, it was still being built. And to that end the guys got stuck into some other bits and pieces that they're now not going to go anywhere near. One day we were tasked by the Force Protection guys because we were near the flight line; we were told to get our weapons and get up to the flight line to cordon a route. So we went out, and the helicopter landed and we literally funnelled a channel back to a waiting truck while they ferried some POWs out, which was quite an odd experience.

One of the days when I'd gone out to recce one of the FOBs for putting a fuel farm in there, with one of the other guys, on the way back we got diverted into an Afghan village, picked up an Afghan guy who had been shot a couple of times, and because there were only a handful of us on the aircraft, both of us ended up helping out the medics. I ended up with my fist jammed in his thigh for the flight back to Bastion, which is not really something I was expecting to be doing. Good news was the guy lived and was able to walk afterwards, but it's not something that gets well publicised – that anybody and everybody of whatever persuasion, if you're in the right place, you're needed.

What that comes back to is training. Admittedly at TSW we do a much higher level than the normal, and we do regular exercises, both internally and externally, where we go fully tactical just to train. So your first aid and your military skills are a little better than usual. But that's important. I'm working with the Army now but that's done me a favour because I'm at the same sort of level they are, skills wise. I've been posted to the Army, on exchange, and it's fascinating for me, it's one of the aspects of my career that I love. What other job gives you opportunities like that?

AIR COMMODORE
BOB JUDSON

COMKAF

Kandahar Airfield is the main staging post for all British forces in southern Afghanistan. As well as containing a functioning civilian airport, it is home to over 10,000 coalition troops and countless aircraft, including the RAF's Harriers and Hercules C130s, Apache AH-64 Helicopters, weapons stores and ammunition. It is the main airport for the UK air bridge from RAF Brize Norton and the administrative headquarters for British forces in the south. Since 2007, the command of the base has been under the NATO flag, with a British commander at the helm.

Air Commodore Bob Judson took up his post as Commander of Kandahar Airfield – known colloquially as 'COMKAF' – in January 2008. A Jaguar pilot for most of his career, it is his first appointment in a NATO role.

This is my first multinational command appointment. I was a Jaguar pilot for most of my career – I did eight years in Germany, a couple of tours of RAF Coltishall, and the usual array of staff appointments. I've had a really interesting time so far and have been involved in a number of milestone events – one of the most memorable was piloting the 100th Typhoon off the production line from the BAE factory at Warton to RAF Coningsby, where I was the first Typhoon station commander. I was also honoured to be the formation leader for Her Majesty the Queen's 80th Birthday Flypast, which was one of the largest flypasts that the RAF has been involved in for many years.

I took up this appointment in January 2008 and my remit is basically that of commander for the whole of Kandahar Airfield. There's a common misconception that it's just the airfield, as in the air operating bit, but actually I'm responsible for the total airfield operation as well as support and Force Protection for everything else, including the garrison. It's a NATO job; the UK took over as Principal Co-ordinating Nation from the US, which was doing it as the lead nation. The difference is small but important I think; the lead nation had almost unlimited liability because NATO's expectation was that whenever there was a problem the lead nation would bale it out both financially and with other resources. The UK wasn't prepared to undertake that, so they created the term Principal Co-ordinating Nation specifically for it. We initially undertook it for a year but the Chief of Defence Staff is quite keen to have it extended – there's a high likelihood that it will be. I think it's a fantastic role in terms of employment opportunities for the likes of me to gain experience in a multinational, joint, combined operation. It doesn't get much more complex than this.

In simple terms KAF is many things. It's an airport of embarkation and disembarkation; it's a deployed operating base for many of the fast jets and UAVs in theatre; a support base and staging base for the majority of the forward elements of Army/rotary, and a garrison with a large number of people based here supporting the forward troops. We also have front-line troops based here when they're not actively deployed on operations. So we're responsible for the airport bit, support and the Force Protection of everything inside and outside the wire within the Ground Defence Area (GDA).

In terms of numbers, the base has had up to 14,000 people in my time and at the moment has 170 aeroplanes of every different persuasion. So we've got fast jets, UAVs, helicopters, transports, and lots of different nationalities, languages, and tactical requirements. We handle about 10,000 movements a month, which is a lot – that's 50 per cent of what Gatwick Airport handles, and it just operates airliners, straight in, straight out; nothing more complicated than that and no threat. Whereas obviously here, we have a fairly significant threat both from surface-to-air fire and from incoming indirect fire (IDF). There's also a threat from insurgents – obviously they'd be mad to come in and attack us at the gates, although there is a clear threat from suicide bombers at the gate that we have to police very carefully.

The predominant threat – indirect fire – is something that we can be proactive about, to a degree. The actual launches are all from within the GDA. It's not surprising when you look at where the population is within the GDA and the tribal mix within that, which is all a bit fractured and mixed up. There are plenty of insurgent links into some of the little local villages around here so it's predictable that they will come from there. The terrain is very difficult in parts because it's agricultural to the north and west – there are fruit trees and they grow vines for grapes to make raisins, so there are 3ft- or 4ft-deep ditches everywhere. They grow their vines on the sides of earth berms, which provide both launch sites, and cover to launch from. There's a lot of intelligence-based work done to try to find where they're getting the rockets from, because clearly, they come from outside the GDA. Who's doing it, and where to do they live? When we find the answers to all of those questions, they won't be doing it any more!

We haven't had any suicide bombers here so far but Bagram Airfield has, and so it's not something that we can ever relax on – this is very much the front line. Security is layered but outside the wire it falls to the RAF Regiment, which does a magnificent job. They took that role on in 2006 from the Romanians who were quite constrained and did very little policing outside the wire. Anecdotally at least, the RAF Regiment has driven down the incidences of IDF by about 60 per cent since they took over, which is an enormous drop and it's all down to presence – basically, being out there with boots on the ground. We've a lot of patrols outside the wire; 18 hours out of 24 minimum we've got guys out on the ground and they do a mixture of very overt and covert patrolling. The overt stuff is designed to win the hearts, minds, and consent of the local population, which is estimated at around 15,000 people in the 400sq km that constitutes the GDA.

When they patrol through a village, they'll always try and talk to the locals, be they kids or the village head. We actively participate in the local district *Shuras* for the two districts that straddle the GDA. We also have a very active civic programme of improvements focusing on proper infrastructure: not so much road building; it's more about wells, power – the sorts of things that are genuinely improving the lives of a lot of Afghans.

I have a mix of resources at my disposal for funding it all. The Americans used to have a thing called Commanders' Emergency Response Programme funding (CERP), where they contributed $100,000 a month, but since NATO took over they've cut that by 75 per cent, so there's just $25,000 per month going in now. The UK has unilaterally funded some work – it put £500,000 in last year and the UK has front-funded some of the contributions for a new Memorandum of Understanding with the other four stakeholder nations in the structure – USA, Canada, UK, France, and the Netherlands.

In terms of actually doing the work to improve infrastructure for the locals, a lot of it is contracted. There are several contractors we use for the sorts of things we want to build, but we're trying to make the process more robust than it used to be – we're basically being a bit cleverer about it. It used to be us rolling up, chatting to the locals, saying this is what you need doing, and it got done. We're now achieving it in a more structured way by doing it through the district chief, who has a clear role in deciding where the money is spent and on what, although we do stipulate the money has to be spent inside the GDA. We now have a better governance structure internally as well – I chair a steering committee and there's a working group on the base that looks at which projects to approve.

We've learned a lot by experience – last year we had some projects that were less effective. For example, if you supply the locals with generator power, generators need maintenance and fuel, neither of which is readily available in some areas of southern Afghanistan, so we're now looking at solar power. We're trying to make the whole process more iterative – my engineers here are actively involved in what we're trying to build because we're trying to control not only what is built but also *how* it's built. For example, we built a very useful causeway recently across the Tarnak River, the idea being it would be useful for both us and the locals. The trouble was, perhaps because we didn't keep enough control of it, we've ended up with something that is a vulnerable point nightmare – we could use it but it would mean lots of checks to make sure it's safe for us to use.

One of the big problems that I face here is that we're delivering a lot in terms of the effect we're producing on the ground. However, in some ways it's in spite of the high-level structuring of NATO rather than because of it, because NATO's high-level structure is predicated on Cold War thinking. It's a 26-nation consensus-based alliance, which is great in terms of getting buy-in for big principals, but that's where it should stop; the nations themselves should be delegating decision-making to a much lower level. The reality is that the nations hold the consensus requirement, in relative terms, for tiny amounts of money for approval of virtually everything. It's very bureaucratic, very process-driven, and very, very slow. Some of the approvals for infrastructure projects, and things like manpower changes, take years, not weeks or months. Here we're dealing with things that are changing almost on a daily basis. To give you a flavour of that, when I took over command here there were under 10,000 people on the base, but that's risen as high as 14,000 since, yet my entire headquarters is sized and structured for a sub-10,000-strong population. When you're dealing with things like Force Protection and support, the sizing is crucial to the size of the organisation you're trying to manage. It's a very difficult thing to combat and it takes an enormous amount of effort.

All you can do a lot of the time is try and paper over the cracks. Obviously where NATO fails to deliver, the in-theatre nations will provide, which is historically how the alliance worked. It co-ordinates things but doesn't really take the lead in them, so what's going on here is breaking completely new ground for the NATO alliance. Running an airfield is not something it would ever normally have done – there would have been a nation doing that with NATO supporting it. NATO is more of a headquarters-focused organisation, working as it did in the Cold War on the basis of an Article 5 collective defence mechanism, rather than getting into the tactical detail of the way we do business here. So they rely on the nations to deliver capability, but it's inefficient because there are plenty of opportunities here right now for more mutinationalisation rather than less. To give you an example, I've got *ten* Role 1 Medical Centres here so people can walk in the door for medical treatment. Having ten different centres performing the same function is crazy; it cannot be efficient.

Every nation is worried about both boots on the ground and money, two very, very key things, yet we're at that level of duplication. Another example is that I have five meteorological offices and that's completely crazy; it's all down to nations saying NATO won't provide one of these so we'll do it. If you want to do it properly, the solution is for NATO to address the problem and get it done on a multinational basis. We're making progress in trying to do that – we're getting working-level agreements to share resources such as police; I don't have enough police officers but each nation does and what we're now trying to do is to make sure we can work all those police together in an international Military Police construct. It would involve them having powers over other nations, at least up to the point of an arrest, because after that you start getting into jurisdictional issues and so on, but that's fine because you can hand over the individual to the relevant nation. Hitherto, we've been in the ludicrous situation where the Royal Military Police will go out doing traffic policing work on the base at the behest of the British commander, but they'll only stop British people, which is absolutely nonsensical on a multinational base.

On a more macro-level, my biggest challenge here is rather akin to herding cats. When I was running RAF Coningsby it had a population of around 3,000 people and I was in command of nearly all of them – I did have a couple of lodger/tenant units that were not under my command but they were still Brits so it was relatively easy to influence all the key decisions. Here, on a base with a population of 14,000, I command significantly less than 10 per cent of the personnel, so the way I have to exercise leadership is quite different to how it would be if I had a command construct that genuinely left me empowered. It's an issue NATO is aware of and is trying to address; they want to give me the authority to effectively match up to my responsibility. At the moment I have to try to get all of the individual nations on the same page and then get them heading off in the same direction on that page, which is largely achieved through consent winning, consensus building, and walking on eggshells, because if I overreach myself in terms of being too direct and alienate the nations, then there is a danger they will just work around me, having refused to do what I asked. That would risk me being left largely emasculated in terms of power and authority for future issues. So it's a bit of a tightrope and I have to walk it on a daily basis.

RIGHT: *SAC Phillipa Williamson, a technician from RAF Lyneham, performs a routine service on a specialist airside vehicle at Kandahar Airfield. Philippa, 22, is on her first overseas detachment after completing her training with the RAF.*
(© SAC Andrew Morris/Crown Copyright)

BELOW: *A WMIK from 51 Squadron, RAF Regiment, drives through a village outside KAF while on a routine patrol. Clearly visible are the .50-cal machine gun (top) and the front-mounted 7.72mm GPMG. Another member of the squadron takes up a covering position on foot.* (© Cpl Scott Robertson/
Crown Copyright)

ABOVE: *The breathtaking beauty of the topography surrounding the Kajaki Dam as seen from low-level in a Chinook. The Helmand River (pictured) which rises in the Hindu Kush and runs for over 700 miles through Afghanistan, is vital to the farmers that have colonised its length.*

LEFT: *A loadmaster takes in the view as his Chinook departs the Forward Operating Base at the Kajaki Dam, which is just visible below.*

BELOW: *Battle weary: the faces of these Parachute Regiment soldiers bear the strain of the intense fighting they experience on a daily basis at their FOB near the Kajaki Dam.* (© SAC Andrew Morris/Crown Copyright)

ABOVE LEFT: *Opium: Afghanistan's only major export and the primary source of funding for Taliban forces in the south. Poppies are a mainstay for many farmers who are reluctant to sacrifice its high-yield crop for lower-paying legal crops such as wheat.*

ABOVE RIGHT: *This young Afghan girl from the village of Mandi Sar, near Kandahar Airfield, sports Kohl around her eyes; this is popular among many young girls and women who live in the desert regions of the country.*

BELOW LEFT: *The face of hope: children, such as this girl from Mandi Sar, represent the brightest hope for Afghanistan's future. When the Taliban fell from power in 2001, there were only 900,000 children in school, all of them boys. In 2008, over 330,000 girls started school for the first time.*

BELOW RIGHT: *RAF Chef SAC Sarah Jones peels potatoes in the 'kitchen' at FOB Naw Zad, Helmand. 'It would take ten hours to do chips because we'd have to wash and chop all the potatoes, and then blanche and refry them.'*

ABOVE: *Rotate: Flt Lt Matt Bartlett lines up his C130J Hercules on the main runway at KAF to begin the take-off run on a night-time air drop to resupply several FOBs in Helmand Province.*

BELOW: *Hunter-killer: the Reaper MQ-9 represents the very latest weapon in the RAF's armoury. This one is being refuelled prior to launch on a 12-hour sortie, which will be flown by pilots at Nellis Air Force Base in Nevada, some 8,000 miles away in the USA. Clearly visible are the Reaper's Paveway II 540lb GBUs and Hellfire AGM-114N Missiles.*

ABOVE: *Sentinel: an RAF Harrier GR9 sits on the pan at KAF. The RAF's Harriers have been a constant in Afghanistan since the earliest days of the conflict, but the heat can have a major impact on the efficacy of its electronic systems. The shelters which house all the RAF's Harriers in theatre provide air cooling to keep the aircraft at a constant temperature.* (© SAC Andrew Morris/Crown Copyright)

LEFT: *Sunrise over Afghanistan: the RAF's fleet of C17 Globemaster III strategic airlifters provide a long-range capability for transporting everything from fighter jets to tanks. C17s also repatriate the bodies of British troops killed in action back to RAF Lyneham in the UK. Here, a C17 crew fly west into the morning, having departed KAF for RAF Brize Norton with a full load of cargo.*

LEFT: *Flt Lt Emily Oliver, an RAF air traffic controller, at work in the control tower high above Camp Bastion, Helmand Province.* (© SAC Andrew Morris/ Crown Copyright)

RIGHT: *'Ring the Bell and Run like Hell':*
RAF Harrier pilots on GCAS at KAF live a
life redolent of that of Spitfire pilots at the
height of the Battle of Britain in 1940.
When the call comes, they have to be ready
to scramble at a moment's notice.
(© SAC Andrew Morris/Crown Copyright)

BELOW: *Flt Lt Frenchie Duncan (second*
from right) stands with Master Aircrewman
Bob Ruffles (left), his co-pilot Flt Lt Alex
Townsend, and Flt Sgt Neil 'Coops' Cooper
(far right) in front of Chinook 575, which
was hit by an RPG, .50-cal and small arms
fire. (© Frenchie Duncan)

ABOVE: *On patrol: members of 3 Squadron, RAF Regiment, on Force Protection in the village of Mandi Sar.*

BELOW: *Hearts and minds: a member of 3 Squadron, RAF Regiment, engages with local children while on patrol in Mandi Sar.*

It's not all political, though; at the end of the day my biggest concern is with regard to the welfare of those I command and, sadly, it's not always as I would like. By a country mile, the single most memorable event in my tenure thus far was the tragic day when we lost SACs Gary Thompson and Graham Livingstone, the two RAF Regiment gunners who were killed in action on 13 April. That was an awful day, as you can imagine. On a happier note, there are numerous things here that have been just tremendous. The job is fantastic fun and because it's so different, so dynamic, no two days are ever the same. People talk about the Groundhog Day phenomenon but that certainly isn't the case for me – everything is different. I've got access to all the different things that are going on here, so the opportunity to learn and be exposed to the way other nations – even the UK – do their business in areas that I've not dealt with before is great. The people are great too – it's great to have a genuinely multinational headquarters; it's really good fun. We work very hard but we try to play reasonably hard as well.

It's difficult to envisage my leaving a single-point legacy after I leave here. One of my deputy commanders made the comment that we're all on a timeline here. This is a long campaign; we're here for the long haul so my individual impact on that timeline can only ever be small. I'll start things, I'll finish the odd thing, but if I start something and finish it, it's going to be something so insignificant it would hardly be worth mentioning. My predecessor did a great job in setting up the structure that we now have – he did a lot of work getting the big contracts under way with NATO, and my role has been to take that to the next level and try to get us to the point where the base is no longer as expeditionary. What inevitably happens on these sorts of operations is everyone arrives, throws their kit down, and gets on with delivering the operational effects. However, the normality of the base just isn't there – it's just a war fighting operation without a robust regulatory or safety structure to ensure it runs smoothly over the long term. That would be fine if we're only going to be here for six months – you don't need to do anything else. But if you're going to be there for 10, 20 or who knows how many years, then it's not enough.

Look at the infrastructure here alone – we're still driving around on gravel roads that create horrendous dust problems, with road signs that are concrete blocks set in rubber tyres that blow over in the wind and get turned around. That is a microcosm of a lot of the underlying difficulties, so my legacy, if you like, will be initiating a lot of work to try to improve that to get to a more normal base structure, with regulation and safety processes with infrastructural improvements that turn it into something that resembles a normal operating base, recognising that we're still very much doing the war fighting operation.

Away from rationalisation and normalisation, the third strand to my work is seeking to establish a long-term development strategy for the Afghans because, ultimately, whatever happens here, this base will revert to Afghan control and be run by the Afghans. The Afghan National Army Air Corps are starting to arrive here even now and will build up to a full Air Wing by 2016. In addition, this will be a very important civil airport for southern Afghanistan. What we want to do is to try and make sure that the work we're doing now is at least not impacting adversely on what the Afghans are going to want for the base in the long term. That is a challenge because NATO as an alliance concept does not do nation building – it leaves it to others to do that and it works heavily on the basis of infrastructural programmes etc, being done to the minimum military requirement. So we are trying to get the Afghans around the table with the various external agencies that they'll need, to help them build up their governance, their infrastructure, their institutions – to ultimately have what should be a great facility in southern Afghanistan. In essence, everything filters down to just three things – normalisation, rationalisation, and strategic development.

There is a major misunderstanding back in the UK, whereby many people who should know better think that the entire British contribution is in Helmand. We get a lot of senior British opinion-formers through here, and I waste no time in telling them that of the almost 8,000 UK personnel in Afghanistan, 2,000 of them are based here in Kandahar. That is often quite a surprise to some of those who constantly talk about Helmand, particularly when you're looking at some of the stuff we were discussing earlier in terms of threat and vulnerability. The emphasis tends to be about what's going on in Helmand, because that's where the main British contribution to the tactical war is, whereas the reality is that the strategic risks all sit here.

Historically, airfields have always been in good-guy land – we've flown out of airfields into bad-guy territory and then come back to the safety of our airfields. We still regard KAF as a pretty safe area, and it is; that's fair enough, but it is in the middle of enemy territory so the security is fragile and we need to preserve it at all costs.

I think the scale of the challenge is in evidence when you get outside the gate here. Sadly, there are a lot of people here who never do; they'll spend four or six months at Kandahar and never leave the security of the base, so their understanding of the issues in Afghanistan are what they see on the television. It's sad but that's obviously how it has to be because the threat's outside the wire and we're not about putting people into harm's way if they don't need to be there. I do go out every couple of weeks with the RAF Regiment, which I see as a clear leadership responsibility for the Force Protection troops under my command. I don't want to hide within the wire while sending them out into harm's way, and I think it's important for me to get out and see the realities on the ground as often as I sensibly can. There's no doubt the guys appreciate that I do share some of the risks with them but equally it's also extremely interesting to interact with the local people and see some of the real Afghanistan.

People often ask if we can 'win' in Afghanistan. Clearly it is a complicated issue but for me at least, one of the fundamental issues is that the Afghans have to want to see real change and they have to be prepared to really strive for that change. Most of the people I've interacted with on the ground are simple subsistence farmers whose knowledge and aspirations are extremely limited and so it's difficult for them to comprehend what we are seeking to enable within their country. A key problem is corruption, which is endemic here in almost every walk of life. If there is to be real long-term success here, the people need to really want change and they have to reduce the level of corruption, never mind the other, bigger, and very well understood problems like counter-narcotics. Because corruption is so pernicious, it filters its way through every stratum and completely destabilises society.

It's a tough life for the Afghans; you see it all the time – you go through the villages and the kids stick their hands out and the one Pashtu word I've heard more than any other is '*qalam*' which means pen – that's what the kids shout at you when you go out on patrol; they all want pens. They're a big status thing but none of the kids can write, so when they get one, they can't actually do anything with it. It's a tough call because if you give them a pen, they just want another one, and another – it's almost a feral existence for some, particularly for the children. And of course they've got woeful problems with health care – we see it here a lot because our hospital here treats Afghans as well as coalition forces.

Our in-theatre medical capability is tremendous. We're saving people now with horrific injuries, life-changing injuries that would have killed people just a few years ago. Some of it's due to the kit – Osprey body armour's very good and we have the ability to get medical cover anywhere in theatre very quickly. With our guys, it's a life-changing, awful experience and I think that often the thing the media gets very wrong – and through them, the public – is that all the publicity is for the people who get killed but there's very little for the wounded. Sky has tried to address that and there have been a few journalists trying to establish the number of people we are sending home with life-changing injuries, but it's still the dead who attract all the headlines.

Our on-base medical capability is first class but it presents a real dilemma for the doctors when they treat badly injured Afghan civilians. We have the ability to, and often do, save Afghan lives following off-base events such as suicide bombings or even road traffic accidents. However, the lack of an indigenous Afghan health system makes the long-term consequences difficult to manage. Having patched an individual back up again it can easily be that you send him back to his village in the certain knowledge that they lack the health capability to look after him in the long term. In the worst cases this can mean you've simply dragged out his death despite having the very best of intentions. It's a tricky one and I'm not sure what the answer is.

I'll take a lot away with me from this deployment, there's no question of that. Certainly, I've learned the need for patience when working in a multinational environment. It's a totally different environment to the punchy, dynamic world within the UK military. There's no doubt that my desires are constantly tempered by the alliance's and the nations' willingness – and to a certain extent ability – to deliver against them.

Consequently, my ambitions for what we can achieve have needed to be curtailed fairly heavily – that's probably the biggest thing. There's a plethora of minor things, like the exposure to so many different nations and the way they do business – some good, some bad – and the way some of the former Warsaw-Pact nations that are now within NATO are really trying very hard. They're doing a great job and they are among the more willing of the nations to step up to the plate, put their people into this environment and deliver. As has been well documented in the Press, their contribution throws the efforts of some of NATO's historic bigger nations into sharp relief by comparison. All in all it can be quite frustrating but that said, when you can only achieve things with what you've got, it's obviously very satisfying when you do.

Squadron Leader
Neil 'Ebbo' Ebberson

NIMROD NAVIGATOR

The Nimrod MR2 is a four-engine, ISTAR (Intelligence Surveillance Targeting Acquisition Reconnaissance) aircraft with a crew of 12 or 13 depending on the role. The aircraft can fly for around nine hours without air-to-air refuelling. The aircraft is flown in Afghanistan by 201 and 120 Squadrons to help provide accurate and timely information to the ground force commanders.

Transitioning from hunting Russian submarines to steering high-profile and highly kinetic operations, the Nimrod is an essential part of the fabric on UK operations in the Middle East, the electronic glue over the skies of both Iraq and Afghanistan. Switching between theatres on a daily basis, crews don't know where they are going until they get into work for each sortie. The ISTAR support provided by the Nimrod detachment is key to the success of ground operations. The loss of a Nimrod over Afghanistan in 2006 made a huge impact on the tight-knit community of Nimrod airmen, and those lost were close colleagues to many of the crews in theatre at the moment.

Squadron Leader 'Ebbo' Ebberson is a navigator on the Nimrod MR2 and has undertaken several detachments to the Middle East.

I'm a Nimrod navigator currently on a staff tour at RAF High Wycombe. I've been married to my wife for 15 years and we've got a 13-year-old daughter. My wife was in the RAF so she understands our way of life and my daughter, having known nothing else, knows that dad goes away for four months at a time roughly every eight months – it's just the way it is. She doesn't think my being in the RAF is anything special, it's just what happens. Dad goes flying, there's his aeroplane; school Christmas party, we all get on a Sea King – it's all just normal to her. I don't think she worries unduly about me being in theatre; it's all she knows, so again, it's just what dad does. Certainly, that *was* the case until we lost an aircraft in Afghanistan on 2 September 2006 with the loss of all 14 people on board. That was hard on all of us because the environment at RAF Kinloss is pretty much unique. There are two Nimrod front-line squadrons and a training squadron there so everyone pretty much knows everyone else. You can go away for two or three years on a staff tour but when you return to a Nimrod squadron, you're home again in Kinloss. That loss hit the base massively and even now, three years down the line, it still hits home.

When it happened, my daughter was at boarding school and I was on leave. I received a phone call on the day of the crash and was told, 'Right Ebbo, you need to come to work – put your No.1s on.' It was a Saturday and England was just about to kick off against Andorra in the Euro 2008 qualifiers. I said, 'There's a football match on!' but it was reiterated: 'No, you need to put your No1s on and come to work – now.' I put 'Sky News' on and saw that one of our aircraft had crashed in Afghanistan so I quickly drove to the base. Before the names of the dead are released to the media, next of kin have to be notified and that task falls to a trained notifying officer; it's not a pleasant task but obviously it's a vital one. And it fell to me and 13 others that day to go off and do the informing. There's never a good way to tell someone that and it was awful because these were people we all knew, people we worked with, mates. Very, very sad.

As I said, that event hit the base massively but Nimrods have been flying over Afghanistan since 2001 so it's a part of our core business; everybody understands that. Aside from the immediate impact of the news on the families and friends involved, it proved a huge wake-up call for the rest of us. Initially you don't realise how far the repercussions of an event like that can ripple – even in your own family. Obviously with two wars going on there is an element of danger there and I accept the risk, but am I right to make my wife and daughter accept it? While my wife hasn't yet said, 'I want you to stop doing that,' there may come a point when she does; there are people whose wives have said it because they don't want to have to wake up and put the news on and see that sort of thing.

As a navigator, I work alongside the rest of the crew on the Nimrod MR2s that we have in theatre. There are 13 crew onboard the aircraft: two pilots and a flight engineer operate on the flight deck, and three Weapons System Officers and seven Weapons Systems Operators who operate the sophisticated sensors, communications and computers that comprise the mission system. Our role in Afghanistan is ISTAR – Intelligence Surveillance Target Acquisitions and Reconnaissance-related roles, which help to support kinetic effects on the ground. In essence, that means providing reconnaissance support to the Army and all ground units in both Afghanistan and Iraq; if necessary we'll vector in Close Air Support and act as a relay from ground to air. It takes a lot of effort and, often, we end up providing 'negative' information – that can be really useful as it prevents ground units wasting effort when there's absolutely nothing there.

One example saw us being tasked to go and look at a prominent building that the Army believed was being used by the enemy. It was in quite a strategic position on a 'Y'-shaped junction in a village around the Musa Qala area. Generally, what we'd do is fly in from our base in the Gulf region and sit there for six hours or so, just getting a feel for what constituted normal behaviour – and therefore, what didn't. We did that over a period of three days and were able to confirm that the building was full of children, and not enemy. The Army commander had been about to call in a kinetic strike, but we realised that the Taliban had moved out of the area and the locals had moved back in. While the enemy *had* occupied that building, after they left, it went back to its previous role as a school. We didn't actually achieve anything in terms of impact with that – that is, we didn't identify something nefarious and vector in CAS – but we did achieve something regardless. You can imagine the negative impact, had the commander called in ordnance because they thought the building was still under Taliban occupation.

The Nimrod MR2 is quite an old aircraft now, but it's hugely capable nonetheless. It's a derivative of the Comet but it's had numerous bits of extra equipment bolted on over the years. It came into service in late 1969 but was upgraded during the Falklands War with air-to-air refuelling capability. It's fitted with radar and electronic support measures but the most recent and, I suppose, the key to us being in both Afghanistan and Iraq, is the Wescam MX-15, a sophisticated day/ night optical system, with a high magnification lens. It works from high altitudes and allows us to provide a picture to soldiers on the ground, their command headquarters, and main brigade headquarters in real time. Think of TV's 'Police, Camera, Action'-type quality and then times it by a hundred – and it's all captured from much, much higher up – there's obviously a threat envelope to aircraft in theatre, so we stay above that. It's a hugely capable piece of kit, no question.

Before the start of a mission, we'll speak with the Army liaison officer, who is a regular presence among the crew, to get a current scheme of manoeuvre from the ground units that we'll be going out to support. Having the Army liaison guy on board brings us huge benefits. It's not that we haven't acquired the skill to talk to the Army units on the ground over the eight or so years we've been doing this. It's difficult to quantify specifically but when the ground units know that one of theirs is on the aircraft – and the Army liaison officer knows that his mates are on the ground – the emotional connection and the trust are already there, whereas if our crews are rotating through every eight weeks or so, they'd have to start from scratch trying to establish that bond again. It's a huge positive for me, a real asset in having the Army guys there.

Generally, once we're airborne it can be a real challenge getting into Afghanistan, due to the political and cultural situation down below; there aren't any radar services as you'd expect with normal air traffic and it's all procedurally flown. Also, the weather in that area, which is influenced by the Himalayas, can have a massive effect on our aircraft. We've had aircraft come back with major physical damage, having flown through thunderstorms the like of which you just don't see in western Europe; the holes in the airframe where hailstones have penetrated are pretty major, paint peeled off the wings, that sort of stuff – that's pretty hairy.

One of the other difficulties or dangers in procedural flying is the chance of an air-to-air collision simply because there's nobody there to deconflict you. The Nimrods have bubbled windows, so you can see pretty much fore, aft, above and below, but not every aircraft has them. On occasion, the radar can be unserviceable and, with the Nimrod primarily being a maritime aircraft, it's optimised to find contacts over the sea. It can find airborne contacts but when you're flying over land it's more difficult to identify them against the backdrop of the mountains, so there have been a number of 'near misses' where we've been close enough to read the registrations of other aircraft, particularly down near Diego Garcia. That focuses the mind a little bit.

I was Detachment Commander on my most recent deployment so I had numerous aircraft and crews to manage. That meant balancing the needs of the various Army 'customers' – it wasn't always easy because I'd have to allocate the taskings based on their bids and each of them would want priority because they deemed *their* mission to be the most important. There are two navigators within the Nimrod crews now; I was a Nimrod captain previously but, basically, you have one routine navigator who gets the aircraft from A to B, ensures there is enough fuel etc, and a tactical navigator who effectively 'fights' the aircraft and takes all of the tactical inputs from the various sensors and directs the aircraft to be in the best possible place to achieve results.

Doing the job in Iraq and Afghanistan requires vastly different skill sets, given the topography and landscape indigenous to each country. Over Baghdad, say, it's pretty difficult trying to track a white Toyota Hilux at 80mph because almost everybody seems to drive one, and at high speed! White cars are popular there, full stop, so if you're trying to track one travelling at speed in a built-up area and trying to second-guess where it might turn off from any given road or motorway it takes a lot of forethought. The narrow, twisty streets of the slum areas and high-rise buildings in the more urban or affluent places also serve to mask your target – not easy.

By contrast, in Afghanistan, there clearly aren't quite so many motorways or high-rise buildings, which in itself provides its own problems because, often, the people we are looking for travel on foot and it's quite a challenge to be sat high above trying to identify a specific individual. It's doable, though, and we can provide information to ground units on anybody we spot on camera – that in theatre can prove valuable, even though it may seem fairly generic. We might spot someone and we'll be able to say that he appears to be acting suspiciously, and he may be carrying something long and tubular, which could be a weapon such as an RPG. Having the Army liaison guy on board is again useful here as he has a repeater screen for the display so will be able to answer queries from his mates on the ground regarding specifics.

We also have an effective electro-optical and infrared camera system. It provides widescreen TV and a narrow image, which means we can pinpoint an individual. We also have an extraordinarily effective infrared camera. In some respects, we can offer a similar take to that of the British Army's Apaches but our endurance is much, much longer. Obviously, if you have an Apache within range, the Taliban are going to know all about it, and although it's an effective tool for identification and reconnaissance of ground targets, it is primarily a very, very efficient weapons platform. On the other hand, if you've got a Nimrod high overhead, it's going to be very difficult for anyone we're targeting on the ground to hear us. If they see us, there is still a lot of civilian air traffic that flies through Afghanistan and Iran so they provide great background camouflage for us to sit in. To anyone on the ground, we're just another commercial airliner.

It's interesting work but you're bizarrely removed from everything up there, even though you're engaged through the cameras; you can feel quite detached. I can remember one sortie when we were flying in the northern part of Afghanistan towards Kabul and we saw a sandstorm approaching, which reached to an altitude of 15,000ft but which was about 60 miles across. I remember thinking it was just like a tsunami of sand and it appeared to be coming right towards us. I thought, 'Right, we might as well go home because we're not going to be able to see a single thing'. The guys on the ground I guessed had all just hunkered down but that worked both ways because if we couldn't see anything, neither could the Taliban. Days like that may be dull, but I see that as a good thing in a lot of respects. If we fly and don't find anything then, to me, that's a good trip – it's not very exciting but if nothing happens, it means none of our guys have been attacked and nobody's died. The exciting trips are those where people on the ground are putting their lives at risk and where we can do some good by giving them the pictures they need to minimise that risk. One that springs to mind was the operation to recover the body of Lance Corporal Matthew Ford, the Royal Marine who was killed in the assault on Jugroom Fort. That became a highly publicised mission because his body was recovered on the stub wing of a British Apache in a daring operation.

The Nimrod had gone on station to support the original assault on Jugroom Fort by 45 Commando and to provide information as to its progress. We did two hours of pre-assault surveillance, came off station, and did air-to-air refuelling from a TriStar, which then returned back to base, and the Nimrod then went back on station to support the actual assault. It was then that Lance Corporal Matthew Ford was fatally wounded, leading his section on an attack, but it was only later that it was realised he was missing, after his commanding officers did a head count. At that stage, of course, nobody was sure if he was dead or alive but a decision was taken that his body had to be found at all costs and the Apache crews conceived the plan to fly four volunteer Royal Marines in, strapped to their wings, to effect the recovery. As I mentioned, the Nimrod's camera is really effective so we knew that we could find Matthew Ford's body if it was there. We found a heat source that looked probable but by this time the aircraft was running low on fuel again.

By then, the TriStar had landed back at base and the crew were just getting off the jet, so we put a call in by satellite phone and said, 'Look, we need to get refuelled again,' and the TriStar crew just filled their jet full of gas and flew back to Afghanistan. The Nimrod came off station, plugged in again and then returned to point out Matthew Ford's body for the Apache crews. They landed, collected the four Marines, and then flew in under fire to recover his body before returning home for tea and two well-deserved medals. I think that illustrates just how far people are prepared to go when something goes wrong. We'll pull out all the stops and work to the limits and beyond the normal rules when unfortunately something like that happens. The TriStar crew were pretty much on the limits of their crew duty and for us the elementary factor for aircraft is that engines need oil. They can only fly for so long without having a top-up of oil and that Nimrod was airborne right up to the limit, so it was a close call. It was a team effort and everybody played their part to ensure that Matthew Ford's family had his body so they could hold a proper burial.

There have been a number of stand-out missions in terms of our presence assisting the guys on the ground. We were doing some surveillance over Lashkar Gah and we received a cue that said there might be an enemy target knocking around some 120 miles to our west. It was a long shot but we were asked to go and take a look. We found a single Toyota Land Cruiser in the middle of nowhere, about three miles from where our cue had come from; there was nothing else around for miles other than this white Land Cruiser which looked a bit suspicious. We then called in ground units based at Camp Bastion and spoke to the Forward Air Controllers, who put some fast air on to it and took out the contact. I like the Navy's phrase, – 'The team works', but that about sums it up; we get some external cueing, we go and confirm it, and then the fast air comes along and does what we need him to. They can't stay around very long and so it's time critical that we vector him in to the right place, but like I say, it works.

During the earlier parts of our time in Afghanistan in 2001/2, lots of times we would use our technology to put soldiers in the right place. For targeting and reconnaissance, nothing happening is good as I said because even something as simple as us finding a dog in a compound can prove valuable information. If that dog hears a patrol go past, then that's the game blown so we'll pass back something along the lines of, 'That compound there has got at least two dogs in it – can't see any humans so you might want to avoid it.' It's just putting those little bits of information into the picture to make sure that our guys don't come to any harm. Most of the time it's just supporting big assaults and making sure that the guys in the command headquarters have got a picture of what's going on, who is going where. Another benefit of us having the Army liaison soldier with us is that if our real-time high-quality video downlink fails, he can commentate and pass on information on what he sees.

As far as the Nimrod is concerned, she's a 40-year-old solid airliner and right up to the point that we lost that one in Afghanistan, I believed that she was completely bomb proof. I've got 4,000 hours flying it and that incident could have happened to anybody, anywhere – it didn't have to be over Afghanistan, it could just as well have been in the North Sea. It's like when you drive a car – accidents happen, but you never think it will happen to you; it's human nature. There was a lot of coverage in the Press after it happened, that crews were afraid to fly in Nimrods and that they were only flying because they had been ordered to. When it happened, I was a senior flying supervisor and in all my time there I *never* ordered anyone to fly – I wouldn't fly an aircraft myself if I didn't think it was safe and I wouldn't order anyone else to. That was a tough time like I said because I had to have some difficult conversations with my daughter. We fly for the same reasons we always have – we have a job to do and there are soldiers on the ground that need our support.

Being on a staff tour now, I miss RAF Kinloss and the guys on all the squadrons, because we're a very close-knit family. There's a lot of banter and constant piss-taking and sarcasm, which is something we employ to full effect to while away the hours when we're airborne. I remember one boss we had was a bit stiff. He knew what it was like once we'd taken off, so he was like, 'Guys, can you stop with the banter and taking the piss – we're doing a professional job here.' We were like, 'Well, yes we are, but while we are looking at two dogs humping in some compound, it is what it is and we'll laugh about it; we're just sitting here being voyeuristic really, but the moment somebody throws a Flash-bang over the wall, away we go in full-on professional mode.' Some of the guys in that crew were very, very experienced – you can take that as 'old' – and they were used to having the piss taken out of them because of their seniority and with that comes experience. We debriefed and said, 'Look, the boss has said this sarcasm within the crew just has to stop.' So two of us agreed that we could take the piss out of each other as mercilessly as we wanted but nobody else was allowed to get involved and they couldn't be offended by what we said to each other. You know what? By the end of our six-week tour, there were only two people in that crew who hadn't joined in taking the piss and bantering with people.

A lot of the missions end up with stuff happening that you just can't let pass without comment. There was one; we were looking at a compound somewhere over Afghanistan that we'd had eyes on for a couple of hours waiting for some British troops to forcibly enter the compound. We're doing our surveillance when the patrol arrives and throws in a Flash-bang, which causes these great, heavy ornate gates to fall in. The troops storm the compound and there are a couple more explosions and the windows and front door fall in. The guys are in there and then we see this Afghan – probably the owner – fumbling by a car and he's there for about 10 minutes. I said, 'What's he doing?' and the Army liaison guy said, 'He can't find the keys!' I said, 'You've just blown the door and windows out of his house and he can't find his keys?! Why don't you just go and get one of the lads from the patrol, I'm sure they wouldn't mind just smashing a window for him!' But they didn't want to damage his car after they'd basically destroyed his house and his entire livelihood. It just seemed so completely incongruous with everything that had gone on around him.

For all the hours I've got flying over Afghanistan, it's never ceased to amaze me what a beautiful and varied country it is. It's a fantastic place where you can almost see the continental plates hit each other to create mountains. That whole bowl in Helmand, further north, and Gardēz where all the original fighting was, is a complete sand bowl, and then out of nowhere rise 18,000ft mountains. And just south of Kandahar there's a bit of desert and then it's almost as if somebody's drawn a line in the sand and this bit is a kind of yellow sand and then there's a reddy-orange – it's bizarre. When I was a kid, I had a crocodile-skin wallet, which my uncle brought me back from Africa. You know the way the ridges are on the skin; the rocks coming through the desert in the orange part, next to Sangin, just reminded me of this wallet. Desert to us Brits is yellow sand and Lawrence of Arabia, camels and great big sand dunes, but the desert there, it's nothing like that, and it's still phenomenal. As you head further south towards the southern border of Afghanistan where it gets squeezed between Pakistan and Iran as you head south, the patterns that the water makes as it drains from the mountains, it's just unbelievable. If it wasn't for the conflict here, it could develop a healthy economy based on tourism. As a future holiday destination, it's amazing.

Our family home is up in the Highlands, in such a beautiful part of the world, and I love the peace and solitude there. That's the thing, though. I've got a nice house but when you're away for four months – and it could be to paradise for all it matters – you're away from your family and that's the hardest thing about deployment overseas. My wife is still going through the same stresses at home while I'm away – paying bills, dealing with teenage angst – and it only takes one word said the wrong way at the start of the conversation and you might as well not have the rest of it.

During my tour in 2007 I led the Theatre Commemorative Service to the crew of XV230, which was pretty tough, as we were still heavily committed to operational flying. So I'd just had all that after I come back and two weeks later, I'm still tense and wound up because when you're away, you're always working to the limit of fatigue because it all comes back to the guys on the ground and if something needs doing, it needs doing yesterday. I know the Army have decompression in Cyprus but we don't at the moment – we're flying sorties in theatre and two days later we're home, so people are still pretty much wound up. So now I come back and I go to work for a week just to kind of get it out of my system with people who know what I've been doing. Eventually, you just get back to a normal way of life but how the Army manages it, I just don't know.

There are many frustrations working in theatre at a tactical level. Afghanistan is a huge piece of land, truly immense, but we've got a touch over 8,000 troops committed to the fight there. Of those, only about 1,500 or so are engaged in front-line fighting, with the rest in support. To put that in perspective, we managed to deploy 27,000 soldiers to Northern Ireland at the height of the troubles, and look at the size of it by comparison – and that in a place where we spoke the same language and weren't separated by culture. We couldn't control NI with 27,000 troops and you certainly couldn't control England with the number that we have in Afghanistan, so how can we achieve what we need to there? We certainly can't do it alone – militarily, it needs to be joined up. All right, we have technology now that wasn't available then but you still need to have a presence on the ground. For me, one of the positives to come out of this is that I do have a better understanding of how our military can work together now. The Army needs us, we need the Army, and we all need the Navy.

My wife would probably say that I'm a lot less tolerant since my various deployments in Iraq and Afghanistan although, personally, I'm not sure that I wouldn't be like that anyway, because I'm turning into a cantankerous old git. The weird thing is, I really enjoy myself out there, and it's a bizarre concept to try and explain to someone who hasn't been there. Once you realise that you can have an effect, that you can do something worthwhile in terms of helping the guys on the ground, everyone moves in the same direction because they're all working towards the same goal and that applies whether you want to be there or not. The banter and piss-taking are a constant theme; you might take the piss out of the Navy – well, we are fighting in a land-locked country 300 miles from the sea – but the *esprit de corps* and the fact that we're all getting on and doing the same thing is great.

People work with a different ethos in theatre, too. The ground crews work their arses off in theatre, especially when they can see that they are playing an important part in helping to save guys lives. Working all hours in unbearable heat to maintain the Nimrod was one thing that never ceased to amaze me – one shift managed to get me to help jack up an aircraft. I said, 'I want that aircraft fixed and you've got two and a half hours to get it done'; they argued the toss: 'But Sir, we need to jack it up, jacking up an aircraft to change a wheel is a big job.' I told them, 'Yeah, well, you've got two and a half hours, the guys on the ground need it.' And fair play, even with my 'help', *whoosh*, it was done in 20 minutes. It was like KwikFit – they were there and it was done before you knew it. To be fair, they could probably have done it a lot quicker without me, but at least *I* felt that I helped!

The thing about fighting a war on two fronts is that it weeds out any coasters within the military. You know, those who might have thought it was an easy option. I don't mind if you're not very good but the important thing is that you *try*. If you're not trying and you don't give a rat's arse then get out of my way because I don't need you here – I'll get somebody in who can. And it may be due to Afghanistan and Iraq but there aren't many people like that in the military any more, certainly not in the bunch that I've come into contact with, because they're all of the 'Right, let's go' mindset and that's important. We're a team and we work for a common objective so let's get the job done. You might not feel much like doing it at 3.00am when you have to drag your arse out of bed and go flying, but it is important and that is why none of us minds.

WING COMMANDER
WILF PUGSLEY

CONSULTANT MILITARY GENERAL SURGEON

Wing Commander Wilf Pugsley is a consultant military general surgeon based at Camp Bastion's Medical Treatment Facility (MTF), which is the receiving point for all casualties airlifted by the medical emergency response team MERT. The surgical team at the MTF stabilise and package patients for further treatment; there are no facilities in theatre for rehabilitation or long-term care. Most of the injuries being treated at the facility are trauma cases, involving bullet wounds or explosive blasts.

The MTF is one of the busiest hospitals of its kind anywhere in the world and is run by the Joint Forces Medical Group. It contains a five-bed accident and emergency department equipped with two portable digital X-ray machines, a CT scanner, and operating theatre with two fully equipped operating suites. The hospital can accommodate up to 25 casualties with an additional 8 spaces available in an intensive care unit.

I'm based here at Camp Bastion on a six-week deployment at the new Medical Treatment Facility. My role is as a consultant military general surgeon and we deal with some 600 casualties each month – some British, some Afghan locals, and even some Taliban. If the MERT is scrambled, we're on the receiving end when they bring the casualties back – the team on the Chinook will have worked to stabilise the patient en route to us and we take over once the helicopter is on the ground, performing any necessary surgical intervention. The MTF only opened in February 2008 and it replaces the tented field hospital that had been used since 2003. It's housed in one of the few solid buildings at Bastion and it's temperature-controlled and consequently better for dealing with the heat, cold and dust that come with the Helmand territory.

I only joined the regular RAF in June 2007, but I was an auxiliary Royal Air Force officer for eight years prior to that with 612 Squadron, which was used to supply individual reinforcements in a variety of operational tours. The first tour I did as part of 612 Squadron was in Kosovo, but we also provided doctors and nurses for Op Telic and now Op Herrick. I ended my time with 612 Squadron as the Commanding Officer (CO), but I couldn't have stayed on. The normal thing is to end the tour as CO and then retire or move into some other area and it occurred to me that I could establish a new role as part of the RAF Medical Services, by taking on a regular commission and doing the work I'm now doing back in the NHS in Wolverhampton, which involves thoracic and emergency general surgery. I did some extra retraining to be fit for purpose in this new role, doing more emergency general surgery and more trauma surgery, and since then I've been a regular officer in the RAF. I'm probably something of an oddity because by my stage in life, most people would have 30-odd years of experience under their belts as a regular RAF officer and be looking at retiring, or perhaps making a move into the NHS, but I've done the reverse. It works for me and it's been a good move.

Effectively, my working life isn't much different to what it was before becoming a regular RAF officer. When I'm not here in Afghanistan, I work within an NHS hospital in Wolverhampton and the mainstay of my practice now is thoracic surgery – lung cancer patients in the main. Every alternate week I spend time on the emergency general surgical take, dealing with emergency admissions as part of the general surgical team. That was designed to mimic the job I do in the military, which is looking after chests and abdomens. The main difference between what I did with 612 concerns how I am deployed. Previously, I was employed by the NHS and I had to negotiate release for my deployments, whereas now I work in the NHS but I'm employed by the RAF. Basically, they tell me where and when I'm needed and I inform the NHS of what I'm doing rather than asking their permission.

Joining the military had been at the back of my mind for many years, but I chose a career in cardiothoracic surgery and that wasn't really something that I thought the military were particularly interested in, so I parked the idea for a number of years. By 1998, I had a very well-established cardiothoracic practice in place, including a Harley Street private practice, but there comes a point when you either say, that's what I'm going to do for the rest of my working life, or else you take on a new challenge. My areas of research of cardiothoracic surgery have always been to do with the generation of micro emboli and that's something obviously very applicable to the RAF. Micro emboli are the little bubbles that come out of solution in the blood – it causes the bends in diving and is also applicable to high-altitude flying. In 1998, I saw an advert for a newly formed surgical squadron up in Scotland, as part of the Royal Auxiliary Air Force. I was also keen to be involved in something new and being involved in a developing squadron at the outset interested me. All these things came together at the same time and that's what led to me joining 612 Squadron.

In terms of surgery here at Bastion, the operating theatres are of a very high standard and we have around 100 personnel on site to deal with the most serious trauma injuries. Most of what we see is life-threatening injury sustained in mine-strikes, explosions, or firefights – blast, fragmentation or gunshot wounds. Our aim is to perform immediate surgery which will save lives and limbs, before swift repatriation to continue care back in the UK. We have two fully equipped operating tables and the radiography department is equipped with state-of-the-art medical technology – there's a CT scanner and two mobile digital DRAGON X-ray machines, which allow imaging within five seconds and, being portable, remove the need to move a patient from the ward, speeding the diagnostic process. The pathology lab conducts blood and sample testing as well as having the capacity to supply blood products for transfusion.

There are two surgeons in an operational theatre – there's the Consultant Military General Surgeon, and that's the role I fulfil (the body cavity surgeon, chest and abdomen), and the Consultant Orthopaedic Surgeon, so we're at the head of the team: two consultants, one interested in the body cavities and one interested in bones and limbs. We also have a General Duties Medical Officer (GDMO) and an

Army major who is a Registrar in Orthopaedics (or an STR as they're called now). Then we have our theatre team with a qualified nurse who assists and scrubs up for the operations, the operating department practitioners who maintain the equipment around the theatres, work with the anaesthetists and may scrub for operations as well and then, of course, we have the anaesthetists themselves. In addition, we have an intensive care unit so the basics of the surgery that we do is primarily about damage control – stop the bleeding, clean up the wound, and then send the patients to the ICU where their general condition is improved. All this together is known as damage control resuscitation and involves the whole multidisciplinary team.

There's no such thing as an average day other than that the hours are long and the workload intense. It's been a very busy period since I arrived and I spend most of each day in theatre, operating. We go and assess patients in the emergency department and then formulate a plan, a sort of priority schedule before we start operating, but there is always something else happening in the ED before we finish a particular operating schedule. So it is always fairly constant. We tend to catch sleep when we can because, often, the early morning call comes in at 05.00, so we're up at that point and then we'll see patients in the ED, go into theatre, get the odd break between operations, but literally carry on operating. We have the occasional quiet day, but they are the exception rather than the norm. We work together, which I think is an important factor – it just doesn't happen in the NHS. Here, we are two consultants either working on different patients but adjacent to each other, bouncing ideas off one another in the same operating room or we're working together on the same patient. Sometimes it is predominantly an orthopaedic problem but there is a good deal of overlap. Take something like a patient with severe leg injuries from a bullet or an explosion – the orthopaedic surgeon will deal with the soft tissue and bony injuries but often there are vascular injuries, too, and that's where my special interest lies, coming from a cardiothoracic background. It makes sense that I'm there to deal with any blood vessels that have been damaged.

Most of the trauma cases that I have dealt with consist of injuries from improvised explosive devices, IEDs – these are 'home-made' but usually highly sophisticated explosive devices which cause blast injuries often going up both legs, so there are severe injuries to both legs going up towards the abdomen. The majority of injuries we have seen have been limb injuries – gunshot wounds, IED blasts. We have had some chest trauma and a couple of abdominal injuries that have required laparotomies, looking into the abdomen, and thoracotomies, dealing with chest injuries, but they are rare. Fortunately, with the increased protection that the Osprey body armour offers, the incidence of major body trauma in British casualties is relatively low. It's amazing the difference that Osprey has made to the sorts of injuries that we see – it has contributed to a huge reduction in the amount of chest and abdominal trauma that we have to deal with. Obviously, a round that hits you full in the chest when you're wearing Osprey is still going to cause blunt force trauma from the sudden deceleration and transfer of all the energy that the round possesses, but very little of it now requires medical intervention. If you compare the situation now, as opposed to say Kosovo and the early days of the Balkans, the number of chest and abdominal injuries has decreased significantly. That is why we are seeing more gunshot wounds to the limbs now – some 'through and throughs', but we've also removed rounds from bone; obviously, the bone fractures and the rounds are retained there so we extract them while debriding the wound.

The mainstay of our surgery is damage control, though. We do the initial life-saving and limb salvage-type procedures and then, with British cases in particular, our emphasis is to package them up and get them flown out by a specialist critical care team (CCAST). I recall one particular case, which was a blast injury to both legs and going up to the abdomen – we did an amputation on one side and a damage-control limb salvage procedure on the other – and I was operating in the lower abdomen and the perineal region to try to access the bladder and insert a catheter into a severely traumatised area. I was also helping the orthopaedic surgeon with the debridement of the soft tissue injuries to the leg. That patient was the victim of an IED and he came in severely shocked – we packaged him and got him ready for a CCAST flight out. I later found out that he was making good progress in Birmingham. Blast effects are broadly similar whether you're in an unprotected vehicle or you've stepped on a mine – the blast goes upwards.

Amputations are sadly something that we deal with on a regular basis but the principals are sound. In old military surgery there was a preponderance just to amputate and sew up. Now we've moved away from that concept and we have to consider limb salvage, but if the limb is not viable and there is a lot of dead and contaminated tissue then we have to amputate, otherwise the patient will develop sepsis (serious infection) with the possibility of life-threatening 'septic shock'. The decision for us out here in the field – the real decision – is do we need to amputate and if so at what level to amputate. We usually take that decision together; two consultant surgeons agreeing a treatment plan. We try to amputate at the lowest level, leaving as much of the limb as possible for the patient but obviously not leaving any dead or contaminated tissue behind. Bearing in mind we can get the patients back to Birmingham very rapidly, certainly within 24 hours, it is appropriate to choose the lowest level because it can always be revised there. For example, if we did a mid-thigh amputation, they would have no chance of offering the patient anything lower than a mid-thigh amputation because we've done that, but if we did a through the knee amputation then there is always the possibility of revision to a mid-thigh amputation in Birmingham if that is shown to be necessary.

Physiologically, it's pretty straightforward – it's muscles, nerves, blood vessels, and bone. We tie off the blood vessels, saw through the bone and cut away the dead muscle tissue. Then again, in the field, we don't try to fashion the amputation stump nowadays, we just leave the skin flap and the muscle open so that when the patients arrive in Birmingham, surgeons there can check and make sure there is no contamination or possibility of infection before they actually complete the amputation stump. Effectively, when we repatriate patients to Birmingham, they are a work-in-progress – this is the concept of damage-control surgery, so that what we do in the field is save the life of the patient, or save the limb or as much of it as appears possible, and resuscitate the patient. What's made the big difference in survival is really this package of resuscitation and life and limb salvage surgery being done in a really rapid way, and then packaging the patient up for early departure to Birmingham.

The most taxing case I've had here so far was a patient – an Afghan national – who had suffered a gunshot wound to the abdomen and pelvis. When he was brought in he was suffering from profound shock and he suffered a cardiac arrest as he was being wheeled into the operating theatre. In that case, the first priority was to get control of the bleeding. It's all very well pouring in a blood transfusion but if the patient is bleeding to death, you can pour in as much as you want – it will just continue to leak out. You can't salvage the situation, so the first part of the operation was to enter his abdomen via a mid-line laparotomy incision and then press hard on his aorta just as it came through the diaphragm. That allowed the circulation to the brain and heart itself to be re-established and the anaesthetists did that part of the resuscitation. Then with somebody still holding their fist on his aorta so that the bleeding into the abdominal cavity was reduced, we were able to determine where the bleeding was actually coming from. The blood supply to the bowel was one source of bleeding and the muscles around the pelvis were another major source of bleeding. We then gained control of that by removing part of the bowel and applying pressure packs to the pelvis itself. We managed to sort out his abdominal injuries and he made a good recovery and left the hospital in good shape. Things like that are a real positive and certainly stand out for me.

In many ways, every patient that we deal with is a really moving story. I mean, most of the forces that come through the MTF are either British or American, and for the most part they are very young guys. It's quite tough when you consider that a large number of them are going to have to go through a whole host of surgical problems and then rehabilitation before they can really fit back into any sort of life – and it's amazing that some of them do actually stay in the military and carry on. Every case stands out in its way and I couldn't pick on any one particular case, but I think it's just the concept of life-changing injuries for very young, fit, healthy guys – it's a tough thing to have to deal with, even for me as a surgeon. That said, it is interesting the number of times that we've had really seriously injured lads that have come in and you'd think they'd be really upset and anxious about their life and what was happening to them, but the first question they ask is, 'Will I be all right to join my unit? Will I be all right to get back to the action?' And you think, goodness me, you know?

I think the lowest points for me, though, are when we get casualties coming through who are beyond help – basically, those who are dead on arrival. I mean, one in any particular day is probably par for the course, but there have been incidences where we've had four or five and there's absolutely nothing you can do. All of our knowledge and skill, all the equipment and the facilities we have available, so many medical staff on hand to do everything they can, and you're completely and utterly impotent. It's immensely frustrating and that's a very low point for all of us, I think. Of the issues that affect us all as individuals, however, there are aspects of the lifestyle on deployment that are frustrating, but they are minor by comparison. I'm divorced now with two grown-up sons, one of whom has a commission in the Royal Marines Reserve where he's serving full-time. I don't have the same ties as maybe some others, so the only things I miss are the small ones like going out at the weekend and enjoying a nice meal and some wine. I'm not saying there isn't any kind of social life here – people do put on various events that are intended to relax, and there's no alcohol admittedly but that's ok, because in theatre it would be inadvisable – but you obviously can't make a choice, for example, to go out on a Saturday night to the theatre or the cinema; there's just no choice.

On the upside, nothing compares to the way you feel when you turn something around and somebody who comes in on the verge of dying is given another chance. Also, I think for me, the biggest plus about this deployment is the teamwork that I've experienced at the MTF – it's truly exceptional. One of the things I believe we've lost in the NHS is the corporate spirit within the hospital – as junior doctors, we used to actually live in the hospital and there was a kind of corporate spirit where we knew all of the other people involved. There was no European working time directive and there was a very definite spirit about the place and that is exactly what happens out on tour. There aren't any petty squabbles or disagreements because we work as a team and we're living within 20 or 30 metres of the hospital and the whole thing revolves around the care of the patients and life within the hospital. In terms of professional experience, we are exposed to vast amounts of trauma; for a person interested in trauma surgery, you get a lifetime's worth of experience in the NHS in just six weeks out here.

One of the things that I find really interesting compared to some of my other deployments, is the increase in survivability that we are seeing among soldiers in this conflict, compared to others in more recent memory such as Kosovo. The difference between the Balkans and here is really quite marked in the sense that we are seeing less body cavity, chest and abdominal-type trauma, and therefore the survivability rate is increased. I think also the introduction of the MERT facility may have made a difference. In Kosovo we had an Immediate Response Team but it was slightly differently organised to the current MERT. The MERT is efficient and brings the casualties 'well packaged' as it were, having had pre-hospital care applied to them. On the whole, when they arrive with us, they're in good condition so that we can get on and operate on them.

There is a combination of factors at play, though – the level of pre-hospital care and the ability to undertake a degree of resuscitation outside of the hospital are clearly a part but so too is the effect of people such as the platoon medics. There's also the introduction of tourniquets for peripheral vascular injuries and a clotting type agent for abdominal, chest, groin and neck trauma. Undoubtedly those have all made a major difference to survivability. In addition to that, the speed with which the patients are brought to the hospital, the hospital facilities, including a consultant-delivered emergency department service, the rapid change from a tented facility to a hard built modular facility with a CT scanner available – all of those things have made a significant difference. But there have been huge leaps forward in terms of the protection afforded by each soldier's personal kit compared to that in previous conflicts. As I've already said, I think that Osprey body armour has made a huge contribution to that and possibly the Mk6A helmet, which replaced the Mk6 in 2005 and according to the MoD, provides 40 per cent more protection. I've been in theatres previously where we had several British soldiers brought in with penetrating brain injuries, but on this tour I've seen none whatsoever.

There is something of a debate going on at the moment as to what kind of doctors should go out on the MERT; traditionally, they don't carry surgeons. Here in Afghanistan it's anaesthetists or emergency-department doctors who go out, and there is a debate about who is best placed to do the pre-hospital care. The doctor has to be capable of doing a rapid-sequence induction – the ability to put a tube down somebody's throat and get them ventilated quickly. The other aspect, of course, is to stop major bleeding, but we have non-surgical techniques to do that, including these haemostatic bandages and tourniquets so they are applied to quell a major haemorrhage until the patient gets back to the hospital.

This is an interesting deployment for me, both at a personal and a professional level, and it's probably changed the way I think about some things, which may come as something of a surprise. It might sound strange, but in your average NHS work you don't actually think about the possibility of death – from a personal perspective that is. I mean, we all know you could drop dead from a heart attack or get knocked down by a car but it's not something that you think about for the most part and it's not foremost in your mind. However, on a deployment I think there is a greater awareness that life is finite and can end at very short notice. You might as well enjoy what you can – that's an overriding, overarching thing that deployments bring out. Obviously, life out here is rather different to back home and you exist in a kind of bubble; you have to because it's so far outside of the frame of reference for one's normal life. But I know from previous experience that I find it relatively easy to switch between the two. I'm helped immeasurably in that by my colleagues in the NHS, and I think I'm very fortunate in terms of how they deal with everything while I'm away. The only frustration is that I believe some of them tend to think along the lines of 'Well he's away and he's just not here, he's on holiday', or something like that, and this makes it a little difficult to readjust when I return, but they're all very supportive in terms of looking after my practice and making sure that when I come back that I'm integrated fairly quickly.

From a professional perspective, the work I do here or back home isn't massively different – that's the theory, anyway. I mean, yes, it's all medicine and it's all about providing care and saving lives, but it's the sheer volume and complexity of a lot of what we deal with in theatre that is the key difference and it's probably something of a problem for military surgeons. We now have vast experience of this kind of work in

Afghanistan and Iraq, and from a surgical point of view it's experience you can't gain anywhere else. Six weeks in Afghanistan will give you a lifetime of trauma surgery experience if you're working in an NHS hospital, so there are huge benefits to the NHS in terms of the experience that people like myself are gaining and filtering down into it. I dread to say this because it could be misinterpreted, but the essence of our employment is that we are employed by the military working within NHS hospitals so that we are ready to undertake these kinds of operational tours. Bizarrely though, Afghanistan has made the situation such that we return to the UK with a vast amount of experience which is then really helpful and necessary to the NHS practices. I'm sure this is all part of the concept of setting up Level One Trauma Centres, something which is just starting to happen in London.

In terms of my own practice back in the UK, I'm not entirely sure there are any immediate transferable benefits from the skills that I have acquired in theatre on this tour because with my NHS work, the trauma cases are so rare. The overarching thing is the damage-control surgery which is the main essence when you get a trauma case – considering the whole patient and doing what is absolutely essential for life and limb salvage and resuscitation. I envisage that I will have some difficulty in applying that to my normal working life in Wolverhampton where it's very much a question of lung cancer cases, which don't conform to that, or general surgical cases, which are emergencies such as appendicitis and strangulated hernias, that sort of thing. But within the context of Level One Trauma Centres, places such as the Royal London Hospital, then this is where the kind of skills that we've got could really be utilised. There is a concept being floated that a few military surgeons might go to work in the Level One Trauma Centres once they're established because it would be good to keep their military practice alive and it would also be utilising the skills that they've gained in Afghanistan and Iraq for the benefit of the NHS. That really would be giving something back.

Corporal
James Taylor

CHINOOK ENGINEER

Keeping the RAF's Chinooks and all their systems functional is difficult enough in England, but translate that to the dust, dirt, and sometimes torrential rain or snow of Afghanistan, together with incoming mortar or rocket fire, and it's an all but impossible task. It's the job of the Chinook engineers to make it happen, though, and keep the Chinooks airworthy.

Corporal James Taylor is based at Kandahar Airfield and had a near miss one night in June 2008, when the base came under rocket attack; a rocket struck the ground next to the Chinook that James and a colleague were working on and ricocheted through the back of their aircraft, taking out vital systems.

I never had any particular interest in engineering when I was younger, but electronics – computers and that kind of thing – always appealed to me. That's basically how I ended up in avionics; well, that and being an air cadet. I knew that I wanted to pursue a career that involved electronics and I'd had an interest in the Royal Air Force for a while, so it seemed only natural for me to join up when I was 17.

I did my basic training at the RAF Defence College at Cosford, the same as everyone, undertook my avionics training and was then posted to RAF Odiham. I'm now an avionics technician supervisor with ExCES, which is the Chinook Expeditionary Engineering Squadron – essentially, we provide on-aircraft engineering activities in support of the Chinooks used by 18 Squadron and 27 Squadron aircrew. My job is maintaining the avionics suite on the aircraft, basically – defensive aids, electronic warfare side, comms side, flight systems side, and electrics as well.

As soon as I got on to ExCES I volunteered to come out here, because I knew it was bound to happen sometime and I wanted to get it out of the way when it suited me, instead of at Christmas or at some other time when, say, I'd had something planned.

Afghanistan wasn't too bad then. Previously, my first ever Out of Area was five months in Iraq on the initial stage of Op Telic. I went out in January 2003 and came back in May that year. That was a big shock, and after that, every year since, as with most of the Chinook guys, I've either done two months out here or four months, as well as UK exercises.

In theory, we're supposed to do a tour, and then spend four times the length of that tour Out of Area but it never works like that – we simply haven't got the manpower to do it, and avionics is quite undermanned in the squadron, so a lot of guys are getting a lot of stints out here. I volunteered to do a couple of short stints close together.

This is my sixth two-month tour out here in Afghanistan, so you could say that I'm kind of used to it now. I've been here a month and a half and I've 19 days left. I wouldn't say that I enjoy it, but to be honest the time passes so quickly here and there's no end of challenges. It's a whole lot busier than being back with my home unit at RAF Odiham, because here we're dealing with the whole of the British Army and the aircraft are being tasked all the time. The turnover is incredible; it's so hectic, especially on the days that we spend at Camp Bastion, because we're dealing with IRT and HRF aircraft there.

Typically, my day is taken up with rectifications on the aircraft after they've been flying, dealing with systems that have gone wrong as well as making sure that the aircraft that are in service are ready for flight. The biggest difficulty we face compared to back home is the heat during the summer months, when it can reach as high as 55°C during the day and it doesn't drop off by much at night.

Temperatures like that really affect your ability to operate effectively and it's a constant battle really – heat like that literally doubles the amount of time it takes to repair the aircraft. It's like an oven in the hangar, there's no airflow. That affects the aircraft, too, as it effectively doubles the number of rectifications we have to undertake. Avionics-wise, the computers are overheating, the processors are overheating; even in terms of normal servicing, oil's leaking, pressure's leaking from everywhere. In this environment, the aircraft are probably stretched the most.

Dust, too, is obviously a huge problem although it's more of an annoyance than anything for us – most of the guys are used to that and they've got their goggles, or sunglasses as most people here wear anyway. It's more of a problem for the aircraft, though, particularly the engines – its fine, like powder, so it gets sucked up easily, but its corrosive so it wears components over time; its such a punishing and hostile environment for the aircraft to operate in and it is going to take its toll.

Personally, this has been the most memorable tour for me due to an incident that happened last week when we came under rocket attack. Obviously, that's a fairly regular occurrence here at Kandahar but I've never experienced anything like this.

It was around 21:00 hours. One of the Chinooks was meant to go on a sortie but the crew had to abort it because of an engine torque problem, I think – they flew around for a bit and then came back down.

They snagged the aircraft for a torque split or a number one engine torque fluctuating as I recall, so myself and a mate went and got the test set and came down to the aircraft. We set everything up, which took about 20 minutes, so it was just starting to get dark by then. We put power on the aircraft; it takes about 20 minutes to half an hour to calibrate the test set for the actual test so, five minutes into that, we were waiting for everything to warm up – and then we came under rocket attack.

Usually when we come under attack, you're fairly remote – you hear the *whoosh* and the explosion, but in the past it's always been quite a way away. You know, you'll be in your accommodation, or in the mess hall and you'll hear a distant explosion. But I've never experienced anything like this – it was really up close and personal. I heard one go past, literally like a firework, and according to a guy on the other aircraft parked alongside us – 895, I think it was – it bounced and failed to detonate. They saw the sparks where it struck the ground. As far as I know it was a 107 rocket.

Like I said, I just heard it go past but someone said it hit the pan somewhere and went over the fence further into the camp. I looked at my mate and said, 'That was fucking close!' and I'd no sooner got the words out of my mouth when '*whoosh*!' – another one and again we heard the rocket noise. We were both stood at the rear of the aircraft by the ramp, facing out – and, at the time, we felt debris shower over us. I just looked at my mate and said, 'Let's just leg it!', so we legged it back to the hangar. I know you get all the drills, like 'hit the deck' and that kind of thing, but it doesn't work that way in practice. And when you're sitting on an aircraft full of rounds and fuel tanks and everything, you just think, 'Let's get the fuck out of here!'

So we legged it back to our little bunker and the guys were like, 'That was a close one!' And, initially, we thought it had hit the gravel to the side of us because we felt debris and heard like the smashing of glass and we just assumed it was the kick-up from the gravel. So we got into the bunker and the guys from the other aircraft said, 'That was really close … we saw the sparks – it was close to 895', and we were a bit in shock and saying, 'No, no it was 673', and they were like, 'No, it was definitely 895.' In the end, we were just sitting there and I was trying to convince myself.

It was dark by now, but just as we heard the siren sounding the all-clear, we came under mortar attack. So first we had the rockets, then the mortars, so we were in there for over an hour. When we were finally given the all-clear, we were all out with our torches and stuff and gave the aircraft the once over.

It's funny how things happen but, obviously, people tend to exaggerate so a lot of the guys thought our story was just that – a 'story' – and everyone was focusing on this aircraft. But when we walked up to the ramp, we couldn't see any debris anywhere, and my mate and I were both thinking, 'We definitely felt stuff.' So we walked around the side – we didn't initially see the left-hand side – and all the guys were like, 'Oh you're full of shit!' And then we walked around to the left-hand side and that's when we saw it – that part of the Chinook was a complete dog's breakfast. And that's when the whole banter side of it just stopped. I was just looking at it and all my mates were like, 'Mate, that's so lucky!' So I came into the aircraft and all the soundproofing had been blown apart in the cab. It was a real mess.

From what we know, that second rocket landed about 5ft away from the aircraft we were on and ricocheted off the pan. Obviously, it failed to detonate, but they really fly those things, and its velocity was such that it penetrated the skin of the aircraft we were on, went through what we call the 'broom cupboard', which is where all the avionics wiring is, across the cabin and out the other side.

It's just so random. To some extent, it doesn't matter where you take cover or what you do, if one of them has your name on it, you may as well just stay where you are. It's just weird – especially when it ricochets like it did here – that and the fact that it didn't explode! Looking back, it all seems so unbelievable and full of 'what ifs …'. We could – should – have been 20ft further up inside the cabin when the rocket struck. What we do when the test set has warmed up is, we have one guy in the cockpit and one guy on the engine, so we'd either have been walking up to the cockpit or one of us could have been there somewhere in the cab, and it's pure chance – there is no reason for us to wait by the test set; we should have been waiting up by the cockpit or something, which is exactly where the rocket impacted.

The next day I came in and JEngO said, 'It's up to you, but do you want to do the repair on it?' and I said, 'Yeah, why not?' I don't think we'll be doing any of the repairs but I did the battle-damage assessment for it, avionics-wise, on the port side; there's another lad on another shift doing the starboard side.

I'm fine, really. My mates here have been really good and I've had other experiences that help to put it in perspective. I didn't tell my dad and I didn't tell my girlfriend, although I guess if they're reading the book now, they're going to know! But at the time, you don't want to put that amount of stress on those close to you – they'll only worry – so I just rang one of my civvy mates. You need to tell someone – so I was telling him about it and he was like, 'Fucking hell.'

I've done Baghdad, I've done Basra, places like that – in Baghdad I had one come through the hangar roof, which lodged itself into the rear of the hangar door – it was a reinforced door. I wasn't in the hangar at the time but I was just outside and that was pretty hectic. In Basra you got used to it because it was like a rocket-magnet. Here it's less frequent, but again you get used to it – obviously that's been the closest.

I remember back when I was in Baghdad – we were at BIAP (Baghdad

International Airport) and there was no hard cover there. That place was always taking rocket and mortar fire and there I was in a little Yank tent – there were hardly any Brits there – and you could hear the *whoosh* as they came in. So I'm lying there, looking at my crew chief – I was 20/21 at the time, so you look at your chief as all singing, all dancing – and he was probably shitting himself as well but he was like, 'Don't worry lads, it's all right, it's all right.' And that's really reassuring at the time.

It's weird really, but I guess the rocket and mortar fire is one of the few things that bring home to you that you're really involved in a war. For most of us here at Kandahar or Bastion, you never get outside the wire. So aside from the heat and the dust, you can become quite detached from what's going on outside and every now and then, the IDF reminds you that, actually, it can be quite dangerous.

And it's odd for us, because unlike the guys at the front, say, you can't fight back. They're armed, they take fire and they fire back, or they'll attack and take the fight to the Taliban. When you're inside the wire at a huge base like Kandahar, though, you have to sit it out and it can feel quite emasculating because you're unable to do anything except react to incoming rounds and hope they land somewhere else.

When you've been somewhere like this for a while, you tend to get quite blasé when you get an IDF. It's the same at BIAP, Basra – anywhere that takes a lot of incoming rocket or mortar fire. You can always tell the new guys – they're the ones with sense. Like last night, we had three rockets hit us, and when you hear the siren, or the first explosion, it's helmet and body armour on and straight into the bunker. It's always a little bit surreal when you're doing that but around you are guys still strutting around like nothing's happened. But when it's like happened to my mate and me, it's a wake-up call.

Even now, there are so many guys here who, if we're getting malleted in the middle of the night, wake up and think, 'Ah, fuck it, I can't be bothered' as they pull their sleeping bags over their heads. Like that's going to make a difference! I'm first in the bunker now – you'd have trouble beating me! And then we all sit in there. It used to be there were guys who'd stand on top of the bunker trying to see where the rockets and mortars hit. It really is just pot luck because the guys firing them aren't aiming at anything specific; they've got only the vaguest idea of the direction. It's not like they've plotted a grid reference or programmed the GPS co-ordinates; they don't know where it's going to land – they just send it and hope, kind of like, 'Let's spark it up and see how it flies!'

There's no question that's been the most memorable event of this tour for me. My highlight, though, is probably working on the IRT. Generally, there's a lot of stick between the Army and Air Force – it's good-natured I guess and it cuts both ways, but the Army guys give the Air Force a lot of stick because they think we're the softies. But, Chinook-wise anyway, when they're in the poo and that kind of thing, the IRT guys love Chinooks; so when you say you're a Chinook engineer, they're chuffed to bits.

Focusing on that kind of thing's good; IRT and HRF – you know that when the IRT goes and you've got that aircraft ready in five minutes or whatever it is, ready to let it go, you know it is going to be really appreciated. It's the same with the HRF, whenever that's taking off to send the guys in. It's a good feeling because it's the one thing here where everyone really pulls out all the stops – the guys at the front rely on us and it's so vital to them, so we all pull together, every link in the chain.

Obviously, you hope it never has to go up and it's certainly not a good feeling when they have to go, especially when you know one of our lads has taken a hit. But when they go, you know they're going in to do something worthwhile. And when the Force Protection guys get off the back of the aircraft, and we're all around it checking it over, servicing it, doing the rectifications on it, they come over to us telling us, 'I love these things.' In fact, on the flight back last time – I was out at Christmas, delayed as usual on a TriStar – I'm sitting on an aircraft full of Marines and they're all saying, 'I hate fucking RAF' and all this stuff. A lad with corporal's stripes turns around to me and says, 'What do you do mate?' And I say, 'I'm in the RAF.' That makes him go a bit quiet so I say, 'I'm a Chinook engineer', and he says, 'Oh that's all right then, we all love Chinooks!'

It's quite amusing in some ways, especially with the Army lads –

they think the Chinooks belong to them! Because these aircraft all come under land command, they see the Chinook as theirs. They see it from a completely different perspective from what it is. I guess it is quite weird, the fact that the RAF operate them; compared to the Americans, the Dutch, and everyone else, where they're all run by the Army. When you do your management courses with the rest of the Air Force back at Odiham, and you've got guys off Tornadoes and it's always their helicopter support guys that are kind of like the off-breed of the real Air Force sort of thing – it's kind of weird.

You try your best to make it homely here for the duration of your tour. You know, your bed space – when you arrive, you've got a cot, somewhere to put your stuff and that's it. So you try to make it as comfortable as you can. And on your down time, there's always the BX or the Green Bean Café, or The Boardwalk – although you don't want to make too much of a habit of the Pizza Hut here!

If you're out here at Christmas, it can be really good, considering. People really rally round, and we're always amazed by how people at home send letters, gifts – just packages from complete strangers addressed to 'A British Soldier, Afghanistan' – there's loads of that. And last Christmas, on Christmas Day, we were wakened by … I think it was a captain or a major, and they came round, kicking the doors in, first Christmas box. Then I went into work, had a bit of a Christmas dinner sort of thing; we had non-alcoholic beer.

Usually, protocol turns on its head and the officers serve the enlisted men dinner, although things were still pretty much as normal for us. Obviously some sections close down, but without Chinooks the guys out at the FOBs couldn't function, so here we're 24 hours a day, 7 days a week, Christmas or no Christmas. We might be at KAF, luxury as it is, but there are still guys down at FOBs, dug in somewhere, who still need water, food, IRTs, etc, so you just do as much as you can really.

I think that each of us here has our own way of dealing with time when you get close to the end of a tour. Because it happens so frequently, I know you're not meant to get complacent, and you don't get complacent with your job, but, when you get into a routine, it flows a lot better and it's good, so it takes your mind off things. I don't think about the trip home, the flight confirmed or anything. Air transport home, I just don't look at it. Everyone else around me is like, 'Oh, who's replacing you?' or 'When is your replacement coming?' And I'm like, 'I don't know, I've no idea.' I just wait until two days before and then take a look around at what's going on.

Other tours didn't change me too much, but this one definitely has. The last two didn't as I was in a routine, thinking, yeah, I've done this before, I've done that before. Telic had an effect too, massively; I was 20 at the time. And then BIAP was the year after. It was strange; although Telic was our main push and supposed to be the big war, I never had one IDF, never saw one drop of blood – it all came afterwards. It was weird during Telic itself and for the first 11 months or so after – during that period and before the uprising of the Mahdi Army in April 2004, we'd been welcomed almost as liberators and, literally overnight, around 10 April 2004, it all changed: IDF all the time, snipers at the BX, rockets, mortars … it was just constant.

This tour has definitely changed me, though. It makes you appreciate things so much more when you go back home – what you can do. I guess that you also notice the absence of what goes on here, too – stuff like IDF, wounded soldiers, or local kids being casevaced into the Royal 3 here – so you notice what doesn't happen. And you think about what people have to put up with here – I mean it's not exactly basic, but there is a degree of privation here. When you think that there are people – our soldiers, Marines – actually living in the FOBs, where they have really basic facilities and they're being absolutely malleted every day, they're fighting back, taking casualties … and you just think, 'Fucking hell.' But there are a lot of people back home – I'm not saying I've fallen out with them, but when I got back, I just thought, 'You just don't know, you have no fucking idea.'

I know it's an old man sort of thing, but you just think, 'You just don't realise how good you've all got it.' Or when all people can talk about is *Big Brother* or *Hollyoaks*, you just think, 'Jesus!' We do watch it out here but you can't take it seriously, not when you see what's happening here. We're sitting here thinking, this is it, this is what people do.

I'm quite a positive person generally and I'm not superstitious, so I think it all helps in terms with coping with life out here. I think it goes with the territory, though, as an engineer, and more especially being a bit of a geek and into avionics, that superstition thing tends to go out the window. Most engineers are quite logically minded. We've had all the, 'Oh, you've only got a couple of lives left,' and all that stuff, but it's meaningless.

There's a lot that you miss about home when you're here, but to some extent you exist in a bubble and you try not to think about it too much. There's lots to take your mind off things, and you get into your own routine, but obviously, I really miss my girlfriend 100 per cent, and I'm not saying it because I have to say it, big time! I can't wait to see her and … you know! But actually, I'm just really looking forward to seeing her. That, and going out – having a good time, being able to socialise, relax, enjoy myself. It's the freedom, I guess, which is such a contrast to here. It's all of that, but I'm really looking forward to wearing civilian clothes as well – something as basic as that – putting your jeans on, or shorts and flip flops; just putting them on and chilling out, relaxing. You just appreciate everything so much more. If there's one good thing that comes out of this place, it's that when you go back you appreciate certain things so much more.

I'm hoping to take my girlfriend to Prague when I get back. We haven't been together that long – we met just two weeks before I came out on this tour – so it's still really new and fresh. This has been a huge commitment for her – and I guess it's far harder for her than for me, because being here, I know what it's like, I have a sense of perspective – it's always worse for anyone close to you, sat back home. They worry.

You do your best to play it down, because when all is said and done, those of us who live at Kandahar or Bastion really have it quite good compared to the lads on the front. I've tried to make it as pink and fluffy as I could, because a lot of people, when you say you're in the Air Force, they assume you're up in the fast jets or helicopters getting shot at and they never envisage anything like this. So I say I'm in the Air Force, I'm in engineering, I'll be all right. I'm technical supervisor for the guys so I'll be fine.

It was funny, when I was speaking to her, I was on Facebook the night that the incident with the rocket happened and she was like, 'How's your day been?' And I was typing and I said, 'Remember this

SAC
IAN 'SETH' SETTERINGTON

RAF FIRE AND RESCUE SERVICE

Contained within Camp Bastion's 10km perimeter are an airfield, heliport, ammo dump, fuel depot, vehicle parks, repair bays, stores, offices, and accommodation for 5,000 soldiers. The protection of these assets against fire is the job of the RAF's firefighters.

One of the hardest jobs they undertake is vehicle extraction rescue – getting soldiers out of their vehicles after they have crashed or been blown up. They deploy to the scene by helicopter with the Incident Response Team – medics, bomb disposal experts, and an infantry protection squad – and they may find themselves working under fire. Equipped with state-of-the-art fire engines, the teams can be at the scene of a plane or helicopter crash at the airfield in less than two minutes, carrying and then pumping 60,000 litres of foam or water on to the fuselage of the plane.

SAC Ian 'Seth' Setterington was coming to the end of his first detachment to Afghanistan when I met him, shortly after he had been scrambled with the Incident Response Team, to salvage and destroy a crashed Reaper UAV.

I'm known as Seth, and I'm with the fire and rescue unit here at Camp Bastion. My home unit is the fire and rescue team at RAF Northolt, but we deploy out to Afghanistan as individuals from RAF bases across the country to form a single unit here.

My primary role in theatre is as part of the duty team providing fire cover for the airfield – basically, that means that there's a team on duty and ready to roll for each and every aircraft that lands here at Camp

Bastion. In that respect, our responsibilities are the same as those of firefighters at Heathrow, Gatwick, or any other civilian airport.

We basically work 24 hours on and 24 hours off. The 24 hours on are spent here at the fire station on the far end of the airfield and like firefighters anywhere, if we're not dealing with calls on the airfield, we're killing time – maintaining and cleaning the fire tenders, our kit, training. We'll sleep here, eat here, and in our downtime we'll keep fit, and there's a pretty cool recreation area at the station here where we can chill out. Our crew room is pretty good too – we've made it feel like home and we've got a big screen LCD TV tuned to BFBS. We've also been adopted by a cat, which has had a few kittens, so they're a regular presence in there and make it feel homely. I've absolutely no idea where she came from – we're in the middle of a desert! – but she's adopted us!

When we're off duty from the team here at the fire station, we're on call for the Immediate Response Team down at the Fire Ops Tent. Basically, if the IRT gets called out, we provide rescue cover. Take a mine strike, or IED; if one of our vehicles takes a hit, or if it's involved in an RTA, our role is to manage the rescue of anybody trapped. We use the same sort of cutting equipment as a civilian firefighter called to an RTA in the UK, except we have to carry everything ourselves, and we're obviously also carrying weapons as we are typically operating on the ground outside the wire in areas where the Taliban are active.

Undoubtedly, the heat is a real factor when we're on IRT call – if we get a shout, we have to be ready to respond within 15 minutes, and that means from wherever we are to the pan ready for departure in the helicopter with all our kit: body armour, helmets, weapons; and all of our cutting equipment and assorted rescue stuff. Often, you're soaked in sweat before you even start, so it's important to be fit.

This is my first deployment to Afghanistan, although I've previously been in Iraq and the Falklands. I was also involved in Operation Fresco during the last firefighter's strike back home, covering Suffolk and then the Midlands, so it's certainly varied. I've been here at Camp Bastion for almost four months now, so I've only got two more days in theatre and then I'm going home.

You have to try and stay focused throughout your deployment here, so you can't afford to slacken off or take your eye off the ball just because you're 48 hours away from finishing your tour. What brings it home the most is that there are people who are in a far worse position than me, and if we switch off then we're potentially putting them at risk. When you think of what the guys on the ground are sacrificing … well, for us to keep our minds on the game for another two days is not exactly difficult. Besides, I've got leave due to me when I get home and I've got a weekend away planned with my fiancée, Victoria. The weekend after that I'm having my stag do, we're getting married at the end of July, and then we're on honeymoon straight after on 1 August – we're going to Las Vegas, Los Angeles, and San Francisco.

Victoria's great, but like many military partners she's never been entirely happy with me going away. That said, it's not a strictly military phenomenon – no partner's going to be happy about you going away for four months at a time. I think after the first month of being here, we were chatting quite a lot and seeing how we were getting on, and we were doing well I think. We got engaged after I got back from the Falklands last year and we said after the first month it would determine how quick the tour would go, and for the first month the time was just flying by.

Time off is at a minimum really. You're on a 24-hour shift up here, then you're off, then you're on IRT. You don't really have much time to yourself because you're constantly working so, when you do manage to get five minutes, you suddenly realise a week's gone, or a fortnight, or your first month's gone. After that, you're almost at your halfway point, then you have your R&R to look forward to, and then after that you're more or less on the home stretch so, as long as you can keep yourself occupied, it's ok. She's busy at home too – she's a primary school teacher – and she's had the wedding to plan so she's had a lot to do.

For me, I think the best bit of all deployments is the people that you work with. You get to meet new people; new guys who are experiencing this for the first time, and you get to work alongside guys with a bit more experience who've been here a couple of times or have been to other places and you get to share their experiences. The camaraderie and the friendships out here are good.

Obviously, it's from a personal perspective, we're in a kind of 'Catch 22' situation because of the job we're in – it's good to get shouts because it gets you excited and gets your adrenaline pumping and you're ready to go, but the flip side is, somewhere down the line, something's gone wrong or somebody is potentially seriously hurt.

Challenges are many and varied. From a personal perspective, it's all the usual ones – like any deployment, it is being away from my fiancée, family, and friends that's the hardest part. From a professional perspective, I think it depends very much on what time of year you arrive in theatre – it's a lot hotter here now than when I first arrived at the beginning of March. So the hardest part for me at the moment is probably dealing with the heat – and also trying to get some rest in too. Because we're on a 24-hour period up here, if there's flying on late at night, you can't get much sleep, and when you've got 24 off, you can't sleep in the heat. During the cooler months it's a lot easier. You can have some down time and not be sat there sweating as soon as you've had a shower!

There are several incidents throughout my tour here that stand out, but one that rises head and shoulders above the others was when we were scrambled do deal with a UAV that had crashed.

Let's take the set-up for a typical IRT duty for the Fire/Rescue team: for 24 hours, you form part of a four-man team and your fourth man is in the ops tent for the evening period. When we got the call, around 3am, I was shaken awake. The fourth man, the guy who is responsible for the phones and radios, sleeps in the control room. He said, 'We've got a shout, we've got to go. So I clambered around my pod, trying to get my stuff, and we all got in the tent. The first brief didn't tell us very much as there wasn't much known at the time. The warrant officer told us that the details were very vague, and that a UAV had crash-landed and we had to go do a recovery job on it. He told us we had plenty of time to get our stuff together as it was going to be a well-planned op over a couple of hours rather than a quick snatch 'n' grab such as we would normally do for the rescues out on the ground for troops, etc.

As the bits of info were being drip-fed to us, we learned that we'd be dropped into a hot zone, that there would be no Force Protection on the ground, that we didn't know anything about the area where the UAV had crash-landed apart from the fact that the Taliban may be aware of it happening, so there may be enemy forces at the site looking for it – just what you want!

Me and the two guys I was with, Pringy and Wiggy, we were looking at each other thinking, 'Do we really want to do this?!' And the warrant officer was saying, 'Look, you're under no pressure here because there are 12 lads, all of whom are eager to get out on the ground.' I was looking at Pringy, who's quite a new SAC into the trade – about nine or ten months experience – and Wiggy's wife was expecting a baby back home, and I'm due to get married, so we were just looking around thinking, 'What do we do? What do we do?'

We had a little bit of a huddle together and just thought, 'Oh, let's do it.' Everybody wanted to do it, wanted to get out there, but I couldn't help thinking about back home. So we had a bit of a huddle, discussed what kit to take, and ended up just taking small hacksaws and general-purpose cutting blades. We took a circular battery-powered angle grinder, which was absolutely useless, and two circular saws. Reapers are fairly lightweight in terms of their construction, although they're very strong, but we knew that we'd be cutting through soft, triple man-made fibre – carbon fibre – which was pretty easy to cut through. So we took basic cutting gear and rescue kit. We took the two circular saws but not the heavy duty cutting equipment, purely because of the time frame that we'd have on the ground and what we were cutting through; we just thought it would be too much to carry and a bit OTT for what we needed. Obviously, along with all that, we were fully kitted up the same as the soldiers on the ground – DPM desert uniform, Osprey body armour, helmet, weapons, etc.

They flew out some RAF Regiment guys on two Chinooks to provide us with Force Protection while we were working and we went out with a couple of the EOD (Explosive Ordnance Disposal) guys and an engineer who knew the layout of the UAV and what he wanted cutting off it. Clearly the whole purpose of the mission was to recover certain parts of it. When we landed, Force Protection went out and formed the perimeter. Then we went over to the crash site.

When we first lifted off on the Chinook, we took off quite high from Bastion and as we were going up and up, a couple of flares went off at the back, and my heart was thumping like mad and I was thinking to myself, 'Seth you idiot, why'd you take this mission when you've got a gorgeous girl waiting back home for you?' And it seemed like no time at all before I looked over at the loadmaster who signalled that we'd be landing in five minutes and I started to panic a little. We were shouting across to the engineer and he was showing us a blueprint of the Reaper and what we were going to cut off, and we looked across at the loadmaster and it was two minutes, then one minute, to landing and soon the ramp came down at the back of the Chinook.

The two Chinooks landed side by side, the Force Protection ran off one and we ran off on the other side, my rifle in one hand and a saw in the other, thinking, 'Now what do I do?' We weren't sure what to do so we hovered around the back of the aircraft until Force Protection went out past us and at the time I was thinking, 'I hope this isn't like the scene from Saving Private Ryan when they run off the boats and all your mates start getting slotted left, right and centre!' When we went down there, I was trying to make myself into the smallest ball possible, with my rifle poking out, and with the Chinook's blades spinning there was dust everywhere and I could hardly see a yard or so in front of myself. I don't really know what was going through my mind at the time. I just wanted to make myself as small as possible and as soon as they've gone out, you don't have to worry about it anymore.

We landed about 50 metres away from the UAV, the Force Protection guys deployed, and then we ran over to the crash site where we were shown what parts needed cutting. When we took off, we were told we had two hours on the ground, but just before we landed we were told we only had an hour and 15 minutes – a total of 75 minutes on the ground. I don't know if it was because there were agencies coming to see what had happened or whether it was because of the fuel in the Chinooks. They had Harriers circling above and the Chinooks took off once they'd dropped us down. So we were in the middle of nowhere, nothing but desert and sand dunes, on our own.

We had parts of the aircraft that we had to work on more than others: the engine was held on by quite a few struts and quite a bit of pipework, so the other two guys who came out with the Fire Service started cutting the engine. They took off the props and the casing and then they had to take off the struts as well. While they were doing that, I was at the front with the engineer and an EOD guy, cutting out different parts from the front, all the sneaky beaky kind of bits which we thought would be easy to take off … they're little clips and a few little screws but because of the crash they wouldn't come out so we had to use a crowbar and jemmy them off.

We had a big kit dump made up of all the parts we'd taken off and all the equipment and there were just mountains and mountains of little black-box recorder-type things, satellite dishes and engine parts – a bit like Steptoe's yard! – and when we got to the hour point and had to get the stuff out, the parts that were black-box recorder size we could just pick up under our arms and carry to the landing site, but the engine was about 250kg so we put strops underneath and around it and dragged it across the sand. But because of all the cutting, there were jagged edges everywhere, so it was bogging down into the sand and it made it feel like we were dragging a half-ton deadweight!

Because of where we were cutting and there was a significant hazard from MMMF [Man-Made Mineral Fibres] dust particles from the body work and the carbon, everybody was on respirators, which nobody likes – you feel claustrophobic, your peripheral vision is compromised and you're sweating like you wouldn't believe. So you're sweating and trying to work away, with your rifle strapped to your back; you've got the saw you were cutting with at the front and the sweat running into your eyes and your mouth, and there's nothing you can do about it because you've got gloves on and the respirator. I felt a bit sick licking salt off my lips.

Then we dragged the engine away from the immediate area and we'd a few of the Force Protection guys help us drag it – it was just too heavy for us to do it ourselves. They told us they'd an area set up for us and all we had to do was drag it to there and the helicopter would land and get it on the aircraft. So we dragged all the bits out and made a kind of pick-up point where all our kit was, about another 50 metres away from the aircraft going out of the crash site. So we had everything set up in one area and the Chinook came back and landed about 100 metres in the opposite direction from where we were, so we started ferrying kit backwards and forwards. This was with full kit, Ospreys, respirator, and absolutely sweating like you wouldn't believe. Once everything was on board the aircraft, we took off again. We were just dying on the aircraft; there were guys being sick in the sick bags due to exhaustion, everybody was just shattered, absolutely drained. All our kit was soaked with sweat, faces dirty with sand, people spitting out sand – chewing gum was being handed round the cab because everyone's mouths were full of sand and no saliva left at all. A few bottles of water were spread about too.

At the time, I was thinking, 'right, get me off this thing and into somewhere with air-conditioning!' When we left the site, and knew what was happening, the whole idea of taking the EOD out was that they were going to blow up the airframe with small charges and then send in a Harrier GR9 to blow it to pieces with a thousand-pounder, just to make sure. But because we'd run out of time and the guys on the ground were saying, 'We gotta go, we gotta get moving now!' we stood back and let the Harriers take it out. We knew more or less what was at stake but not the whole story. We knew an aircraft had crashed-landed off-site and we had to go and recover some parts from it. But when we came back we knew we'd done a really big thing and it dawned on us then that what we'd done was a lot bigger than what we'd realised at the time. A lot of people gave us a pat on the back – a job well done kind of thing, and that's when we realised the importance of what we'd done.

They're not all like that, though; I've been involved in two non-starters while on the IRT. We've been called and told we were going out on a shout, we've got to the back of the IRT Chinooks and then told they'd had enough men on board. Just recently we've had quite a few shouts, with guys trapped in vehicles from mine strikes and such like, but they're the only ones I've been out on. It can be a bit frustrating when you're scrambled and it comes to nothing. Obviously, if we're not going out, it can mean we're not required, so nobody is seriously hurt. It's exciting to get the call and go but then when you think about what you've got back home and the thoughts that are going through your head about what your missus would say if she knew what you were volunteering to do … sometimes I'm glad I didn't go – but I'm kind of glad I did the Reaper shout. I'm thankful really that I haven't been called out to anything else.

After the Reaper crash, when they'd finished the investigation, the

AOC of 904 EAW gave a commendation out to the three of us on the ground who had done the recovery and the cutting, so we had a photo taken and a bit of an award ceremony at the fire section here.

It was an RAF-led operation right the way down to the Force Protection – the FP guys were brought up from Kandahar and were RAF Regiment rather than the Army guys who were based at Bastion. I believe the thinking was: this is an RAF drone [UAV], so it's going to be an exclusively RAF operation to get it back. So we were all RAF on the ground, the RAF flew us there and back, and the RAF blew the thing up. We wanted to recover every important piece of the UAV rather than to risk it falling into Taliban hands and I think the fact that we blew up one of the remains of our own UAV rather than let that happen speaks volumes. A lot of people were very happy that it had been a successful mission, so it's quite a high point of the tour for me.

FLIGHT LIEUTENANT GARRICK HILL

REAPER PILOT

The RAF's Reaper MQ-9 UAVs (Unmanned Aerial Vehicles) are the future face of aerial war; flown by pilots from 39 Squadron based in Nevada and Afghanistan, who operate from remote terminals based in darkened rooms some 8,000 miles away, they can launch devastating attacks against Taliban forces using Hellfire missiles or Paveway Laser Guided Bombs (LGB).

This is war with a difference. The RAF pilots live and work near Las Vegas but go to war in Afghanistan. When they finish, they drive home again to their wives and families, and undertake normal family activities such as shopping at the mall, eating out, or hanging out with friends.

Flight Lieutenant Garrick Hill is a Reaper pilot with 39 Squadron deployed to Kandahar; the drones are launched from there by Garrick, after which he hands control to his colleagues back in Nevada. At the end of a sortie, he again takes control and lands the Reaper, at which point ground crews in Kandahar maintain and rearm the UAVs for their next sortie.

My home unit is the recently reformed 39 Squadron, which is based with the USAF's 432nd Wing in Nevada at Creech Air Force Base. I was a Nimrod pilot for most of my career – I'm 48 now and I've got about 4,500 hours on that aircraft – but my role for the past few years has been flying Predators and MQ-9 Reaper UAVs. I've lived in Nevada for over four years now, I got remarried there, and it's where I call home. You can live quite comfortably because your money goes so much further; when I go back to the UK it's quite a shock at how quickly I can get through a £20 note! The standard of living is much higher in the US, so materially, you're better off, although whether you're happier or not depends on you. Las Vegas is such a unique place to live, though.

I'm here in Kandahar on a four-month deployment as a Reaper pilot, but in terms of the landscape, it's not a lot different from home; it's 44 degrees here today, bone dry and sunny, so the weather's largely the same as it is back in Nevada. This is my second deployment from Creech to operate the Reaper; I did the first four months when we took delivery of these in September 2007, went back to the US for four months and here I am back again. It seemed like a very short four months at home, but we're short of people. The RAF's UAV capability is relatively new in the great scheme of things and as with most new kit, there's a very high technical aspect to it so training is a problem. At the moment, there's an insistence on only qualified and experienced current pilots being allowed to fly them so that can create a bottleneck. They are fully integrated into air operations and often fly missions alongside manned aircraft so I suppose it makes sense from that perspective.

The MoD purchased MQ-9 Reapers from the USAF to provide an all-weather, persistent ISTAR capability 24 hours a day, over a wide geographical spread so they provide our troops with a better picture of activity on the ground. Often, FACs will have real-time access to the video feed from the Reapers on their battlefield computers and they can call in the strike, which will be executed by the operator in Nevada, or occasionally by us. The original Predator UAVs were principally used in the reconnaissance role but the MQ-9 Reaper is a hunter-killer UAV designed for long-endurance, high-altitude surveillance. They're equipped with Hellfire missiles and Paveway laser-guided bombs, which is pretty much the same payload as one of the USAF's F16s. Unlike fast air, though, which takes time to get on station and might only be available for 60 minutes, the Reaper flies in 12-hour shifts. It gives the RAF a real 'deadly persistence' capability, with its ability to fly over a combat area night and day waiting for a target to present itself. In this role an armed Reaper neatly complements piloted strike aircraft because while a Harrier, say, can drop larger quantities of ordnance on to a target, the Reaper, which is much more economical to operate, can be kept on station almost continuously, with ground controllers working in shifts.

The Reapers are maintained, armed, and launched by two of us here in Kandahar – a pilot like myself, and a sensor operator – using radio antennas which link the aircraft to our ground-control centre. Once airborne, the link is severed and reconnected via satellite to Nevada, where it is piloted on screen by my colleagues at 39 Squadron for the duration of each mission. At the end, they'll hand control back over to me for the landing. It's a very difficult aircraft to fly, very unforgiving because you're isolated from the real world as it were. We fly the aircraft from a console inside an ISO container here. The controls aren't a million miles away from what you'd expect to see in the cockpit of any aircraft, with the usual instruments, throttles, etc and several screens. Aside from our instruments, though, our only way of 'seeing' is through a fixed camera lens in the nose of the aircraft that provides a view of about 30 per cent of the sky, so you have almost no peripheral vision or awareness. You really have to think yourself into the cockpit and even though I've now got 2,000 hours flying Reapers and Predators, it still requires a lot of imagination.

The workload on approach is quite challenging because aside from the visibility issues, it handles differently to a conventional aircraft in many respects. The UAVs themselves are delivered in boxes brand new from the factory and they arrive here on the back of a C17. The boxes are rolled off, the guys put it together, and a few hours later, it's ready to fly. The pilot console here is a mobile version, which we just unloaded from a C17 and plugged in to get it up and running. It has all the instruments and screens you'd expect of any cockpit so the rest is down to me and my 'co-pilot'. We have two consoles with similar controls so either can be configured to fly from, but in front of me I have a head-up display with all the usual instruments, head-down displays and the various screens that give me navigational information, maps, routes, etc. There are several levels of automation available, so you can have it on a pre-programmed mission where all the parameters are handled by the autopilot; I can then have it where the autopilot is flying set speeds, headings, and heights or I can remove the autopilot altogether and fly it directly, through a stability augmentation system.

When I'm flying an approach, my co-pilot – he's a flight sergeant at the moment, we worked together on my last deployment – will back me up with speeds, heights, calls, radios, weather, etc. The interface is difficult to work, so I'm operating pretty much at maximum capacity and he's backing me up, checking everything, and calling it all. Another difference from a conventional aircraft on landing is that there are no audible warnings from the radio altimeter telling me my height – with the Reaper, I just get a warning beep and height calls from my flight sergeant, so that would be an enhancement, certainly. We've a phone in here and that can go while I'm flying the approach, which isn't something that happens in a conventional aircraft landing! Take-offs bring their own challenges – the Reaper's fin, or the rear stabilisers on the Predator can impede your take-off and ground out if you're not careful. It requires a very gentle angle of climb on departure. It's an operating hazard but it doesn't cause problems and although it looks like they sit low in pictures, they do sit up a little when the engine's running.

The Predator predates the Reaper but the two have very similar characteristics. The Reaper is bigger and heavier, so it's the more stable of the two, but the Predator is more affected by thermals, winds, and variations, just like a motor glider. The Reaper has more bulk, more inertia, so it's better on the approach, although they're both equally tricky on the last few feet. Looking at images of the two, it's easy to see how one grew into the other – the Reaper was originally known as the Predator 'B' and its wingspan is a massive 66ft and it weighs in at 10,500lb when it's fully armed, fuelled, and loaded. It's a turboprop so it's got a lot more power available, it can do 250 knots and it can climb at quite a respectable rate, too. In UAV terms, it's quite a high-performance aeroplane. Remarkably, it is capable of flying in excess of 24 hours and has a high operational ceiling of 50,000ft so the possibilities are pretty much endless. Both aircraft look the same – same basic principle, same functionality, but on different scales and with differing capabilities. The Predator is slower – half the speed, double the endurance, a fifth of the weight; it was built to loiter because of its reconnaissance role. They've evolved; they started as drones really, a basic reconnaissance asset and have developed over time into hunter-killers. Now they're the poster aircraft of the counter-insurgency wars and they've really made a huge impact.

We're hot and high here in Kandahar, so we have to allow for that when we are launching the aircraft, although in cooler weather, in winter time, you can get airborne in a shorter stretch of runway. It all depends how much you hang on it; I mean, if you start hanging all the bombs and missiles on it, it does need a lot of space. When we flew it clean, it would leap into the air and soar off skywards and it really didn't need very much at all. It needs a long runway for landing as it's difficult to slow down. Once airborne, we'll climb to height; I'll set the aircraft up and turn on the return link for the satellite. We transmit from the aircraft and it ends up in Nevada, they see it and configure their aeroplane, they then activate their command link, take over control of the aircraft and off I go for however many hours. At the other end of the mission I'll come back here and do the opposite procedure.

Once airborne, the Reaper has the ability to range over the entire country – we're not limited by the line of sight transmitters and we have a small forward footprint. To be honest, all we need is a small satellite dish out here and we could fly the whole operation from here, but why bother when every man here needs to be flown in, fed, guarded, and accommodated along with all the rest of it? It's pointless when you can have just two people here and a whole squadron back in Nevada, so the way we do it is much more resource friendly. This way, if we need to move somewhere else from here, it's doable because we just move this portion of the unit and the rest can stay fixed. It's all about flexibility.

If there's any residual fuel once control is handed back to me, I'll undertake supplementary tasking; I'm available, there's fuel available, so we can fly extra missions and get as much out of it as possible. It's value added because if we did nothing, nobody would be upset, because they've got out of it what they were contracted for, but if we do extra, then it's a bonus. One of our strengths is that we're here in theatre so Intel will be fed to us and if it's close in, short-range tasking, I'll undertake it. There's a lot of action out on the ground round here so if there are two or three hours of fuel when I regain control of the aircraft, I'll undertake two or three hours of line of sight operations in the local area. If we have eyes on, we have authority just like every other aircraft – if there was a Harrier out there, the procedure to strike would be exactly the same.

So far, I haven't come across any situations where we're being told locally to do x, y or z, and we've had to remind them that we're not principally here to do that, but that not's to say it won't happen in the future. We'll only undertake our line of sight operations providing that they don't obstruct our primary one, and for the most part people understand how it is. When the aircraft is under satellite control, it's more flexible – you can go anywhere with it and you have all the connectivity and all the mission support you'll ever need. Here, it's obviously a little more limited, its range is less etc. The idea is that if there's an aircraft fuelling out on the dispersal and it's loaded with weapons and there's a crew available to fly it, then we'll fly it, if we can. The primary tasking is run from the US, but we've still produced a decent amount, so we're quite in demand here.

When I first got here I was teamed up with an American who's since gone on to Balad, in Iraq – the USAF have a Reaper team there – and we were doing some residual line of sight taskings. On this particular day, as we took control of the aircraft, I saw ten people in a field taking up fighting positions in a building, but we didn't get clearance to engage them because we couldn't get positive ID on their weapons. Then we were cued in to a field where we saw two guys laying a mortar. We were still trying to get permission to engage them when they left and we tracked them to a tree line. We managed to get a positive ID on an 82mm recoilless rifle that they had with them. One of them had secreted it under his clothes before but then teamed up with his friends to attack friendly forces. That's when we engaged them with an LGB.

There are accounts that from the ground, an inbound 500lb bomb sounds like a steam locomotive heading in towards you at high speed. Personally, I can't say, but there were five guys on the ground when that LGB was launched and we got four confirmed kills so there's a fifth man walking around out there somewhere who knows for sure and, doubtless, he's spread the story of what happened to all his friends. You'd think that would send a message, wouldn't you? You know, if this is what you engage in, this is what happens. Obviously, not everyone learns, do they?

We operate the Reapers well outside the threat envelope normally. Its endurance, armament and reconnaissance capability all add up to a pretty potent and capable platform. If the conditions are ideal, then we'll be high enough that we're not visible or audible from the ground, although sound perception is a very complicated thing. It depends a lot on background noise really – you can shout in a concert and nobody will hear you, but if you whisper in a field then people a long way away will hear. It's really complicated, so you have to look at all environmental variables before you could actually say that it's silent; if you're in open desert, with no wind, you'd be able to hear aeroplanes at 35,000ft, but in a city street you won't hear what's going on around the corner, so it all depends on your perspective. Mind you; that said, it doesn't really matter – the range of the camera and the weapons mean that if someone spots it, it's too late for them to react anyway.

The whole US/UK mash up is quite interesting in that for almost everything, we're completely interchangeable. As I said, there are US crews here, US Reapers and Predators and the one RAF Reaper – so it's a question of whoever is on shift will fly whatever is available or tasked. The maintenance engineers here in theatre are all from General Atomics Aeronautical Systems, who build the Reaper, whereas in Creech it's all contracted out. We have RAF engineers back in Nevada but they're all on the Predator programme still. I'm sure that'll come because we have to develop engineering expertise, but this is still very much the early stages so to get it quickly we just buy in the servicing and the training and do it that way. We've had RAF engineers on the Predator system for four years or so now but you have to bear in mind that it's a new technology; it's new, it's novel, it's leading edge.

Regardless of the duality of everything, one major point to bear in mind is that I still have to operate the Reaper within the UK's Rules of Engagement. We don't lose our nationality, so that has to be observed at all times with each of us working to our own national rules. In my case, it's me, not the aircraft, which defines the RoE, so even if I was flying a US Reaper, I'd still be working to the UK's RoE.

It's not so bad here, but it's a bizarre existence sometimes back in Nevada. I can be flying missions over Afghanistan and engaging the Taliban while I'm at work, but at teatime I'm back home with my family, chilling out, or visiting with friends. You still have all the normal life stuff, like going to the shops, cooking, paying bills, but instead of heading off to an office, or flying halfway round the world to deploy, you head off to the base and fly combat and reconnaissance missions over Helmand province. It's been described as armchair warfare, or remote control warfare, which isn't a saying we're very happy with, but it does describe the reality to a degree. Some people argue that because we're so remote, we're detached, shielded, and immune from the full horrors of the effects of any weapons we fire, like the Hellfire, unlike infantry soldiers who are up close and personal to witness the effects of their weapons. It's not like that, though; the Reaper's high-definition cameras play out everything in real time so you aren't denied any of the effects.

Although it's an RAF squadron and based in Nevada, 39 Squadron is comprised of personnel from all three UK services: RAF, Royal Navy, and the Army. There are probably about 90 of us in total, about half aircrew and half engineers. Our mission is to provide persistent ISTAR and, where required, offensive support to UK and Coalition forces involved in operations but, as I said, the squadron was only reformed in 2008 and it's based with the USAF's 432nd Wing. There's little practical distinction between crews – when I finish work here today, the RAF Reaper will continue flying and a US crew will come in. I fly USAF Reapers too – it's just the way shifts work out. Basically, it doesn't matter if it's the US or us, here or back in the US – they can fly the RAF Reaper and they do, we all just get it up and launch it. Obviously, different nations do some things differently and some of the edges might need smoothing over a bit but it's an efficient system and we help each other out. I think the whole project is very successful and the Americans have been very pleased with our input and support, while we're very pleased to get access to their technology, facilities, and infrastructure. So I think we've put a lot in and got a lot out. Both sides are very happy.

I think it would be fair to say that I'm agonising about where I go from here. In my first year flying UAVs, I was desperate to get back to manned aeroplanes – I wanted to be a pilot; I wanted to fly something real again. Now, I'm so accustomed to the enormous capability and the positive benefits that I can do that to leave it would create a big hole. I'm not flying as I've known it throughout my career, I'm not actually in the aeroplane so I miss being airborne and flying hands-on and the whole experience, but I can do so much more with this aircraft than I could with any other type of aeroplane. That's what it's all about: you've got to shift where you get your satisfaction from, and I've been doing it for so long now, I wonder if I might just be stuck here.

On the whole I enjoy it. I get a lot out of it and I get a lot out of the system. It's interesting that people refer to aircraft like the Reaper as UAVs – *Unmanned* Aerial Vehicles because they're not unmanned at all. The only aspect that is actually unmanned is the air vehicle, which is only one portion of the entire system. This is a global system that is manpower intensive – it is most definitely *not* unmanned. I suppose 'remotely piloted' would be more correct. All the human interaction skills and team-working skills are still there and it is immensely satisfying when a team comes together and works well. Because 39 Squadron was only reformed earlier this year and it's been reborn, it's still growing, a few people have wondered about whether we should have the letters 'UAV' after '39 Squadron' to designate what we fly. My thinking is, well, why would you want to? We provide the same service and with similar equipment to other squadrons, with the only major difference being that we fly the Reaper from some place other than where it is.

You see mentioned in the Press every now and then that all military aircraft in the future will be UAVs, that the pilot is the weak link in the chain, but it's not something I see happening, certainly not in the foreseeable future. What I think we'll see is the same thing as happened at the very birth of aviation, where aircraft started off basically as reconnaissance platforms and then, by the end of the First World War, they were shooting, bombing, and doing everything in between. I think UAVs will develop in the same way; they started off as reconnaissance platforms, now they're hunter-killers and eventually they'll just pick up more roles. There are UAVs that do a lot of Close Air Support, others do reconnaissance; who knows where it will all end. Air transport will probably be the last because there's no benefit to going 'remote piloted' unless in doing so, you bring added benefits; there's no point in doing it just because you can. So the idea of the unmanned airliner? No. I mean, why go to all the trouble when it's easier and people are happier to have a pilot in there?

WING COMMANDER
EILEEN BUCHAN

BRITISH EMBASSY COUNTER-NARCOTICS TEAM

Afghanistan's only significant export is heroin. This illicit £1.5bn industry warps the entire economy, fuelling corruption and bankrolling the Taliban, while giving a huge number of the population a vested interest in maintaining the instability. With drugs the mainstay of the Helmand economy, which single-handedly supplies 20 per cent of the world's heroin, British commanders cannot afford to alienate the populace by being associated with poppy eradication. However, it is equally clear that there are increasingly close ties between the Taliban and the drugs mafia.

I met Wing Commander Eileen Buchan at Kandahar in July 2008, but she is based at the British Embassy in Kabul where she is seconded to the FCO's Counter-Narcotics Team. She works with Harmid Karzai's Minister for Counter-Narcotics and is at the forefront of Afghan efforts to reduce opium production in Afghanistan.

My home unit is RAF Honington but I'm currently serving in Afghanistan on secondment to the Foreign and Commonwealth Office (FCO) in Kabul. I previously worked as OC Support Wing at RAF Honington, which provided all the life support services for the RAF Regiment. My role here is as the military representative on the British Embassy's Counter-Narcotics Team, which means that I'm an interface between various agencies such as International Security Assistance Force (ISAF) and Task Force Helmand and the FCO in delivering counter-narcotics efforts in Afghanistan. While the military campaign and counter-narcotics efforts have previously been mutually exclusive, ISAF and the wider international community are becoming more and more aware that the two strands are inextricably linked. Narcotics revenue is one of the underpinning funding mechanisms for the insurgency; moreover, the narcotics economy prevents the spread of good governance because it fuels corruption.

Part of my job is to support General Khodaidad, Harmid Karzai's Minister of Counter-Narcotics who is responsible for the National Drugs Control Strategy (NDCS). His Ministry is accountable for counter-narcotics policy across the whole of Afghanistan. As Britain is the lead partner nation for counter-narcotics we are a key interface in the international community. We work with all nations to synchronise efforts in terms of what we deliver across Afghanistan. It's one of those jobs that goes from tactical, where I can be in a poppy field helping support the efforts of the Poppy Eradication Force and de-conflicting them with the efforts of a task force, to the strategic, where we work with the wider international community to support the Afghan delivery of all strands of the National Drugs Control Strategy.

It's against the law to grow narcotic drugs in Afghanistan, therefore the UK's role, and that of the wider international community, is to support Karzai's government in delivering law enforcement. How they do that is multifaceted; in part, it's through the elimination of narcotics, and that's a vast continuum of everything from drug demand reduction to encouraging farmers to grow something else such as wheat, corn, grapefruits, pomegranates – all sorts of things. This strategy has eight pillars: Public Awareness, Criminal Justice, Institutions Building, Law Enforcement, Alternative Livelihoods, Demand Reduction, International and Regional Cooperation, and Eradication. While the strategy focuses on all eight pillars, people often think that the only action arm is eradication but that is not the case. It is, however, the part of the strategy that receives the most publicity and is perhaps the most controversial. It is law enforcement at its most brutal and is conducted by the Afghan Police, who are mentored by DynCorp. Eradication is conducted in the early stages of the poppies' growth so that farmers have an opportunity to replant with something else. The window of opportunity for eradicating poppies is at the 'cabbage' stage, when they appear as little more than green fuzz in the fields. This allows farmers to opt to grow something else. That's an area where ISAF has been very good; supporting governors across Afghanistan with the eradication, helping the Afghan government to do what they need to.

British forces in theatre follow UK policy on counter-narcotics, which means that they support law enforcement and its delivery, but our soldiers aren't involved in the physical eradication of the poppy fields. There are many ways we can assist Karzai's government to deliver its counter-narcotics law. Just last week they managed the biggest drug seizure ever, one of the biggest in the world – Afghanistan's drugs forces captured the equivalent of 31 double-decker busloads of hashish. It's a massive tonnage, something like 190 tonnes, and it's one of the biggest hauls they've ever had. They managed that in part because they tend to have intelligence-led operations, and intelligence is one of the areas we're working with them to develop. At the moment we're helping several provinces so that they can work on their own intelligence development. They are working at it and they're good at picking up chat. Here, that gossip is good intelligence as it tends to come from good sources. The counter-narcotics force is working with mentors from other countries so that it's able to do its own interdiction and it's currently one of the most well-developed forces in Afghanistan. ISAF support during the 2007/8 season was pivotal in ensuring the safety of the UN verifiers, who audit the scale and shape of the eradication, and of the Afghan National Police (ANP).

The biggest difficulty for me on a day-to-day basis is getting the international community to buy into the counter-narcotics effort. Everyone tends to focus on eradication but the national drugs control strategy is built on eight pillars of activity. Each one is structured to support the development of good governance, a solid structure of institutions, and an ability for the government of Afghanistan to conduct law enforcement. When that's all put together, they'll be able to deliver a coherent counter-narcotics policy. Part of that policy is supporting alternative livelihoods that could assist people in choosing not to grow poppies, or with the security of main supply routes so that people can get their crops to market. One of the main reasons farmers choose to grow poppies in Afghanistan is that they cannot get crops to market without getting taxed at illegal checkpoints. Opium dealers on the other hand will come to their home and collect the opium.

One of the main factors preventing farmers from growing other crops is that opium crops have attracted a premium over, say, wheat. Then you have the attitude of farmers who say things like, 'I can't do much with wheat, except make bread – I wouldn't make enough money to do anything else.' The farmers' resistance to abandoning opium poppies is common across many provinces because the history of its cultivation is so deep-rooted; opium has been a staple of trade in Afghanistan for centuries. Progress is being made, though; the farmers are being forced to reconsider the balance of risk involved in growing opium – they might get slightly more for opium, but how will they pay their landlords if the crops are eradicated? Some of the governors offer incentives in return for the farmers abandoning opium, such as development projects like roads, or more recently, the food zone programme. If they grow poppies, they don't have room for wheat and grain, which drives up the cost of feeding families and livestock. If their crops are eradicated, they get no profit at all. The Taliban also levy taxes on opium production in some areas, plus poppies are a really labour-intensive crop to harvest; each poppy has to be scored four times on separate occasions to get maximum yield and that has to be done by hand. Imagine scoring a poppy in two or three areas, and you have to do a whole field – that's very labour-intensive, and it costs somewhere in the region of $12 per day to hire someone to do that in Helmand, so that in itself is costly. You then have to process it and after all that, you still have to get it out. Grow a legal crop and all of those legality risks are taken away.

Turning a farmer with no formal education against opium is not as difficult as you might imagine, even if his only interest, in the short term, is to have enough money to feed his family. A lot of Afghan farmers don't want to grow poppies – if you look at the north of Afghanistan, the vast majority is poppy free. This is due to good governance and a means to licit livelihood. I mean, you see five-year-old children who are heroin addicts; if you know that could happen to your own kids, that alone is quite a compelling argument. The health risks inherent in opium abuse are massive. Farmers know it's illegal so they know it's a risk. If you keep heaping on the risk pile while making the alternative livelihoods more attractive, you assist the farmers in making the business decision to stop growing opium.

More and more, we're starting to get convictions for people who are involved in the drugs trade so that adds to the risk for a farmer. If you've got 3 wives and 20 children and you get carted off to jail for a couple of years, your family is not going to be a cohesive unit when you come home. So all these risk choices are being fed to farmers and we do a massive outreach programme in terms of public diplomacy and the government of Afghanistan getting its message out. This is the time of year when the farmer makes his choices as to what he's going to grow, so we're working with the government of Afghanistan and the PR agencies in ministries, such as the Ministry of Agriculture and Ministry for Rural Affairs, to inform provincial leaders and farmers about support to grow legal crops and what is likely to happen if they elect to grow opium.

We monitor progress and measure successes through a partnership with Cranfield University back in England. They have satellite imagery on what is grown, where and when. They've got historical records on the areas where cultivation is greatest and they serve as a useful indicator of where we really need to focus our efforts. When you look at Helmand, it had 105,000 hectares of cultivation at its peak and we're hoping to see a decrease. That will be a positive step for us because it will indicate that we have started to eat away at the attitudes of those growing poppies. We find that where governance and security prevail, the Afghans are more likely to grow licit crops. However, where there is neither good governance nor security, narcotics are rife. For example, in provinces like Nimroz, which is adjacent to Iran, there is no ISAF presence and limited rule of law, and as a result poppy cultivation has flourished.

We are having an effect but you have to put it all in perspective, because really the government of Afghanistan cannot cure this problem in a short time frame. If you compare it to Colombia, which is relatively secure and the counter-narcotics police are well established, it has taken some 30 years to get on top of the issue and that's in a nation with good governance. Here, they're building a government *and* a law enforcement force *and* trying to secure the country. All that, and they are fighting a massive battle against narcotics in a place that is the number one producer of opium in the world, so that's going to take time. If we were doing this in the UK – starting an operation and bringing it to fruition – we'd probably spend a considerable amount of time in surveillance, building an intelligence picture of the entire narcotics industry. In Afghanistan we are only now just getting to the stage where the intelligence picture can be best utilised. We know how networks operate from our experience in the UK – we'll look at a network, how it runs across a country and know where to take the nodes out and focus our efforts to achieve best effect. Contrast that with an operation in Nangarhar where the CNP seized all the ledgers from the area financial system. The removal of the ledgers meant that the economy in the area seized up because no one could borrow or lend money. It was like shutting down the equivalent of Lloyds, HSBC, and Abbey National all in one day for that province – in the end we had to give them back to the Provincial Governor so that normal business could resume.

The parallels between the Taliban insurgency and counter-narcotics are undeniable and there is evidence that the Taliban uses the narcotics trade as a source for funding; they draw huge amounts of cash from it. You only need look at the level of attacks on the poppy eradication force – they are four times what they were previously. Last year it was the farmers who were attacking the eradication force, whereas now it's insurgents. They recognise that they are being targeted as people of influence and they're being targeted in terms of their revenue source. The two are so closely linked that you really can't fight one without fighting the other.

I'm very lucky in that my post at the Embassy has enabled me to travel widely, both officially with ministers from Karzai's Cabinet and with other agencies that work in the country. West, east, north and south; I've gone as far as Herat in the west, to Orūzgān, Helmand, and Kandahar in the south, and up to the north to Balkh and Faryab. I can't imagine I'd ever have seen as much of Afghanistan in any other role and I've been able to see the real differences in this country. It's just a phenomenal geographical masterpiece, from the heights of the

ABOVE: *A C130J Hercules touches down at Camp Bastion. The Hercules is the RAF's workhorse, transporting troops, ammunition, and equipment between KAF and Bastion, as well as making air drops and resupplies across the whole country.* (© Crown Copyright)

BELOW: *Members of the Joint Helicopter Support Unit based at Camp Bastion prepare to attach an under-slung load to an 18 Squadron Chinook for a resupply run to Sangin.* (© SAC Andrew Morris/Crown Copyright)

ABOVE LEFT: *The office: the cockpit of this GCAS-ready Harrier GR9 will have been set up in advance by the pilot to save time in the event of a scramble.*

ABOVE RIGHT: *Fast and low: the view from the cockpit of an RAF Chinook as it flies over the Green Zone on a 'routine' sortie at 90 feet above ground level.*

BELOW LEFT: *Lonely planet: an RAF Regiment patrol in the vast prairie-like terrain that lies outside the wire at KAF.* (© Crown Copyright)

BELOW RIGHT: *Section Commander Cpl Scott Evans from 3 Para, encourages Pte Danny Berk to enter a compound door just after he has thrown a grenade on Operation Oqab Tsuka at Kajaki.* (© Sgt Anthony Boocock/Crown Copyright)

RIGHT: *Pre-flight: Flt Lt Eleanor Lodge, on IRT duty, fires up her Chinook in readiness for the arrival of the rest of her crew after being scrambled to recover a wounded British soldier.* (© SAC Andrew Morris/Crown Copyright)

BELOW: *A soldier from X Company, 2 Para, based at FOB Zeebrugge, patrols into the head of the Green Zone at Kajaki. X Company is based next to Kajaki power station to maintain security so that engineers can continue to provide electricity to the local population of Southern Afghanistan, and relies on the RAF's Chinooks for resupply and transport.* (© Capt Tom McShane/Crown Copyright)

LEFT: *Light relief: an RAF Regiment patrol stops to engage with a local villager. Note the adobe wall to the right of the picture. Made from sand, clay, water and dung, these constructions, which are common throughout Helmand, are extraordinarily strong and Taliban positions made from this can require Hellfire missiles to penetrate them.* (© Crown Copyright)

MIDDLE LEFT: *Good to go: Wg Cdr Andy Lewis, OC 1 (F) Squadron taxies his Harrier GR9 out for a routine mission over Helmand Province. The 'nose art' painted beneath the cockpit depicts ordnance dropped per sortie* (© SAC Adam Houlston/ Crown Copyright)

BELOW: *Soldiers of Patrols Platoon from A Company, 3 Para, engage in fighting with Taliban forces concealed in the tree line. Shortly after this photograph was taken, Sqn Ldr Matt Carter called in air support from an Apache AH-1, which neutralised the threat to UK forces.*
(© Matt Carter)

ABOVE: *Hercules procession: two USAF Hercules return to base at KAF after a sortie in Afghanistan. KAF handles 10,000 air movements a month, some 50 per cent of Gatwick Airport's traffic.*

RIGHT: *Si Scholes took this photograph of some of his friends from 3 Para taking a break during a lull in fighting at Sangin on 18 August 2006.* (© Si Scholes)

BELOW RIGHT: *A soldier provides top cover with the GPMG as the sun sets on the village of Mandi Sar.*

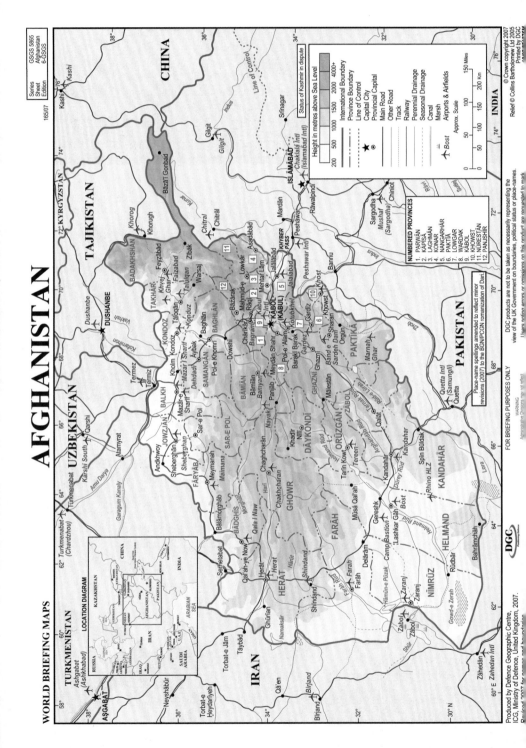

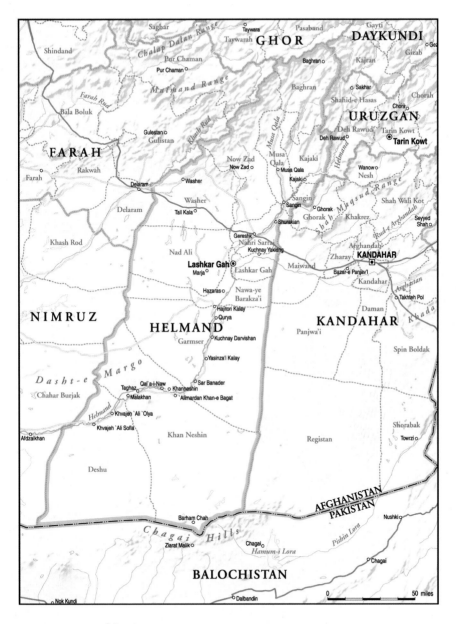

OPPOSITE PAGE: *Afghanistan.* (© Crown Copyright 2009. Crown Copyright material reproduced with the permission of the Controller HMSO)

ABOVE: *Helmand Province.* (© Crown Copyright 2009. Crown Copyright material reproduced with the permission of the Controller HMSO)

ABOVE: *Rear gunner: Sgt Anna Irwin mans the M60 rear machine gun on a Chinook as it flies over Helmand Province.* (© Phil Coburn/Crown Copyright)

LEFT: *Air bridge: the aircrew of an RAF TriStar prepare for a tactical landing into Kandahar Airfield.*

BELOW: *Flt Lt Jules Fleming and Sqn Ldr Nikki Thomas fly the supersonic Tornado GR4 on close air support missions from their base at Kandahar Airfield.* (© Crown Copyright)

mountains that I've flown over in a Huey where the tops are snow-capped and beautiful, to the lush vegetation where we've landed and you just think, 'What a fabulous landscape.' You go to places like Kapiśa and Bamiyan and realise it is a truly beautiful country – you could almost say you're somewhere in a gorgeous Italian rustic setting because the ground is so lush. It is so productive; their irrigation systems were built by USAID in the 1960s and '70s and they are second to none, still fully functioning and still very well cared for in terms of management. Afghanistan has the opportunity of being quite a successful country if they could just get the security squared away.

It's been such a fascinating opportunity for me, with so many highs – and the odd low. We went to Marjah, which is a part of Helmand, where ISAF troops hadn't been for more than five years and the Afghans were able to target eradication on a former corrupt official. With the aid of the satellite imagery from Cranfield we were able to identify who had grown what, where, and with information from the Land Registry, we were able to piece together who owned the land and what the effects would be of eradication. The biggest difficulty the people of Afghanistan have with central government is that they believe it's corrupt. They don't believe it will take action against anyone except the poor or those without influence. So with Afghans delivering eradication – which in terms of the Afghan legal system's robustness is almost as good as a conviction here – the Afghan government showed it was willing to extend law enforcement to people who had previously operated with impunity. That was a real positive. One of the negatives for me was going to a drugs clinic in Lashkar Gāh and seeing the absolute desperation of patients who suffered from addiction and had been abandoned by their family. Thousands of people are on a waiting list for a 24-person clinic, and they are at their lowest ebb, which just drives home to you how important it is that all the elements of the counter-narcotics policy are brought together.

I really love this secondment and it's one of the benefits of being single that I was able to stay here for 12 months. It wasn't originally 12 months but I was asked to stay longer and I said yes without any hesitation. It's the variety – I get to work with the Afghan Minister for Counter Narcotics almost on a weekly basis; I'll be right down to working in the coalface of a poppy field. You can work right across that continuum so it picks up every skill set you can bring. I would say to anybody who was offered the same chance to grab it with both hands because it's so different from anything else we do. What's really good is that you get to see the military from the outside in and it's an interesting reflection – you see yourself as others do. It's been an extraordinary opportunity, absolutely fantastic. It's one of those jobs where you read the job spec and think, 'Yeah, that sounds ok – strategic plans in the British Embassy for Counter Narcotics?', but it belies so much depth and variety. There's so much involved in it. I've done eight months now so I have just under four to go – I know I'm going to miss it.

It's interesting how there's so much cultural variance between military and diplomacy, particularly when the two so often go hand-in-hand. I've had a lot of discussions with my boss along these lines, particularly about the FCO doing nation building – that's not exactly a skill set that comes immediately to mind when you think of the FCO but that doesn't mean they are not delivering because they are. They are great at diplomacy, phenomenal – I watched some of my colleagues working in an international meeting and you sit there and you have to think in syntax – I mean, what exactly are you saying there? Somehow, without being in the slightest bit rude or harsh, they can deliver a hard message to a foreign government using words and inference that you or I would never even consider. It's that punch wrapped in a velvet glove and it rallies them into appropriate action without even the slightest ruffle of a ministerial feather. Their ability to démarche and lobby and get decisions made is second to none, but I think one of the ways in which they differ from the military is that we come with a culture of organisation about planning, execution and delivery. Maybe that's why it works so well for them having a military strategic planner like me in the Embassy – they can come up with the innovative ideas and I can perhaps contextualise and operationalise them in a way that makes them useful and useable. It's that balancing of skill sets, to be honest.

Obviously, there's a degree of personal risk involved for everyone working but I think we are well protected. The nature of our work means we can plan exactly where we want to go, exactly who we're going to be with, and our security is layered accordingly. My duty of care is slightly different from the FCO's in that I carry my own weapon and can be responsible for my own security if needs be. I'm still first and foremost a military officer so if I'm out with a minister, I can't stand back whenever he goes somewhere dangerous – it just means I'll be walking down the street in body armour and with a side arm – it's swings and roundabouts. My view is that me choosing to do my duty is my risk to take and I wouldn't want to let my service down by saying, 'You all put yourselves at risk and I'll watch out of the windows.' That's not what we're here for and the guys on the front line put themselves at risk every day. I didn't join up to stay at home. It has meant at times that we have been able to get a British presence in an area where otherwise we would have not. In addition, the Afghan Government expect us to go where they go and if we say sorry we can't attend they tend to feel a little disappointed. But putting this in perspective, the risks I have faced pale into insignificance when they are compared with the front-line troops who face the Taliban on a daily basis.

I don't always wear my uniform in this post; more often than not I get to wear civvies, which makes a nice change, although it depends very much on what I'm doing. If I'm working with Taskforce Helmand in an operational context in the field, then I will generally wear my uniform and General Khodaidad likes having, as he calls me, his 'British colonel' on his staff. Sometimes he asks me to wear it to meetings; he likes having a military presence, he's a big military man. He's a Hazara and he's a really lovely chap. He was trained by the Russians and was formerly a Para in the Afghan forces – he's one of the only Hazaras in Karzai's Cabinet. Historically, the Hazara people of Afghanistan are its most culturally distinct, and most persecuted. Facially, they have gentle Mongolian features that set them apart from other Afghans, as does their adherence to the Shia sect of Islam. By appointing a Hazara to this role, counter-narcotics gets a cultural balance you're looking for; it's all about where the balance of power lies. The Deputy Minister for Counter Narcotics is General Mohammad Daud, who is Pashtu. He brings a lot to bear, and him and General Khodaidad work together.

Some people assume the Afghans don't know what they're doing but that is a foolhardy assumption. They have such huge cultural heritage and their history is littered with outside nations getting involved in their affairs. They have seen so many people come and go through their country so you can understand why they think that we're not here to stay. The last 30 years here have been such a tragedy in so many ways. This used to be a vibrant and developed country, some would even say decadent, with a pretty western outlook and way of life, which was interwoven with the rich cultural heritage. Almost overnight, everything changed when the Russians arrived, and from that point on, it's been almost constant fighting. I think people make a mistake in viewing Afghanistan as a whole, when in fact it is a collection of diverse and unique provinces. There are 34 provinces in total and each one has its own culture, tribal balance and economy – what suits Nangarhar will not suit Helmand. Therefore, the security and development plan for each province needs to be developed to suit that province – there is no one-size solution where Afghanistan is concerned.

I'd be lying if I said that I didn't have some concerns coming into this role in terms of how the Afghans would deal with me as a woman. Obviously, women in Afghan society don't have the same opportunities as we do in the West, and the way in which we are perceived here by the men is different. That said, though, they're actually more open than we perceive them to be because they have female MPs and ministers, so they are progressing. I think that one of the reasons that General Khodaidad likes me to wear a uniform is that, as soon as he introduces me to an Afghan as Colonel or Wing Commander Buchan, the whole ambience changes. It works only so far, though – if you don't add any value, they would soon dismiss you. It's really a case of my uniform having sometimes served me well in getting the door open, but after that it's up to me to keep it open and deliver, otherwise they will close it very quickly.

I look at other people from the RAF deployed out here and I know we'll all have different memories of this place because we're all different people with different jobs; but I feel really privileged at some of the things I've seen and experienced here. One of the things that drives that home is when I travel through Kandahar, which I stage through regularly. There are 12,000 people there and, for most of them, their enduring memories of Afghanistan will only be what's inside the wire. That's just dreadful, because the Afghan people are so generous, so full of heart and courage, and I think that if everyone got to meet more of the Afghans and learned a bit more of what they wanted and needed, then their mindset might be slightly different. You never know, but if we could do that, the way in which we deal with things here might be different too. You can't always do it from a bespoke viewpoint.

SERGEANT
SIMON SCHOLES

FORWARD AIR CONTROLLER, RAF REGIMENT

Sergeant Simon Scholes is a Forward Air Controller with the RAF Regiment and was deployed to Afghanistan with the 3 Para Battlegroup in April 2006, as Flt Lt Matt Carter's second-in-command. Whilst in theatre, he deployed to Sangin with A Company, 3 Para; their mission was expected to last no more than a few hours at most – they were there for three months and engaged in firefights on a daily basis with Taliban forces.

A short time later, Si deployed to Kajaki with A Company. Again, they were involved in regular contacts with Taliban forces and, in a high profile incident, several members of 3 Para lost limbs when they walked into a minefield. It was during this particular incident that Corporal Mark Wright was killed and posthumously awarded the George Cross.

Throughout his time in Afghanistan, Si Scholes was responsible for calling in a phenomenal amount of ordnance, a lot of which was Danger Close.

I'm known as Si and I'm a sergeant in the RAF Regiment, trained as a Forward Air Controller or FAC. I was in the Air Cadets at school; I joined when I was 13 and went straight into the RAF from there when I was 17. I did my initial basic training and then went to II Squadron, RAF Regiment – the Para squadron. That was 25 years ago, so it's all I've ever known really.

At the time of Operation Herrick 1, I'd been attached to 16 Air Assault Brigade for seven years as an FAC. There were three Tactical Air Control Parties (TACPs) in the Brigade, each consisting of four people: an officer in command, a sergeant as his 2i/c and two SACs. The officer and sergeant are both FACs, the two SACs are signallers. I was with the brigade when they deployed to Bosnia, Sierra Leone and Kosovo, so it was an interesting period for me on a professional level. Then in April 2006 I deployed to Afghanistan with the 3 Para Battlegroup on a six-month tour. I went out as Flight Lieutenant Matt Carter's 2i/c in the TACP, but in the event, our jobs were broadly the same on a day-to-day basis.

We spent a week acclimatising in Kandahar on arrival, and we then went forward to Camp Bastion, which was still being built when we got there. We were attached to I Battery, 7 Royal Horse Artillery – 7RHA are all Para-trained – and my role was to set up the Fire Planning Cell (FPC), which involved all the artillery people, the mortar teams and FACs. I was basically controlling all the air space around Bastion; there were no air traffic controllers there at that stage but there were Hercs and C17s flying in, Apaches flying over, UAVs as well, so I'd be speaking to everyone. It was a steep learning curve; you have to remember that back then it was very different to how it is now – 3 Para were the first British forces to be deployed to Afghanistan in any sizeable number, and there were a lot of people doing a lot of things that were not in their comfort zone. It was a massive responsibility because there's no margin for error – get stuff like that wrong and people get killed, it's as simple as that.

Although my home unit is the RAF Regiment, to all intents and purposes I was with the Parachute Regiment – all my mates, the guys I worked with on a day-to-day basis, were Army, so I was a lone RAF man in an Army world. As an FAC though, that's how it works and I loved it. I was with A Company, 3 Para, so wherever they went, whatever they did, I was with them. I was part of what's called a Fire Support Team (FST) and it consists of an FAC – me – to handle the air; a Mortar Fire Controller (or MFC) to handle mortars and signals, and a Forward Observation Officer (or FOO) to handle the artillery.

My first experience of being under fire came in June. Basically, A Company – at that time around 90-strong, plus me, the MFC and FOO – was deployed to secure Sangin following Taliban activity in the area the week before. The operation was only supposed to last for a few hours – certainly no more than a couple of days – so I packed only essential kit along with a toothbrush and a change of socks; 3 Para ended up staying until the end of their tour and, for my part, I was there for two months.

Our 'home' was the 'district centre', or DC, a rundown compound half a mile from the town centre, which also housed the local government offices, and a contingent of ANP. We carried out some rudimentary fortifications consisting of foxholes dug round the perimeter, sandbags reinforcing the compound walls, and we built 'sangars' up on the roof. It was pretty basic accommodation, though; the compound was poorly built, constructed from roughly-plastered breeze blocks and mud bricks. We had no running water or electricity, no beds and only a handful of plastic chairs to sit on. My 'bed' was a piece of cardboard that I found in a skip after a couple of days, laid on the concrete floor – not that we ever got much sleep. We'd arrived in 'light scales' – what we needed to live and fight for one day. We were on compo rations for two months and were rationed to just a bottle of water each, which was for drinking; we washed in a channel that ran off a river through the compound, but shaving went by the board from the off and we all ended up growing beards.

At first there was no contact with the Taliban, although we knew we were being 'dicked'. But the attitude of the inhabitants towards us was reasonably sympathetic; we were even able to undertake patrols into the city without interference from the Taliban. That all changed quite abruptly on the 27th though, after a raid nearby during which two soldiers – Captain David Patton and Sergeant Paul Bartlett – were killed. Literally overnight, the attitude of the locals changed and the Taliban started attacking us soon after, sometimes six or seven times a day – that's called a TiC, or 'Troops in Contact' – and it was relentless. They malleted us with small arms, rockets, RPGs, mortars – you name it, they threw it at us. So it was my job during a TiC to get some air cover – Apaches, A10s, B1 bombers, Harrier GR9s, F16s, F15s, F14s… whatever was available. Basically it was like the Wild West.

All the roads were cut, so the DC was effectively under siege for the whole time we were there – not that it stopped us launching patrols outside the compound. We were reliant on Chinooks from Bastion for re-supply, although sometimes we'd go as long as five days in-between as Taliban fire was too intense for the choppers to come in. Eventually, a unit of combat engineers worked under almost continuous fire to encircle the entire compound and the helicopter landing pad with a double rampart of Hesco barriers.

Each day in Sangin involved maybe a few hours of us doing bugger all – we'd read, write home or play draughts or backgammon, but then the Taliban would start on us and there'd be four hours of sheer madness although, bizarrely, they seemed to like starting contacts around 14:30 and again at 22:00 – there were lots of night-time contacts. Although we had time to sleep, nobody ever did – not properly, because you were always on edge. You could die, just like that, so all any of us did was cat nap; I don't think anybody had a proper deep sleep for the whole two months. There wasn't always any plan to us coming into contact, either; whenever the Taliban saw us, they'd shoot at us. You'd go to the river for a wash and you'd hear the 'whoosh' or the sound of a round ricocheting as they shot at you. So you'd have soap all over you, but you'd have to grab your weapon, armour and helmet and go running up to the roof in a state of undress. There was no let-up.

It was a mad time, Sangin. On the one side there was us – Paras and support troops, with all the best equipment and technology that money can buy, the best training and a fantastic bond between all of us in it together. And we're fighting a load of men in pyjamas and plastic sandals and flip-flops, each and every one of whom seemed to have a death wish. At first, they aimed sporadic small-arms fire at us in the compound, although that was no indicator of what was to follow. Over the time I was there, they acquired and used a whole arsenal of kit – mortars and 107mm rockets, RPGs and heavy machine guns.

Of course we didn't sit idly by and have them malleting us to their heart's content – we fought back and hard. There was one occasion – they'd obviously got one of the Taliban commanders down to plan it – that they tried storming the compound and we really gave them what for. We slaughtered them – the guys were directing artillery and mortars and I was up on the roof calling in air support from a B1 – a US Cold War bomber designed to drop nuclear warheads on the USSR – to drop Danger Close. One night, they got within 30 metres of the compound wall and we were throwing hand grenades at them – that worked! After that, the Paras protected their positions by placing mines outside the walls and the mines took out ten Taliban in just one night when they tried to creep up on us. We had sniper teams on the roof – three two-man teams – and they slept up there after a while to save time running up the stairs when we started taking fire.

It's difficult to single out any particular contact because looking back it seems like it was just one after another for the whole two months I was there. It was like Groundhog Day. There'd be a TiC going on up on the roof, we'd be under attack. So I'd go upstairs, get comms, call in an aircraft, drop some ordnance and that would be it, every single day, twice a day. I think I only fired my weapon once because I was too busy every time trying to spot which one of the houses that surrounded us was being used by the Taliban. It's been well documented since that we experienced the most intensive and sustained combat of any British troops since Korea. I think something like one in seven of the original company as deployed was killed or wounded; 1st Platoon lost almost a third of its fighting strength.

There's one incident that I remember well. At the end of a single-storey row of shops on the other side of the wadi to us, there was a place called the pharmacy. It was a hospital and it doubled as a dispensary before all the locals in Sangin packed up and left. The doctor that operated out of it had become an ally, but he was threatened by the Taliban who took him away to treat their own. They said if he refused, they'd torture and kill his family before killing him. The Taliban then moved in and used the pharmacy roof to launch RPG, rocket and small arms attacks on us. On 1 July, they launched a 107mm rocket, which scored a direct hit on a small room on the roof of our DC, killing three men sleeping there – Corporal Peter Thorpe and Lance Corporal Jabron Hashmi, and an Afghan interpreter.

One afternoon a week or so later, we started taking heavy RPG fire from the pharmacy roof; the RPGs were impacting against the compound wall, but it only needed one to mess things up for us. We'd had enough, so I called a TIC in and was told I had two Dutch F16s inbound from Bagram. At that time, I was told we couldn't hit any hospitals or schools so I made a judgment call. Our guys were taking hits, there was an RPG on the roof so I said, 'Right, the target's a pharmacy, we need to take it out.' We had two 540lb bombs available but on the FAC training course in the UK, you're told that the safety distance for one of those is 800 metres; I was calling these on to a target that was maybe 100 metres away at most and, on occasions, I'd dropped bombs and rockets just 50 metres away from us – real Danger Close.

The first one I dropped demolished the roof. The second one came in with a two-second delayed fuse, so it went into the crater left by the first one and exploded inside the roof. I was asked by Kandahar why I did it, so I said, 'With all due respect sir, I was there, you weren't. It was my call.' And then the firing stopped. For me, personally, I think that was the best I ever did. I did things there that I would never do again but they were dictated by circumstance and it was my choice. You get so psyched up on making sure the bombs are on target and that our guys aren't hit; it's a case of Band of Brothers. I would just do anything to stop our guys from taking fire and to make sure there was no likelihood of fratricide. It's a different world there; it's them or us.

Looking back now, it seems like everything I dropped was Danger Close. Technically, it's defined as Danger Close if we call in ordnance within 100 metres of friendly forces. Obviously, it depends on the weapon being delivered – a 2,000-pounder at that distance is going to make life very uncomfortable compared to, say, 30mm cannon. If I'm calling something in though, and it's Danger Close, then I'll give the pilot my name and initial; I then say, 'Read back', and he'll repeat my instructions. If he drops a bomb on our guys then, it's my fault so I know that every time I do it, I have to make a massive judgement call. It's a real balancing act.

Every FAC uses a radio, which enables us to speak to friendly forces on the ground, each other and any air assets in our area, as well as ops back at Bastion and Kandahar. It's good, but it weighs about 40lbs what with batteries and handsets, although it's since been replaced with a much smaller and lighter model, which is a bonus. Basically, as soon as we came under fire, I'd get on the net to Camp Bastion and advise them we were in a TiC and I'd then speak to Kandahar to ascertain what aircraft were in the sky or were likely to become available. Sometimes, there would be nothing airborne or loitering when I put the call in, in which case they'd have to scramble the Harriers from KAF, which could take a while to reach us. That said, if we were under a heavy contact, even an hour was better than nothing; CAS makes such a difference when you're on the ground and taking fire. The quickest time we got air was within 30 seconds of me putting the call in; there were two A10s just passing by so I called on them and they did the job. The longest I ever had to wait was half an hour – I had to get two Dutch F16s from Bagram.

Once the CAS was inbound to us, the pilot would check in with me and I'd tell him the grids of the target area from the map and GPS. I'd also advise him of the location of all friendly assets on the ground nearby and ask him what he was carrying – that could be anything from bombs, missiles or rockets, to a Gatling gun and 105mm Howitzer in the case of a Spectre gunship. Once the pilot had confirmed my instructions and read them back to me, I would then say something like, 'You're clear hot to drop a 1,000lb bomb on this set of co-ordinates here, you're cleared hot.' It's my call; if the bomb lands on our troops, I'm mega in the shit.

If one thing sticks in my memory from that tour, it's the death of my mate Mark Wright, who was a corporal with 3 Para. It was a lot later on in our tour – early September – and a few of us had deployed to Kajaki once we were eventually relieved in Sangin. Fifteen of us were up there on the mountain and I was the senior rank. There was me, my SAC signaller, and the rest were 3 Para mortars and Milan platoon.

On 6 September a patrol left our OP to investigate a Taliban checkpoint that had been established in the town below. Ordinarily, we'd have launched a few mortars, but it was out of the question in this case because of the number of civilians around, so we dispatched a sniper team with the aim of attempting to pick off any Taliban that they spotted. Lance Corporal Stuart Hale, one of the team, wanted to get closer because the checkpoint was just out of rifle range. He took up his weapon and walked down a small sand dune and suddenly he was flat on his back, badly injured. He'd stepped on a legacy mine and eventually he had to have his left leg amputated.

We heard the explosion back at the OP because we were only about 400 metres away. We first heard a bang and then I saw some black smoke and at first we thought we were being attacked. Mark Wright rounded up a party of medics and stretcher bearers and he and eight others headed down the path to meet up with Stu. While the medics worked on him, Mark and a few others prodded the ground for mines so that they could clear a path to a flat patch of ground a few metres away where a helicopter could land to casevac him. Suddenly Stu's oppo, Stu Pearson, was blown up. He'd set off another mine.

That changed everything because the guys realised they were literally in the middle of a minefield. I'd scrambled two Blackhawks from KAF because they had winches on and they would have been a much better bet than a Chinook for getting the guys out, but they were half an hour away and a Chinook was en route to us already from Bastion. Although Mark had marked the HLS with smoke, the Chinook put down several yards away, in the minefield. That meant that the medics couldn't get off and our guys couldn't cross to it, and after a bit of confusion one of the guys managed to convey to the loadie that they should take off. Obviously, the Chinooks kick up a shitload of dust when they take off and land, so as it's going up, the guys bent down to shield themselves from all the crap they kick up.

Mark must have overbalanced or something because he put his hand out to steady himself and touched another mine. Mark lost his left arm and took a load of shrapnel to his face, neck and chest and the blast caught Alex Craig, one of the medics, too. Another medic – Tug Hartley – managed to reach Mark safely, and Andy Barlow, who was a machine-gunner, stepped back to give him some room. He too stepped on a mine and the blast also blew Tug to the ground and hit Dave Prosser, one of the other Paras. After what seemed like an age, the Blackhawks arrived and winched the guys up. Poor Mark never made it; he died on the chopper on the way back to Bastion. I was gutted about that.

Once the guys had all been casevaced or extracted, the Americans at KAF ordered me to drop a bomb on the minefield. Basically, the guys had left all their kit there as they were pulled out and there were weapons, radios, webbing, day sacks, Bergens – even morphine, because a lot of the first aid kit was still there – all lying in the minefield, and I guess they were worried that it would fall into the Taliban's hands. So I dropped two 500lb bombs and a 1,000lb one from a Harrier to destroy it all.

I must admit, I found that whole episode really tough to deal with. I could see the minefield from where I was at the OP, so I'd watched everything happen, but I was completely helpless. Because the guys in the stretcher party had witnessed the other guys getting blown up, they were rather traumatised to be honest, and they had to get sent back for a bit of R&R. I stayed on at Kajaki, though, because if the Taliban had launched an attack there'd have been no air cover. There was simply nobody able to cover for me so I stayed; I just soldiered on. Unfortunately it was just another bad day in Afghanistan.

Another thing that stands out for me was the action for which Bryan Budd won his VC and in which he was killed in the August. Bryan was a corporal in A Company and 3 Para. He led a patrol to investigate some compounds and identified a number of enemy fighters ahead. In an attempt to outflank them, the element of surprise was lost and the patrol took heavy fire and a few of the lads got hit – a good mate of mine got shot in the arm. One guy got shot in the face and another took a round through his leg – and took cover. Bryan knew that if they stayed where they were they'd be overrun, so to regain the initiative he rushed the Taliban position alone and that was the last time he was seen alive. When the guys recovered him, he was surrounded by three dead Taliban.

After the battle in which Bryan died, I had to scramble two Harriers from Kandahar. The flight time was ten minutes and when they arrived, a pilot from 1 Squadron checked in with me. I gave them the co ordinates of the map and GPS and said, 'Right, you're clear hot. Drop a 1,000lb on this position.' The Harrier came in, and the bomb landed short by about half a kilometre. I said, 'Good splash, but you missed. I want a second bomb half a K south-east of the first one.' There's only one bomb left and it's a Mark E2 air-burst bomb so it's going to explode in the air. So, it's clear hot, it came in and landed about 3 metres from me – it was a dud. I honestly thought it was all over. Even without exploding, it's a bloody shock when a 1,000lb bomb hits the deck next to you. But if it had gone off I'd have been dead – actually, if it had gone off, I'd have ceased to exist – that close to a 1,000-pounder and you're going to be no more than pink mist. The Air Force wasn't very popular that day – if that bomb had exploded, it would have taken off the entire roof of our compound, which consisted of me, Major Jamie Loden who was the OC of A Company, the MFC and FOO. I found out from 1 (F)

Squadron's OC the next day that there was a problem with the pilot's cockpit sighting system, hence the bomb landing where it did. We never found out why it was a dud, though.

We eventually came back in November 2006, although for those of us on the ground it's not a case of leaving the front line and boarding a TriStar back to RAF Brize Norton. That's too dramatic, so the MoD psychiatrists have devised something called decompression. It's supposed to act as a buffer from front line to your front room, so that you don't find yourself taking fire and watching your mates get blown up on Friday, and finding yourself back home with the wife on Sunday. We got two days in Cyprus as a unit – I was there with A Company – and everything was free. Wine, beer, brandy – all the booze was paid for. We had an all-day session, there were massive barbeques and loads of fights – I think the guys were just getting it all out of their systems, settling scores and rivalries, sometimes just letting off steam. I suppose decompression is like a pressure valve, a way to let out some of the aggression that has been your constant companion for six months. After that, we all flew back to England and I got sent on two months' leave. When I arrived home, I found it hard to adjust.

Before I went to Afghanistan, I wrote off to the *Sun* – they were offering to put soldiers out there in touch with pen friends back home, and I received post every day that I was out there from single mums, young women, divorcees. They sent me books, parcels, sweets… everything.

Afghanistan has completely changed me as a person. I find now that, even at work, I get bored and restless very easily. Out there, you're on a high 24/7, either from adrenaline or from stress. I'm a lot quicker to anger now, a lot less calm – I find that people wind me up very easily and I have to walk away. My wife's a nurse so she's been a huge help, talking me through it all, that sort of thing. I think PTSD is a real issue for a lot of the guys in 3 Para who fought in Sangin when I was there, but many of them won't seek help because they may see it as a weakness. I'm quite sure that today, just as in the Falklands or Northern Ireland, lots of people have it but they are just keeping it to themselves. Still, for me, there's one small consolation – if I have a bad day at work now, I say to myself, 'It could be worse, I could be back in Sangin getting shot at!'

You wear earplugs in training as an FAC and you're supposed to wear them in operations too, but whoever came up with that gem of health and safety legislation has obviously never had to call in 2,000lb bombs Danger Close. Sure, you can wear ear plugs in training, but in a place like Kajaki you just can't do it because you'll die. I'm taking fire, I'm on the radio to the pilot of a Harrier who's about to drop Danger Close and I'm shouting and taking instructions from my mates who are shooting at the Taliban. What am I supposed to do? Shout, 'Time out guys, I just need to put my ear defenders on and oh, sorry, I can't hear the radio now so is it okay if the pilot just drops where he thinks the bomb needs to go?'

I enjoy my job now and it's a long way from Afghanistan, but I feel like I'm using my experience there to best effect. I'm based at RAF Cosford now and I train those who are due to deploy to theatre on the IRT. I train all ranks – the highest so far has been an air commodore, but we have officers on it, aircrew, nurses, and doctors. Basically, the course teaches them tactics, how to survive a minefield, weapon training, convoy drills, contact drills, all sorts really. I also teach combat stress on the course, which means I can draw on my own experiences. We have a PowerPoint slide on combat stress which is devised by psychiatrists in theatre but, what they think people get and what I got are like chalk and cheese. So I tell the course in my own words what I got – they're a good audience.

I've done 25 years now, so in five years I'll have done 30. I'll be able to leave and get a proper job. Fortunately my house is paid for, which is a massive bonus, to be honest. My pension is ok, so if I get out in five years I'll be 47, so I'll probably join the Prison Service … who knows? Anything more sedentary and less stressful than what I experienced in Afghanistan is good for me!

WING COMMANDER
ANDY GRAY

CHIEF OF STAFF, 904 EAW

No 904 EAW is directly responsible for air support to Operation Herrick. As such, it incorporates Close Air Support by the resident Harrier squadron and all air transport and resupply missions undertaken by the Hercules C130 fleet, as well as tactical air command and control. As Chief of Staff, Wing Commander Andy Gray heads up the Executive Staff, which directs the activities of 904 EAW and acts as an interface between the Wing and the other national and international groups at Kandahar Airfield, Bastion Airfield, and wherever needed throughout the operational area.

I'm the Chief of Staff of 904 Expeditionary Air Wing (EAW), I'm on a four-month tour and I'm currently three months in, but it looks like it will be extended. I don't mind if it is. I volunteered to come out here, and enjoy it, so a couple of extra months won't hurt. Despite being COS of 904 EAW, my background is as a helicopter pilot – mostly Puma and Chinook, but I have also flown the Merlin, Gazelle, and Wessex.

I joined the Air Force from university in 1985, as a direct entrant, and joined 33 Squadron at RAF Odiham for my first tour as a helicopter pilot. I had a fantastic time and I must have gone to something like 26 countries in 3 years. I did multiple tours in Northern Ireland and spent eight months in Belize, as well as exercises all over Europe. I then went to RAF Shawbury to become an instructor, returning to Odiham after a year to join the Puma OCU. I had three great years teaching, although looking back I think I learned more than my students. I then swapped to Chinooks straight after the Mark 2 entered service. Transferring to a new type was a challenge that I needed and the Chinook is an awesome aircraft to operate; it is so capable. Again, I spent a lot of time away with 7 Squadron, including the Falklands and Bosnia. In fact, I have spent a lot of time away throughout my career. My 'best' year was 297 days away, but I suspect I averaged somewhere between four and five months away over the first ten years of my career. It's interesting that it has become such an issue now, a lot of effort is taken to track days away and to keep them within 'guideline' limits, but it has never been any different within the helicopter force. Perhaps now that it affects a wider spectrum of people it is taken more seriously.

My last role was, at various times during my tenure, Officer Commanding Operations Wing, Deputy Force Commander Puma and Merlin Force, and Chief of Staff, Puma and Merlin Force Headquarters. Whatever the title, being given a command appointment within the Royal Air Force is an honour; not everyone gets to do it, and ultimately you are trusted with several hundred people and several million pounds worth of equipment. However, even though I recognised this, it was still a job that initially I did not want. As a pilot, the only job I wanted was to command my own squadron, so I was disappointed at 'missing out'. This thinking was a product of how the RAF is constructed; the primary fighting unit is the squadron, therefore commanding one is the prime post. I did ask if I could turn the job down and take my chances in future squadron commander selection. I was told in no uncertain terms that declining the appointment would ensure that I would never be considered for command in the future, or indeed any other job I might want. This made the decision easy. I joined the RAF to fly, but I stay because there is nothing that can compare to the challenge and satisfaction of being in command. So, my ego took a blow, I got grumpy at being second best, and then took over one of the best jobs in the world.

Despite my initial misgivings, I had a great tour, it was challenging, exciting and deeply fulfilling, proving that you never really know how things are going to turn out. Or perhaps just proving those preconceptions are often false! It was also draining at times. We had far too many funerals. The Puma Force suffered a relatively high fatality rate during my time at RAF Benson. It was hard on everyone, as each loss is deeply felt, whether you work closely with the individual or not. We are a close-knit team and losses hurt and anger. However, it never stops us getting on with the job. What we do is inherently risky, and once you are engaged in operations those risks increase. There is always a balance between the risks of the mission or sortie versus the benefits that might be gained – either operationally or in training. The risks and benefits are constantly changing and it is for the commanders to assess which outweighs the other. Sometimes the risks pay off, sometimes they don't. It's inherent in everything we do and I think it's something we all accept.

I volunteered for this deployment because I was curious to see how different Afghanistan was, having seen so much of Iraq. From my perspective, it's not that dissimilar on a day-to-day basis, but when I first arrived and got off the TriStar I was amazed at how dusty it is here, and just how much it stank. The open-air sewerage pond, known variously as Emerald Lake or Poo Pond, hits you right between the eyes and defines your first impression of Kandahar. We were driving through camp from the passenger terminal and I could see about 50 metres through the dust and I felt like gagging, the stench was so overpowering. I remember thinking, four months of this is just not going to be fun. Basra had a similar reputation in the beginning due to sewerage problems; there were open sewers there in places but this seemed worse.

I have since found out the smell varies depending on the wind, temperature, and I presume various noxious chemical reactions in the 'Poo Pond'. You also get used to it – something I would never have believed possible. The dust, however, rarely goes away. It is fine talc-like dust that gets into everything. The vehicles kick it up off the roads, which aren't paved despite thousands of vehicles using them every day. So we have 20kph speed limits to try and minimise it. Even with the dust there is a good side. Given that we can't change the dust because it's part of where we live, I think if I had one wish about where we spent money it would be to get rid of that sewage farm – it would improve morale no end. However, a dust storm moving across the airfield at 50mph, obliterating everything from view is a sight to behold. This is another reason why I would never change being in the military; I have seen things that I would never have seen in most other jobs.

Our mission here at 904 EAW is to support the precise and timely projection of air power and influence in all forms when, where and as required. The EAW concept has its origins during the Second World War when Wings were established so that the RAF could project Allied air power around the world, whereas today, the concept reflects a move away from static forces and the home-defence posture of the Cold War, and a need to be more agile, adaptable and focused in the delivery of air power. EAWs allow personnel to train together before deploying as a fully integrated force, thereby engendering a greater sense of purpose. The benefits are fourfold: delivery of a more focused operational effect from the outset of any deployment; a more cohesively trained body of manpower; a broader understanding of air power capability; and a more inclusive formation identity, both at home and on deployed ops.

I had a three-day handover from my predecessor when I arrived in theatre, but I've changed this job quite a bit during my tenure – I think that's one of the beauties of the four-month roulement. Some people curse it because you don't have continuity and you get this collective amnesia as everyone changes over, but the flip side is that you can make quick progress as there's very little inertia. This job was known as OC Ops previously and it was very much just a support function, just making sure that the force elements – the Hercules and Harriers – got what they wanted. We weren't really operating, in my opinion, as a war-fighting headquarters. My previous appointment as Commander of Joint Helicopter Force (Iraq) meant that I had experience of how helicopter and brigade headquarters work. Luckily, I had a boss who agreed with me that the role needed to change to that of Chief of Staff. So, for the second tour in a row I transitioned away from airfield support into war-fighting support.

You don't get much time to settle in and get used to your new job. The handover is quick and can't really tell you what lies ahead. Operations are about firefighting, fixing current problems. The situation is highly fluid and dynamic. How do you hand over anything of substance when you have no idea what the next problem will be? So the best handovers are those that tell you where the files are in the computer, who the best people are to talk to, and a very comprehensive contact list. As with everything it is the relationships you build with your colleagues that count and sadly those can't be handed over. There is also always a natural time constraint. Very few people wish to spend time in theatre unnecessarily, so the newcomer will try and come out at the last possible minute, while the incumbent will be trying to get out on the first possible TriStar. There's no malice or unprofessionalism, but that is human nature.

What I'm trying to do is, first of all, run a headquarters that actually looks at operational output, not activity. This is not easy. We do not have a ready set of terms that describe the effect we are having or an easy way of measuring it, but we have to try. Everything we do should be assisting the commander achieve his campaign plan. In some senses it may seem counter-intuitive. A mission where fast air goes to support ground troops is a success if by dropping a weapon it stops the engagement and protects soldiers' lives. However, against another measure it is a sign of failure – we are not here to bomb Taliban or other insurgents. By dropping weapons we are affecting the local view of us and perhaps affecting their willingness to support our campaign. The fact that we are having to drop weapons could be seen as a measure of how our campaign is not moving as we would like.

It is a similar story for the Hercules. Traditionally their contribution is measured by people or tonnage moved. It might look a very impressive day if 1,000 people have been moved around theatre, but can we say what effect it produced? Why did they need to be moved? Did they achieve their aim? More importantly, could the same effort have brought about greater effect? Instead of moving these people should we have moved mosquito nets to the local population, thus reducing infant mortality, thus increasing popular support and widening the gap between population and Taliban? An over-simplistic scenario, but the principle stands. It is very difficult, but we need to try and quantify what effect each of our actions brings and do our best to make sure that they are positive.

The HQ must also offload the force elements to get on with their job. Let's imagine that the Harrier Force is having a problem interacting with the headquarters at RC South, Task Force Helmand or Task Force Kandahar. Instead of having them worry about how it's going to be resolved, I'm trying to put the headquarters in the way to do that for them so I leave them doing their day-to-day tactical job. We at headquarters should be stepping in far more and trying to smooth the path and integrate what the RAF does far more into the land manoeuvre operation, and I have a team of four highly qualified aircrew who are dedicated solely to this task. One of the advantages I have is that because I've spent most of my life working with the Army – that's what happens when you fly support helicopters – sometimes I can be more easily accepted in the brigade headquarters as I have met many of the people there before. I work for LAND Command at home and therefore I'm not quite an outsider. I'm not seen as being truly Air Force. I think that as more of the RAF is exposed to operations, and indeed as more brigades get to work closely with the RAF, these barriers are already becoming anachronisms, but we need to make sure we keep working on eradicating them.

I have two major pressures. One is trying to get my colleagues in the UK to understand what's going on, which basically means me trying to persuade them that what I'm seeing is actually ground truth and that they need to adapt their policy and thought process to it. This is a healthy tension, the rule book should not be thrown away on operations, but equally lessons and experience have to be fed back into the system to make the regulations contemporary and relevant. It is very difficult to run Bastion Airfield in the way that I would run Benson at home; I just cannot maintain the same safety regulations. However, it would also be wrong to disregard the principles of the regulation. I have to make an assessment of the operational requirement and then take appropriate sensible risk. This dialogue normally takes place between myself and desk officers at Air Command, although there are many other interested parties. I think the process keeps us both honest and delivers the best operation balance – although it can be a robust exchange of views at times. In the end all the information is given to the boss and it is his call – another 'benefit' of command.

The other one is just trying to make sure that 'Air' is considered and built into the programme. It's very easy, for instance, to view a Hercules as 'All they do is move people.' You get narrow thinking so you don't get any innovation – there's no entrepreneurial spirit about it, nobody thinking, 'What could we be doing? What should we be doing? How can we affect this?' So internally, my problem is getting all my staff, and people in other organisations, to understand that we are all here to move a campaign plan forward – if you are just moving people, you can't measure how that's helping because you measure it and say, 'Ooh look, it's really good, we have 50 seats, we have 50 people moved.' Well, that's only useful if the 50 people (a) needed to move and (b) if they got where they needed to be.

It's the force elements of 904 EAW that give me the least trouble because they're so good at doing their jobs. That sounds quite bizarre because that's why we're all here, but it's the bit we're really good at so, in terms of the Harriers going in supporting a land unit or flying a recce task or anything else it runs like clockwork. There are lots of people who know what they are doing and are very good at it, so I try and leave them alone. The same as the Hercules programme – whether it's doing air dispatch or moving troops or JCBs, it doesn't matter – they know how to do their business; so apart from the general overwork, trying to make sure that no one works too hard, which results in people being run ragged and making bad decisions because they are too tired, I can leave that pretty much to them. It's the interaction with other agencies that causes friction.

We are very comfortable in Kandahar, certainly when compared to the FOBs (Forward Operating Bases), but there's always a desire for more. The biggest perceived gap is in the welfare area. We don't have widespread wireless internet access and you have to pay for what little there is. My generation are used to writing a paper 'Bluey' from the Falklands or Belize and not getting an answer until 20 days later. Phone calls might happen twice in a tour if there was an emergency or an anniversary. But that's not the expectation of the young people who work for me. Their expectation is that they will be able to sit down whenever they get free time and chat using Skype or MSN. They are used to real-time universal communication and it has a disproportionate effect that something they take for granted at home isn't available in the same way here. They do have access to the internet and to telephones, both a huge step forward, but it is still not the connectivity that they take for granted at home. In one way I'd like widespread wi-fi, because it would go a long way to meeting these expectations; therefore they'd be happier and hopefully more efficient. In another way, it would provide an added distraction. Productivity is always higher on operations because there are so few distractions. Consequently, making it more like home might not be entirely beneficial.

Sadly, I think my abiding memory of this deployment will be the repatriation last week of the five Paras who were killed in two separate incidents. I've done far too many in this tour, but that was the first one where we had that many coffins – it's usually one or two. We spent a whole day rehearsing with empty coffins to ensure that we knew how we were going to get them into the airframe – it was a really tight fit logistically, as we had 41 people to board as well as the coffins, because of the bearer party, escort party, and everything else and a Hercules isn't really that big. It's memorable for me because I had so many mixed emotions tied into it. You work hard to make it work for the unit so there's a degree of satisfaction in being able to do it properly, but it's an odd emotion to take satisfaction in moving five dead bodies. Sitting in the back of the aircraft once the bearer parties, escort parties, and everyone else had gone, it was just 904 headquarters staff – I used my headquarters staff to do the transfer – with five coffins all with the Union flags over them. Very, very humbling.

There are so many mixed emotions. No one I took on that flight would have known any of the dead soldiers, but it becomes an individual and personal contract; you want it to be absolutely perfect. We have a short brief before we go; it's always the same from me – I tell them that it doesn't matter whether the protocol is followed precisely, because something will always change, something will always happen that we weren't expecting. What does matter is that everything is done with dignity and decorum and that you do your best for those people in the coffins, whether you're religious, spiritual or not. I haven't seen anyone it doesn't affect. In the back of your mind there are also the unseen people, the families, and you want to make it right for them. You get an immense sense of pride in being able to do it properly, but it is also very humbling because you are carrying five people who died for 'Queen and Country'. They deserve nothing less.

The bearer parties will nearly always come from the losing unit, so you have to manage things bearing in mind that soldiers who have just lost their colleagues in battle won't be thinking practically. They won't be worrying about anything beyond carrying the coffin; the dangers involved in being around a running aircraft, the noise, the limited space available, are all irrelevant to them, so we look after them. They just care about their comrade and, quite rightly, they want to see respect and dignity. It's not quite showmanship, but I think in some way, all areas of ceremonies have a degree of presentation. The commander of 904 or myself will always be in the aircraft; we salute them as they come on and again as we hand them over on landing. The process of securing the coffins, making them safe for flight, is done behind closed doors, but with no less dignity. However, it takes a lot of people to do it properly in the time available and I use the HQ staff for this.

I am exceptionally proud of the way they handle themselves. When we did the repatriation for the five Paras, we landed back here at a time of day when we often get IDF attacks and I asked everyone, 'Right, what are we going to do if, when we are taking the coffins off the aircraft, we get an IDF attack?' Every single person said, 'We're just going to ignore it and carry on.' So they are willing to recognise the personal risk, and accept it, in order to get the decorum, dignity and process right, which I think highlights how important it is to everyone – that you're willing to just stand there while a rocket comes in. That's speaks volumes about human nature, doesn't it?

Morale obviously takes a dip as soon as we hear that somebody's been killed. We hear quite fast, as our connectivity with the rest of theatre is very good. The mood becomes subdued – I wouldn't say that anyone gets overly depressed about it, but you're aware that someone has just lost their life. I think that thought is more marked because of our escort duties in the aircraft. Certainly, for the team I've got here, there's a deep understanding that this is just a 'consequence of what we do'; it's a phrase I've used a lot with people under my command. We are an armed force, we are on operations, and as soon as you put both those things together, you are going to get casualties. What you can't afford to do is get into a downward spiral of introspection. This is what we signed up to do, this is our job – now move on. It doesn't in any way diminish the sacrifice of the people that have died, but we all know, if they had been able to articulate it, they wouldn't want it any other way.

I spent quite a bit of time in Iraq on Op Telic, so it's interesting to be able to draw comparisons between there and here. Take the command chain; this is a NATO base with a NATO command structure, whereas I had a Multi-National Division [MND] above me in Iraq so the flavour is different. Much more is done by consensus here as opposed to directive, which is sometimes disconcerting for me. We are here as an alliance, but each individual nation decides what it is prepared to do and how it wants to operate. The nature of the campaign is different; it felt like we were playing catch-up in Iraq to conditions that were set very early on after the war. Here, the situation is far more open and still within our control to win or lose. The solution isn't entirely military – I'm a firm believer that we're just an arm of government and the only way this situation is going to be resolved is through every branch playing its part. The buzz phrase is a 'comprehensive approach'. Unless Afghanistan can be built as a cohesive, coherent country we will not have succeeded. The military can't do this on its own. The military can create the conditions to allow other people to do it – you need teachers, lawyers, and a judiciary to name but a few. But militaries shouldn't install judiciaries; if they do, beware!

I feel, certainly with Afghanistan, that initially there was a great deal of understanding and support from the population back home compared to the war in Iraq, but over the course of the last 18 months or so, it seems to have evaporated and a great degree of ignorance appears to exist now as to why we're actually here. People seem inclined to draw parallels that I, personally, can't see. I think the average citizen would find it difficult to distinguish the causes, effects, and rationale behind two campaigns, and the media simply doesn't have the space to devote to it, as the interest just doesn't seem to be there. You get headlines such as, 'British soldiers killed in roadside bombing' and that's all that people are interested in. Certainly, people deployed here seem to be happier about being here than they were in Iraq, but it's interesting how the Taliban campaign is evolving towards the same tactics used by insurgents over there, although the IDF threat is considerably lower here than it was in Basra.

I think IDF and IEDs really affect people's psyche, as well as being a physical threat, because they are so indiscriminate. There are pluses and minuses to that. Firstly, people think it's not going to happen to them – that's why people drive without seatbelts – so it gives them a 'get out' clause. There are people, though, who can't cope with the fact that no matter what they do, it might be them, and it's the sense of helplessness – 'It doesn't matter what I say or do, if that rocket hits me then that's my time up.' I guess it depends on how fatalistic you are on whether you cope with that or not. It's an interesting tactic from the enemy's point of view – it's an easy way of creating disruption but I'm not sure that we really understand how it affects our people because it's too subtle, too nuanced. I gave a Para JTAC a lift to lunch the other day and during the conversation he explained that it was his second tour and said, 'I've got no trouble with the fighting, but I hate driving around because of the IED threat.' He went on to explain that, 'There's nothing I can do, I just drive around waiting for it to go "Bang" underneath me. When I'm out fighting, when I'm in a contact, it's about how good my tactics are against theirs.' It was control that made the difference, having a say in the outcome. Statistically, he might be more at risk once he is in a firefight, but it's not about risk, it's about control.

I think the shift in the Taliban's tactics is largely due to our successes here and if we're to carry on having the successes, we need to carry on adapting faster. RAF Air has to come to terms with that. We understand the whole concept of troops in contact – when we turn up, we can massively affect the fight in a very small period of time. It's measurable – the firefight started, then ten minutes later we turned up and it stopped. But how do you do that with pressure plate IEDs? Because you have such a low rate of success finding them per hour flown, does that mean you stop looking? Do you make it a priority, it's recognised as the biggest threat? If you make it a priority, what do you do about the time when you don't turn up and you lose paratroopers? It is dilemmas such as these that keep me, and people far cleverer and highly ranked, awake at night puzzling over the best use of airpower in a counter-insurgency campaign.

We can't do what we did in Northern Ireland and simply move everyone by air. There are a lot of people and not many things to move them in. Unlike Northern Ireland, there is also a distance part to the equation. In Northern Ireland, the average troop lift was probably about ten miles, taking six minutes; out here it is in excess of 100, taking an hour. So to do the same job you would need ten times the lift, or using the same number of helicopters you could move 1/10th the people. Neither is feasible. Another issue is engagement. If we fly everywhere, if we cede the ground to the insurgent, then what have we achieved? Perhaps a type of occupation, but not an insurgent-free Afghanistan. We cannot reassure the local population from the air, nor can we easily protect them; we would be viewed as a mechanised, remote occupying power. Currently, the only viable ways to combat the threat of IEDs is to have good tactics and procedures on the ground and take away the support base of the people planting them. The first can never be universally effective and the second takes time and effort, but that's what winning hearts and minds is all about. The local population will always know what is going on in their area; the trick is to get them to start telling you. For this to happen they have to trust you and be free of fear of reprisals. Easy to say, very difficult to do.

There are lessons to be learned here from our experiences in Iraq – it's what I meant about our response being constrained there by early decision making. Iraq had a professional army that was by and large respected by the population, so maybe disbanding it wholesale wasn't the smartest move. Here, we've got an Afghan army which is, again, professional. It's pretty well respected and they're doing lots of operations on their own. So we've now got an Afghan security provision to an Afghan problem. I think the more that we see foreign fighters involved in this war, be they Pakistani, Syrian, Chechen or whatever, the more they will erode any support from the local population. Afghans are tribal people, quite insular and bound by loyalties: small group loyalties at that. To them, an outsider can be someone from another district, but if they're from another country, then that's not really going to play well with them.

I've got this premise that, actually, most families have the same base requirements: they want shelter, food, kids, and opportunities for those kids that they didn't have. The important thing is they will ostracise people who challenge all that. They'll ostracise us if we challenge it but they will also ostracise the Taliban because they threaten all their aspirations. It's a question of how you get them to that point in the 'needs' structure, because to be worrying about your family structure you've got to be content you're going to live through the day, so there has to be a degree of security before that.

If there's a problem it's probably that there's not enough intellectual debate going on about what counter-insurgency means. It's a very easy expression to use, but what is the most important thing in that counter-insurgency? Traditionally, from an Air Force perspective, fast pointy things that drop bombs have been the top of that hierarchy, but here it may well be the transport, it may well be the fact that we can get the Afghan National Army somewhere. It may well be that we can help in some way in a humanitarian aid/reconstruction role – there are all sorts of things going on and, for my part, I'm trying to nurture an Afghan Army Air Corps because that's *really* going to start making a difference. If you can get the ANA flying around in helicopters, doing patrols and being seen to be able to do that organically – not being helped by people outside but doing it themselves – that's where we've got to go. We are going to be here a long time anyway but if we try and do it any other way, then we're not leaving and I don't know that we've got the stamina for that.

The trouble with any organisation is that it selects and promotes an image, and that's fraught with danger in terms of being adaptable and survivable. Are we really getting a philosophical thesis? The people in charge of the RAF that dictate its persona, it's ethos as an organisation, left school 40 years ago, so one could ask the question, how are they constrained? You could argue that for some, everything they've done in their formative military careers was defined by the Cold War; the RAF had a different role and purpose then. The defence of the homeland was a real issue, then it went away, and now it's come back with the terrorists' strikes, but how adaptable are we as an organisation when we could be seen as being moulded in an image that is already 40 years out of date? Conversely, we obviously need some stability, but from an organisational perspective, where's the ability inside the MoD to take the 25-year-old entrepreneur and push him into that direction, which commercially you would do if you had someone who is delivering? You'd keep pushing as hard as you can because you'd want them as high as you could get them, as quickly as possible, whereas we need to temper the balance between the time served in each rank to gain valuable experience set against actual performance or results gained, and you can compartmentalise it so that by the time you are 32 you know what your service ceiling is at 55. For it to work in the military you've got to strike at the heart of what we think is important, which is experience, so does intellect outweigh that? That's the key question.

For me time here flies by, there never seem to be enough hours in the day. This might be a benefit of rank. The beauty of being higher in the command chain is that you've got other people to worry about, so it becomes much easier to shut yourself off from home because you have a bunch of people that you're responsible for and worry about. It means that there is always something to do! But I think it is true for most people to one degree or another. Life is simple and busy. It's the parents, wives, girlfriends, husbands, boyfriends who have the hardest time because they are living a normal life with a bit missing, which serves as a constant reminder to them that you're not there. Here, there is no normality, you have no reminders. This helps us with our compartmentalisation. I think we all become masters at dealing with the current 'reality' and preventing the two lives – operations and home – from mixing too much. It keeps us sane. One of my female officers has just gone home for R&R but she was apprehensive about it because her real life was about to intrude into her bubble and she wasn't sure how she would react. That's why I don't like R&R. I think it's a strange concept – you just get to say goodbye again, which is the most painful part, so what's the point? Compartmentalisation can cause other problems, though, because we expect our lives at home to have entered some sort of stasis, we expect things to be as they were when we left. It is the small things that catch you out when you return, like cutlery being in a different drawer. The instinctive feeling is, 'This isn't my home any more.' It is very dislocating and can make the transition back to 'normal' life very difficult. In my most extreme case, I returned to a different house than I left, having moved 'in absentia'.

I'm no longer current on any helicopters; you have to fly regularly to be competent and I have been behind a desk too long. It's strange because although I don't miss the actual flying, I do miss doing the job. I talk to crews on the helicopter force out here and they tell me about

RPG attacks, of tracer going between the aircraft, and I want to be part of it again. It's all about proving yourself, proving you can do it. I know a lot of people who feel the same and if you've done it, it's incredibly seductive. We go through a lot of training and like facing challenges. We like proving ourselves. That's a feeling you don't get in many jobs.

I genuinely believe that being in the military is one of the most challenging and rewarding jobs on the planet. When I leave I know I am going to miss the pressure, the immediacy of it all, and I love the fact that I don't get to sit in an armchair and watch the news – I get to make it; that's such a buzz. We're not shy, retiring people, so there's no point in pretending we are – to be making history instead of watching it is a phenomenal motivator. That's why I volunteered for another operational tour; I enjoy it. That might make me odd, but for me this is my job, this is where my professional competency is proved, not back home.

Because of that I don't really miss much from home. When I finish this tour, I'd like it to be cold at home. I love the sunshine, but after the heat here – it's averaged 45 degrees for the past month – I want to be cool. I was lucky and managed to time my deployment to fit in with my lifestyle, so I came here after I'd been skiing and I'll go back in time for the start of the football season, although I missed the end of the last. I'm a Chelsea season ticket holder and I'll go back the day before the first game – I'm not missing that! I also get to catch the end of the Proms – a strange mix of pastimes I suppose. Some privacy would be good – in fact I think privacy would have to be top of the list of what I'm looking forward to. We're all good at getting on with each other out here, even if we don't have much in common. We have to; we work together, eat together and, in the non-biblical sense, sleep together. No one in this HQ has a private room, apart from the boss. So having time to yourself, both professionally and personally, becomes really important. I miss privacy. I miss the ability to be on my own.

FLIGHT LIEUTENANT
ALEX 'FRENCHIE' DUNCAN DFC

CHINOOK PILOT

Flight Lieutenant Alex 'Frenchie' Duncan foiled an assassination attempt on Britain's most important political ally in Helmand province by refusing to land his Chinook helicopter, even after a Taliban rocket took out part of its rotor blade. He saved the life of the province's governor, Golab Mangal, by battling to keep his helicopter airborne. Mangal's support for UK forces in Helmand and his hard-line stance against corruption and the poppy trade have made the governor a prized scalp for the Taliban.

That incident was just one of two within a week for which Flight Lieutenant Duncan was awarded the DFC, the air equivalent of the Military Cross and one of the highest awards for bravery. The citation notes Duncan's 'bravery and stoicism' and says he 'displayed consummate professionalism and strength of character' throughout both incidents.

I'm 32, married, and we have a young son who is 18 months old, and two dogs. I'm known by everyone as 'Frenchie'; my mum is French and my dad's from Scotland so I was brought up in France 'til I was about 20 and only came to England to join the Royal Air Force – French is my mother tongue, English a second language. I'm based at RAF Odiham, so that's where we spend most of our time when I'm working, but I also have a home in Paris and I like to escape there whenever possible. So I have two homes really.

I've been based at RAF Odiham since doing my basic flying training on helicopters at RAF Shawbury. I'm in 27 Squadron now but started in 18 Squadron so I've flown with both of the RAF's Chinook squadrons. I'm currently training to be a flying instructor so I'm doing the QHI course here at Shawbury and I'll be back to Odiham in three months' time to start training students on the Chinook. I've enjoyed my career of operational flying so far but I'm ready for this job now – I did one tour to Iraq but I've been to Afghanistan four times.

My first tour in Afghanistan was with 3 Para, in the summer of 2006. It was a particularly difficult period between May and July of that year and my first really bad experience of coming under fire would have been around 11 June, when Flight Lieutenant Craig Wilson got his DFC – I was his co-pilot that night and we got shot at repeatedly. It was very strange because it was scary afterwards but I don't recall being scared while we were taking fire. I remember landing on this HLS where we'd been just before and the enemy had already targeted that site so they had it zeroed; we were on the ground, rotors turning, waiting for a British casualty to be loaded on and I remember thinking, 'If an RPG hit my head now, would it hurt?' It was a very strange thought and it was dark so I had my NVG goggles on. I was looking out, wondering how painful it might be and that was all I could think of. That was probably the scariest time.

We took a lot of fire but we didn't actually take any hits that night – nothing that impacted the aircraft, anyway. We even had one rocket fly between us and an Apache during the transit from Bastion to the target area! Initially, I thought it was a shooting star. The first time I got hit, though, was in June 2008, on my last detachment – I'll come on to that later.

I think all aircrew have a similar feeling – you know, 'It'll never happen to me.' I think we worked 25 hours the night that Craig won his DFC – we did a day into night into day. We lifted from Bastion to go up to Kajaki to pick up an ANA who'd been shot in the foot. We got him back to Bastion and it was getting dark when we landed. We went back to the IRT tent and, almost immediately, we got a call saying that a UAV had crashed in Sangin. They'd sent a patrol to recover it but they'd come under contact and a British soldier took a hit, so off we went.

There was a clear window in the contact – it was night by then and we'd obviously studied which way we were going to come in. We went very low, at 150ft and Craig flew the most perfect landing. The ANA were guarding the HLS and they'd made a circle that was so tight you could literally only just fit a Chinook inside and when the dust cleared, bearing in mind it's at night, I had one ANA guy looking at me from under the window and Craig had one on the other side and there was a ditch right behind the aircraft – there was no room to spare! That was the most perfect landing and it had to be otherwise we'd have killed some guys and probably lost the aircraft.

So we picked the British soldier up and he survived, thankfully; he'd taken a round between his shoulders, it had come out via his back plate and missed his heart by no more than a couple of millimetres either side. He was a very lucky chap. We took him back to Bastion and there was a Herc there within minutes to take him on to the UK.

Meanwhile, reinforcements had been sent back to try and help the patrol we'd just recovered the casualty from. They became pinned down under intense fire and one of the guys got out of his vehicle and an RPG hit his arm, almost taking it clean off. He was a British soldier, so we were told we had to go back in. By now, the Taliban had zeroed the landing site so we had to have a diversion. We held off while an Apache rained fire on to the ground to keep the enemy pinned down. They fired a lot of ammunition into the ground to sanitise the area and we held on as long as we could until our fuel was literally just above the minimum we'd need to make the return flight – then we *had* to go in.

According to the doctors, the guy's arm was hanging on by the muscle. The medics on board worked brilliantly to stabilise him and we hit the gas and flew him straight back. By now, we'd been on duty for 20 straight hours and the word back at base was that another contact had started up and reinforcements were needed to hold the ground. The boss asked us if we wanted to do it and we said we might as well as we were already broken in – there seemed no point breaking in another crew. That was a dawn launch. We flew the assault and inserted the reinforcements and by the time we came back we'd done about 25 hours.

Those sorties that we flew when Craig won his DFC were tough, but it was more of a marathon than a sprint; a long day with a lot of flying. For me, though, it was an event on my last detachment in June 2008 that is most prominent in my memory. In effect, we became the first – and so far, only – British helicopter to be 'shot down' in Afghanistan, but it took eight miles for the aircraft to give in, although it wasn't quite that simple! It was by an RPG – I think I dealt with the RPG all right … but it wasn't just the strike … it was the aftermath and I feel I dealt with that situation ok.

On the day in question, I was captain and my co-pilot was Flight Lieutenant Alex Townsend, a new guy – I think he'd been on the squadron for just eight or nine months. In my rear crew I had Master Aircrewman Bob Ruffles, a very experienced guy with about 5,000 hours on Chinooks, and Flight Sergeant Neil 'Coops' Cooper, who again had a lot of hours. So my co-pilot Alex, although not very experienced, was very competent, and in the back … well, you couldn't get any more experience than that. We were to be the number three ship in a three-ship formation made up of us, the Flight boss Jonny Priest – JP – as captain on number two, and Flight Lieutenant Rich Hallowes as the formation leader.

Rich Hallowes was based at Kandahar, JP and me were at Bastion, so the plan was for JP and me to meet up with Rich over Lashkar Gah. The tasking was for the three of us to do a couple of runs to Lash, fly on to Musa Qala and then back to Bastion. So we launched early in the morning with an Apache providing overwatch for us and flew up to Lash. We met up with Rich and each of us picked up a load from there, together with some VIPs in the back. Once we were loaded up, we launched together and off we went as a three-ship.

We flew over Gereshk and out into the desert but as we got there – I think we were probably about five miles north of Bastion – Rich's aircraft had a problem which precluded him from carrying on any further. So he peeled off towards Bastion and we just carried on towards Musa Qala as a two-ship with JP as formation leader.

On the run in to Musa Qala, the Apache passed us information on enemy activity in the area, but I didn't think too much of it. So, like I say, it was there at the back of my mind, but I didn't give it too much thought. Anyway, we landed the aircraft, got our people out, and lifted off again with JP. On the way back, we called Bastion just to be a bit proactive and JP said, 'Look, Rich's VIPs are stuck at Bastion so we're gonna do the tasking for his aircraft and take his passengers to Musa Qala.'

First, though, we both needed refuelling so we stopped off at Gereshk, which was our refuelling base at the time. It's pretty straightforward normally, but as our tanks were filling, JP's aircraft had a massive fuel leak – and I mean massive; I've never seen anything like it! The Chinook has tanks on each side and they've got these vents – well, one of the tanks basically decided to overfill itself and the valve didn't shut so the fuel was just pouring in and the only place it had to go was the vent and it was literally jetting out of it. Nicely atomised in the air, just by the engine so it could have ignited at any time and we were right behind it, still attached. We couldn't move, we couldn't talk on the radio, because it could cause electrical discharge from the aerials and ... boom, game over! We were panicking in the cockpit and the crewman was there, just refuelling and chatting away to his mate and there was a Niagara Falls of fuel behind him! Eventually he turned around and saw it, gasped and started to panic. He stopped refuelling and obviously, that was it. So, over the radio, I told JP that I'd do his tasking for him and what had started out as a three-ship tasking suddenly had just my aircraft on it.

So it's now just us flying, with the Apache in support. I'd been due to return to Bastion after refuelling and resume duty on the HRF but I now had the tasking to do – the VIPs that were still on the ground at Bastion. I radioed to JP, 'I'll get an armourer for you when we land because you've got fuel on your flares.' You don't want to fire flares with fuel on them. So when we got to Bastion there was a further delay because sometimes when you pass messages to Bastion they don't always understand what we're trying to achieve and it's a headache. We were on the ground for an hour and I had to radio them to tell them to pull their fingers out because all my hydraulics were going over the limit, everything was going over the limit. In the meantime, I also had Rich's VIPs, although I didn't know who they were at this stage, but they were very well dressed and very pissed off. Not surprising, as they'd been waiting for the best part of an hour and then waiting for a further hour in my aircraft.

In the end the armourer came across, on to the jump seat, and I said to him, 'Don't worry mate, I will pick you up in 45 minutes – put the flare box on JP's aircraft and I will be back to pick you up in 45 minutes.'

So I dropped him off at Gereshk and off we went towards Musa Qala.

On approaching Musa Qala, we contacted the Apache, which had gone on ahead, and we were advised that something big was afoot – there was an indication that the Taliban were preparing to have a go at our aircraft and were moving weapons around. Just like in 2006!

At that point the hairs on my back *did* go up – call it a sixth sense, but there was an instinct of self-preservation setting in. I said to the guys, 'I'm not going to stop a mission for that but we have to be a bit careful about this.' The Apache then asked me to hold but I told the boys I didn't want to – I said we'd go along to FOB Edinburgh and pretend that we were going to unload there so if anyone was dicking us, they'd think that we were unloading there and stand down their weapons at Musa Qala. Edinburgh and Musa Qala are close enough together that it would have fooled anyone dicking us. Bob in the back said, 'These people in the back are very well dressed and look very pissed off – and I'm not sure that half a ton of sand is going to improve their mood!' It's really dusty at Edinburgh and the cabin fills up when you land there. So I said, 'I'm going to do a low-level orbit over FOB Edinburgh and use terrain masking so they won't see us at Musa Qala.'

So that's what we did. We were flying a figure of eight and we got called in. Now, our biggest threat comes from RPGs so if we're fast and low and someone's aiming at us, we're not only harder to hit, chances are the head won't arm. So normally we would fly a CAD, or Concealed Approach and Departure. At first, everybody who does CAD training will learn to fly at a speed commensurate with height to ensure aircraft safety, ie low and slow. In my view, at that time, the safety of the aircraft was paramount, so we had to get as fast and low as possible. We set our altitude warning systems very low; X feet on light out and X minus a bit on the noise. What that means is that if I go below X feet, a light will come on and at X minus a bit the noise comes on. The non-handling pilot has the noise and the handling pilot has the light. So I told Alex, 'We're gonna go as fast and as low as we can.'

Obviously, wherever we fly, it's to a fixed site, and we're into the same LZ every time; you can change your routes, your angles, but it's to the same destination and the Taliban know this so they'll sit and wait. When we landed at Musa Qala earlier that day, I'd flown in from the south-west and JP had come in from the west. So this time, I decided to come in from the north-west and make a totally different approach. The Apache told me that apparently the Taliban were moving weapons on the south-west so that only reinforced my idea. I told Alex to put us four miles north from the point – there's a deep wadi there and I wanted to be well in that wadi, at max speed – I didn't want to come down just a mile off the target. He did that very well, got me just where I wanted – down the wadi we went and I was flying. Basically, I was just trying to get the light on and no noise, just flicking on as I flew down in the weeds.

A short time later – perhaps 30 seconds – I saw a Toyota Hilux with a man in the back alongside the wadi; the Hilux is popular with the Taliban, although it later transpired that this wasn't one of theirs. As it turned out, though, it probably saved our lives by being there. I told Bob, 'Get yourself on the right-hand Minigun, there's someone looking dodgy!' and I jinked the aircraft hard left. At that point, our flares went off and Coop shouted, 'We've been hit!' so there was hardly any time to do anything. As he said that, the aircraft lurched up and right, even though I'd told it to go left. Then Coop shouted, 'We've lost a piece of the blade' and I thought that was it – we were going down for sure, because the aircraft had just done something I didn't ask it to do and there's nothing worse than that for a pilot.

For some reason, though, we'd gone up and right, not down and right, which at 20ft would have been the end for us. So I pushed the stick forward and left again and it responded – I was quite happy I had a response and all I did from that point was a wing over to get out of the wadi. Suddenly the mobile phone tower filled my view through the cockpit window and just zoomed past; somehow, we'd just turned inside it! That thing is on the site of an old Afghan fort and stands 260ft over the Musa Qala district; it provides mobile phone coverage to the whole of that part of Helmand Province so it's of key strategic importance. The Taliban are forever launching rocket attacks against it – 27 in the past three months at that point, so it's well defended by us and I almost brought it down on my own!

Coop said he'd seen a massive piece of the blade come off and the aircraft was shaking like a bastard. The pedals were shaking, all the controls were shaking – it was basically the rotor head telling me that it was missing a piece. I considered I should really put the aircraft down immediately, but then I thought, 'We're still in the kill zone; I have 16 civilians in the back, we have four rifles between us to defend them and we're maybe 400 metres from the firing point – we've got no chance.' Training takes over to be honest, and I was manoeuvring the aircraft as we'd been taught for when you're under contact. Then another RPG came by and more rounds and we were taking fire again. The aircraft felt completely wrong as I was trying to fly her; the rear end was skidding – a real sign of a big imbalance at the back. Obviously, at that point, I didn't know an RPG had gone in, I thought it was small-arms fire because you'd think a bloody RPG would take the aircraft out completely; I considered maybe a .50 cal round had shattered the blade. I decided to carry on and I said to the boys that I'd stick it to the floor and follow the terrain. The aircraft was flyable but any problems and I'd just slam into the ground.

In the meantime, Alex did brilliantly because I was flying the aircraft and it was hard to fly, so I had no spare capacity, but he did all the actions. We lost our number two hydraulic system, so he had to secure that; we lost the AFCS – Auto Flying Control System – it's an auto-stab that helps keep the aircraft straight and level, so he had to secure that. Bob put a radio call out to Crowbar, the radar station at Bastion. Alex had tried but I told him to chin it and just put a Mayday out so anyone could pick it up; that was the only bit of spare capacity I had at that point. Coops in the back was busy securing all the guys who were obviously very scared.

In the back of my mind I knew I had the option of putting the aircraft down, just throwing it in. I was really worried about losing the blade and I made myself little targets – you know, 'I just want to make it to there!' Every time I made one, I carried on and just kept telling the guys we'd make it to Edinburgh and I'd do a baby basic dust landing – basically, minimise any control movements which would damage the blade further. I wasn't going to mess around and try to put it anywhere specific, just right in the middle. So I did that, and as soon as the dust cleared, I ordered the guys in the back to get rid of the passengers. When the crewmen came back I asked them if they'd be happy to move the aircraft again because once we shut down, that'd be the LZ out of action until the aircraft had been repaired – we were right in the middle of it. They were ok about it so we lifted to hover again, moved to the edge, and landed; then I shut down.

I remember Coop saying, 'Fucking hell, you wanna see the twist on that blade!' and I still couldn't picture it because I still thought it was a .50 cal round. But there was nothing left of it apart from the leading edge and the blade was just twisting as it was shutting itself down; a massive chunk of it had completely gone. Coop then said, 'Fellas, we've been hit by an RPG.' And I remember looking at Alex and he was absolutely in shock. I know I was surprised but his face went bright red and his eyes nearly popped out – he was in absolute shock. Then Bob was laughing but he's always laughing. I think that, though, was nervous laughter; we'd survived – and I then found out that our cargo of VIP passengers included Mohammad Golab Mangal, the Governor of Helmand Province; the First Secretary to the Ambassador; and the entire senior staff of the Province Reconstruction Team (PRT) from the Foreign and Commonwealth Office, along with their bodyguards.

The Taliban somehow knew who we were carrying, they knew where we'd be, and they'd brought the RPG guy in specially – he was an expert, one of their senior guys. They'd obviously practised what they did because they'd put three weapons systems into the aircraft; when I inspected it after shutting down, I couldn't believe how she'd stayed aloft. As well as the RPG passing through the pylon and taking out part of the rotor, we'd taken a significant degree of shrapnel damage, seven or eight rounds of .50 cal, and some 7.62mm. The angle at which the RPG had gone in probably saved our lives because it was heading square in, but because I'd seen that Toyota Hilux, I jinked to the left suddenly, which put an angle on it. Funnily enough, the firer was identified and killed in a subsequent operation.

In later analysis, the RPG was identified as being first generation – we were able to tell via cut marks on the pylon, which showed the round as having four fins. One of the problems of the Gen 1 RPG is that they need to hit a target square on. If the outer casing touches the inner casing before the percussion cap impacts with the target, it becomes inert and the fuse doesn't detonate; that's the only reason it didn't explode when it hit us. The head of the RPG went through the pylon then it deviated into the blade and when it hit the blade it disintegrated.

Boeing, who make the Chinook, told us that the blade whipped it back round so we were effectively hit a second time by the RPG and some of the shrapnel damage we took was caused by its outer casing coming in. It was that which nicked a hydraulic pipe – just the tiniest bit. But the hydraulic system is pressurised to 3,000psi, so we lost the lot within a second; there you are, half your hydraulics gone, just to make life a bit more interesting! Also, one of the .50 cal rounds hit the gearbox but it hit a big round nut and didn't go in – it just bounced off and disappeared. If it had hit straight on, it would have jammed the gearbox and destroyed it.

We were so lucky; I'm not at all superstitious but there were so many bizarre twists of fate that not only put us in that position in the first place, but also allowed us to escape. In another bizarre twist, our aircraft 575 took rounds in Iraq. Perhaps unsurprisingly, I couldn't sleep that night. Every time I closed my eyes all I could see was the phone tower passing by the cockpit. It cracked me up because my crew were all snoring and I couldn't sleep. I went to the tent, I think I was half-cut because someone had a bottle of Jack Daniels that he said he was keeping for a special occasion, and I said, 'Right, this is a special occasion!' I've never drunk on det before, or since – that was the only time I did. I thought it might put me to sleep.

What happened, though, wasn't the scariest moment of my tour; that was still to come. About two weeks before the end of my tour JP asked me if I wanted to fly again; I was keen to get back up sooner rather than later, so I did a routine HRF tasking into FOB Edinburgh where I had to land beside the aircraft that, just a short time before, we'd been shot down in. We were really well looked after by the FAC who was in charge of Edinburgh's HLS. They have nothing at that FOB; no running water, living in dust, and they have no magazines or anything, so we loaded up the aircraft with Coca Cola and magazines like FHM and dished them out to them. And they were really happy with it all and I said, 'Well, you looked after us really well, it's the least we can do.'

The next day, the boss said there was an op coming up – a four-ship assault on two villages – and he wanted me on it; he asked if I felt happy with it and I did. The mission profile was for a two-ship to go from Bastion to FOB Gibraltar at night and collect several platoons of Paras, and for another two-ship to follow five minutes later; then we would insert them at the two villages for the assault. The first two-ship was led by JP with Flight Lieutenant Hannah Brown as his wingman; I was leading the second formation, flying with Alex as my co-pilot and Rich Hallowes as my wingman. It was all worked out; JP and Hannah would be four minutes on the ground and we would land one minute after them.

Take a step back, and the frame of mind I was in was that I was pretty scared. Remember what I said earlier, 'Air crew always say, "it'll never happen to me".' Well, my balance had tipped the other way now and I was thinking, 'It *does* happen to you.' I was so close to going home at the end of my tour by then and I remember walking to the line with Hannah. I said, 'You have no idea how deep I'm digging … I'm scraping the bottom of my well of courage.' I was shit-scared of getting airborne that night, an emotion that was remarkably prescient as it transpired. Everything went wrong from the off; JP went five minutes early, we were on time. And even though he had ten minutes to do the pickup, the troops were slow in loading so we had to hold up. They finally lifted and in we went; we picked up our troops but we had problems with them loading, too, so we were eight minutes behind the timeline lifting off.

JP and Hannah went for their drop off at the first village and we were eight minutes behind them; they were calling 'Contact' as they came into the HLS; first tracer, then actual contacts. They were flying all sorts of evasive manoeuvres and I was thinking, 'Oh my God, this is not what I want. Here we go again.' I was really scared but I couldn't show it because I had to lead my crew and another aircraft in there. Alex, bless him, never voiced his own fears either but he asked questions, which is out of character for him – it was just because he'd been exactly where I had. We were thinking, 'Should we put the aircraft somewhere else?' but we couldn't, we *had* to put it in the hot LZ because our Paras were needed to support those who JP and Hannah had on board; we *had* to go in there. We had eight minutes to think on that, and it was the longest eight minutes of my life. It seemed much longer than when I nursed 575 down at Edinburgh after being hit, I can guarantee you that.

When we got to the target area, more tracer fire started coming up … and suddenly, it just stopped. So our two-ship got in, we inserted our troops, and as soon as we got the signal they were clear, we lifted off. The plan now was that we would fly to FOB Inkerman and pick up more troops there for insertion at the second village. So we transitioned, flew across a wadi, and just as we were about to cross the other side of it, I saw a massive flash on the left, out of the corner of my eye – and I saw an RPG flying straight towards my aircraft. I sat transfixed – it's such a cliché, but time becomes completely elastic – and I watched through the glass panels below the rudder pedals as the RPG flew straight under my feet. It was so close I could've put my hand out and grabbed it. I remember screaming at the guys in the cockpit and Alex was just looking at me because he hadn't seen it, but it was so close I remember seeing the back end sparkling and jetting purple fire that reflected on the instruments; I instinctively lifted my legs off the controls. Then Rich, my wingman, called an explosion to the right of the aircraft and he shouted 'Contact!' but we didn't see the other one and it exploded just behind us on the ground. The Taliban had two firing points; we were both low and slow, and they missed the aircraft. I'm thinking, 'Oh my God, this is horrendous.'

Anyway, we went to Inkerman, and there were issues again with the troops because they were trying to push a quad with a trailer and the trailer was really heavy; it wasn't coming up. Then Stu Haig, the captain of the aircraft to my left, said, 'Contact, three o'clock!' So I looked right and I'm seeing tracer going up five miles away. I've honestly never seen anything like it; the weight of fire seemed like the opening scenes to *Saving Private Ryan*. There was so much tracer and rocket fire going up you could have walked on it. The crewmen in the back of the aircraft were all firing Miniguns; they fired an entire can of ammo on the M60, some 200 rounds into targets. I still don't know how they escaped but they managed to bug out by the skin of their teeth and miraculously there were no rounds in any of their aircraft; there'd been firing from everywhere! But JP is a great tactician and he'd had us all practising tactics and formation flying throughout our tour; we were using them now. All this practice made me decide at the last minute during the pre-flight brief that we would depart the target area almost the way we came, as it was a quiet piece of desert to fly over. We lifted from Inkerman, got to our next target without incident, and it was quiet, no fire at all. But as we transitioned, Stu again called, 'Contact!' He said he had an RPG miss him when he was doing 40 knots; it just flew right by him – he was transitioning, so low and slow again and really vulnerable. A Chinook is 99ft long, so it's a big target – how they missed him is unbelievable. This was the only contact we received for this target area.

Then we went straight to do another mission where we were extracting these British soldiers and they'd been in almost constant contact, taking a lot of fire, for the best part of two weeks. It was an extremely dusty HLS, but we'd to fly in there and get the troops. JP went in first and he left a massive cloud so we had to orbit until it cleared. But we got in – it was a pretty violent landing – got the troops, organised deconfliction so that JP could get out of Bastion and we wouldn't meet each other on the way back, and he called on the radio which, as I said before, was very unusual for him, but he must have felt what we felt because he said, 'Black Cat 22; Black Cat 23, are you ok?' And I just looked at Alex and said, 'That's so not like JP, he must be shit-scared for us – and he's worried.' And I came back with the words: 'Shaken not stirred!'

And then we did another pickup and that was the end of the night; it was the most amazing feeling to land that aircraft; I shut it down and felt so … alive! We walked back to the line to meet the other guys and, you know what it's like, 'I did this' and 'I did that' – that fear of dying just fell away at that point. I think it was the adrenaline rush I had talking about what we did. But, don't get me wrong, it came back the next morning.

The last few days before the end of my tour were tough. I had a few more routine flights and, funnily enough, my very last sortie was a test flight for 575 once it was fixed. I did that and a couple of days later, was back home in England trying to readjust.

I've mulled over what happened extensively since I got back; all of us have. You try and look for explanations and I still can't believe we survived after that RPG hit us – you don't even want to think about the fallout if we'd gone down, the PR cost to the Government, but more importantly, the strategic impact on the guys in theatre. Our Chinooks in Afghanistan are being flown relentlessly – losing one would be an absolute nightmare. The only way I can rationalise it is that it was down to my training; had I not flown the way I did, had I not been trained the way I was, we'd have been killed, full stop. I made the firer's job so much harder by flying so fast and low – if I'd been any higher, he could have put two RPGs in the aircraft. I don't think it was luck – it was professionalism and training.

As far as I'm concerned, there's nothing I did that any of my friends wouldn't do, or anyone else in the RAF. I just did what I had to do, and then got on with the next mission. A lot of talk is made about courage but I'm not sure what that is. Perhaps it is about forgetting about yourself and doing what has to be done; it's only afterwards that we seek to pin labels on our actions, when we see the consequences of our actions on other people. I've heard courage talked about as being like a bank balance before; that each of us has a finite well to dip into before it runs out, but I don't think it's like that; I think sanity is the thing that runs out. Courage will always be there, but every time you dip into that courage fund, your sanity fund gets depleted and doesn't come back up. I think courage is there or its not but it doesn't go down if you have it. I know that my behaviour is not what it used to be before the last tour.

A few months after I got back, I was at work one morning and I'd been given a really crap job that kept me grounded. The 2i/c came up to me quite early on and said, 'You have to go and see the OC at 11:00', and I came out in a cold sweat because on the Friday before, we'd had a massive dining-in night and I got home at 05:00 on the Saturday morning. I thought I might have said some things that had upset a few people and I honestly thought I was in for a proper bollocking by the OC. So at 11:00, I went in and I said, 'Right sir, if it's anything I said on Friday, I'm really sorry but I don't remember a thing,' and he stopped me there before I embarrassed myself and told me semi-officially that I'd won the DFC. It came completely out of left field, my legs went to jelly, and I had to sit down.

The official announcement before the media came a few days later and I couldn't believe it because my parents were over from France on a visit at the time, which meant they'd be there with me. It was completely serendipitous, a rare coincidence but all to the good. They were delighted! So on the Thursday, I managed to blag the squadron Range Rover – it's pretty cool, a 4.2 Sport with all the toys, so with Ali and my parents, I drove up to 16 Air Assault Brigade's HQ at Colchester for the media announcement. We were all called forward one by one, where our citations were read out by Lieutenant General Sir Graeme Lamb, who made one of the most amazing speeches I've ever heard. After that, a quick round of interviews and photos and we headed back home. The boss had organised some drinks at the mess, Ali came with me, and I can't say I remember much of what happened the rest of that evening!

I feel enormously proud and privileged to have been awarded the DFC, but to me, it's recognition for the crew, too – they were as much a part of it, and also it's huge recognition for 27 Squadron and our involvement in Op Herrick. I think 18 Squadron have been awarded four or five DFCs since the start of ops there, but as far as I'm aware, this is the first for 27 Squadron since the Second World War. Now, I'm looking forward to my colleagues who were in theatre with me coming back from Afghanistan, because they're out there again – I'm looking forward to having a few drinks with them and after that, I'll be heading to Buckingham Palace for my investiture. I'm really looking forward to that and, hopefully, I'll be able to use my three tickets to bring the three members of my crew who were involved in the incident at Musa Qala with me.

Everything that's happened throughout the numerous tours I've done in theatre, particularly the last one, has changed me and I'm a different person now. I'm still working through it but my attitude's probably not the best at the moment. I think my values have shifted in terms of what's important. I think people place too much importance on too much crap now. I have sleep problems, too – it's like my brain doesn't shut off. I can sleep for 12 hours straight through but I'll wake up feeling like I've been on the piss and had just three hours. I think I appreciate life a bit more; I'm more sensitive than I was and I'm more in touch with my emotions, which is weird compared to the person I was. But I'm a lot less tolerant than I used to be, I have less patience; my fuse was never long, but it's even shorter now.

It's the little things you do that help you to stay grounded – spend time with the family, walk the dogs. I look at my family differently now; they are far and away the most important things to me. A lot of things I do now I stop and think, 'God, you take this so much for granted.' I remember something as simple as tapping an email the next day, saying I was fine and thinking, 'God, how lucky am I to be able to type that email?' It makes it quite hard going back to Civvy Street or a teaching environment like I've been doing at RAF Shawbury – it's so far removed from the front line it's almost a dot. I have to say that Afghanistan is behind me now and I just want it to stay behind me. I will go back, no doubt, but now that I'm doing this new job I can pick when I want to go and I won't be going between May and September, which is when the Taliban are at their peak. In wintertime, it's like a different place – the Taliban melt away and go back to looking after their opium.

POSTSCRIPT

Over two years have passed since I first put pen to paper on this project and much has changed since I added the last full stop and submitted the manuscript to the MoD in March 2009. At that time, we had 8,300 troops deployed to Afghanistan, 1,500 or so of whom were engaged on the front line; a total of 150 young soldiers had been killed in action, or had died subsequently from their wounds, most as a result of being shot. Chinook helicopters were in short supply and their crews were flying hours that were way outside of what is mandated as safe in peacetime, in an effort to try and take up the slack.

Yet as I write now, almost one year on, all the signs are that we are becoming more deeply committed in theatre than was ever first envisaged in 2006, when the then Defence Secretary John Reid announced the deployment of the 3 Para Battlegroup to provide security for reconstruction efforts. US President Barack Obama has announced his long-awaited strategy and another 30,000 American troops have already begun to deploy in Afghanistan, supplementing the 70,000 US soldiers already in theatre. Britain, already the second largest provider of troops to the region, has sent a further 1,200, so there are now 9,500 British troops in Afghanistan, with the vast bulk – 6,200 – in the southern province of Helmand.

The overwhelming majority of the fighting takes place in the south and east of the country, predominantly in the provinces of Kandahar and Helmand, which is where the Taliban are most active; much of the fighting is at close quarters. The violence is the worst it has been since the Taliban were removed from power in 2001, and 2009 has proven to be the bloodiest year so far for British soldiers, a trend that is also reflected among coalition troops and civilians. That fact, perhaps, represents the most poignant figure of all – in the ten months it took for my manuscript to be cleared for open publication by the MoD, a further 105 British soldiers died in Afghanistan, bringing the total since 2001 to 255.

One of the biggest changes to take place in the past year is the increase in the use of remotely detonated explosive devices, which are being used to target foreign forces across the country. Around 80 per cent of British deaths in 2009 were as a result of IED explosions, evidencing a change of tactics by Taliban forces, which suffered extensive losses in conventional firefights against the better-trained and equipped British and US. According to figures from iCasualties.org, ISAF deaths attributed to IEDs rose from 41 in 2006, to 275 in 2009, an increase of 571 per cent.

A book like this can only ever be a snapshot of a particular timeframe in the war. People, aircraft, places – and indeed, the tide of battle – all can change over time. When I visited Afghanistan to research and write this book – first in June and July 2008, and again in December the same year – the RAF's Harrier GR7s and GR9s provided Britain's fast-air capability; these have now been replaced by Tornado GR4 bombers. Two RAF Chinooks have been lost in crashes in the past few months, placing further pressure on the remaining fleet, but they have since been supplemented by the deployment of six Merlin helicopters. In addition, eight Chinook Mk3s – grounded for years due to software certification problems – are being reworked by a Boeing-led team to Mk2A standard. The first of those aircraft has just come online for training in the next two months, enabling an increase in deployed Chinook numbers if required.

Many of those whose accounts have been featured in this book will have moved on since I interviewed them; some have been promoted or recognised for gallantry awards, and two or three have left the military altogether, but even more have returned to theatre since I met with them there in 2008 – in some cases, up to four times. Such are the demands of life in the modern RAF.

The war in which they are engaged is unlike any other we have faced in modern times. An asymmetric conflict in which the well-equipped and trained professional forces of the coalition fight an increasingly bitter war with the Taliban, a group for whom the Geneva Conventions are anathema; even journalists are a target. When I covered events in Iraq throughout 2004, I was clearly identifiable as a member of the media; the soldiers with whom I was embedded wore their camouflage desert-pattern battledress, whereas my own body armour and helmet were in the now familiar 'journalists' blue', used since the Balkan conflicts to delineate the distinction between journalist and soldier.

That distinction is important because in journalism, objectivity and independence are all. In previous wars, journalists would report from the field without depending on western forces for support, without the consequent colouring of perspective that is a consequence of only being able to see and report from one side. The kidnapping and barbaric murder of journalist Daniel Pearl by al-Qaeda in 2002 changed everything, though, and made truly independent reporting of events in Iraq difficult – journalists in that conflict were being deliberately targeted by insurgents. It's a lesson that hasn't escaped the Taliban – already particularly media-aware, if a distinction exists to them, it's that killing members of the media will garner bigger headlines than the more familiar and frequent deaths of military forces. This blurring of the lines was driven home to me when I embedded with UK forces in Helmand in 2008; I was given the same kit to wear as the soldiers who I patrolled with, on the basis that I wouldn't stand out to Taliban snipers.

This was brought into sharp focus again recently when the sad news broke of the death of *Sunday Mirror* defence correspondent Rupert Hamer, 39, who was embedded with the US Marine Corps when his vehicle was hit by a bomb near Nawa in Helmand. Hamer was the second journalist in two weeks to lose his life to an IED in Afghanistan; Michelle Lang, a reporter for the *Calgary Herald*, was killed in December when the vehicle she was travelling in while embedded with Canadian soldiers was blown up in Kandahar. In August a US journalist working for CBS, Cami McCormick, was injured when the armoured vehicle she was travelling in hit an IED. And as I write, a UN report has just been published stating that the number of civilians killed as a result of the armed conflict in

2009 was higher than in any year since the Taliban were ousted from power.

Yet despite the rising death toll, most Afghans are increasingly optimistic about the state of their country, according to a poll commissioned by the BBC, ABC News and Germany's ARD. Of more than 1,500 Afghans questioned, 70 per cent said they believed Afghanistan was going in the right direction – a big jump from 40 per cent a year ago – and of those questioned, 68 per cent said they now back the presence of US troops in Afghanistan, compared with 63 per cent a year ago. For NATO troops, including UK forces, support has risen from 59 per cent to 62 per cent. The other significant theme which emerges from the figures is growing antipathy towards the Taliban. Some 90 per cent said they wanted their country run by the current government, compared with 6 per cent who said they favoured a Taliban administration; 69 per cent believed the Taliban posed the biggest danger to the country, and 66 per cent blamed the Taliban, al-Qaeda and foreign militants for violence in Afghanistan.

Chief of the General Staff, General Sir David Richards has said that he expects fewer British casualties in Afghanistan from the end of 2010, despite anticipating a 'tough year' ahead. The head of the British Army said that the mission would benefit from more soldiers, mainly US forces, and a larger Afghan army and police force, but that it might be possible to reduce troop levels in about 18 months. In an interview for BBC *Radio 5 Live* recently, he said, 'I personally anticipate as we get this business of mass right – the numbers of boots on the ground, a result of Allied enhancements and a growth in the Afghan army and police – that I would see a diminishing level of casualties from the end of this year, but it could be a tough year until we reach that point.'

The Government is keen to point out that this isn't a war without end, although nobody is prepared at this stage to say when that end will come. And nobody could have foreseen the way that events have unfolded in Afghanistan over the past 12 months, particularly the astonishing spike in the number of British dead and wounded. General Richards' words may yet come back to haunt him, but if we are to achieve our objectives, we must stay committed and not lose focus.

With what we have invested to date, this is not a war we can afford to lose. Whether we ultimately prevail will largely depend on continuing public support. As General Richards said last October, 'It is a war very much worth fighting, for our sakes and our children's sakes, and the price of failure hasn't been understood.'

Antony Loveless, February 2010

GLOSSARY OF TERMS

2i/c: Second in command.

.50 cal: British L1A1 Heavy machine gun, .50 inch (12.7mm) calibre. Usually vehicle mounted to provide top cover.

Apache AH1: British Army Apache attack helicopter fitted with Longbow radar. A more powerful version of the US AH64 Apache.

Bowman: The latest generation tactical communications system used by the British armed forces, currently being introduced into service.

CAS: Chief of the Air Staff or Close Air Support, depending on context.

Casevac: Casualty evacuation.

CCAST: Critical Care Air Support Team.

CDS: Chief of the Defence Staff.

CGS: Chief of the General Staff – the head of the Army.

D&V: Diarrhoea and Vomiting is a perennial problem on deployment and no matter where you go in any base, you're never standing far away from a bottle of disinfectant hand gel or a sign, drumming into you how serious and incapacitating a bout of D&V is. It spreads like wildfire with predictably debilitating results for operations.

Danger Close: Proximity to a weapon's effect considered to be the minimum safe point when wearing body armour and combat helmet. Also a term used by Forward Air Controllers to indicate that friendly forces are within close proximity of the target. The close proximity distance is determined by the weapon and munitions fired.

DC: District Centre

Decompression: A project launched by the MoD in 2006 to act as a buffer between fighting on the front line and being at home. Front-line personnel deployed to Afghanistan for four months or longer fly from theatre to Cyprus where they spend two weeks 'getting things out of their system'.

Démarche: A formal diplomatic representation of the official position, views, or wishes on a given subject from Government to another government.

Det: detachment or deployment, military term for time spent in theatre.

DFC: Distinguished Flying Cross, awarded in recognition of exemplary gallantry while flying during active operations against enemy forces.

DfID: UK Government Department for International Development.

Dicking: A term coined by British soldiers in Northern Ireland during the 1970s, referring to terrorist surveillance of location and movements of military forces or assets.

DUSHKA: Nickname of the DShK, a Soviet heavy anti-aircraft machine gun firing .50 cal (12.7mm) rounds. Nickname 'Dushka' (lit. 'Sweetie', 'Dear'), from the abbreviation.

DZ: Drop Zone.

EAW: Expeditionary Air Wing.

Fast air: Offensive military jet aircraft such as the Harrier GR7/9, Tornado GR4 or F16.

Flechette: 85in tungsten darts fired from a rocket travelling at Mach 2+.

FOB: Forward Operating Base.

Force Protection: Military term given to a range of measures designed to preserve the combat power of our own forces.

GBU: Guide Bomb Unit or smart bomb.

GPMG: General Purpose Machine Gun. 7.62mm Light machine gun, which is the mainstay of British forces.

Green Zone: Lush habitation of irrigated fields, hedgerows, trees, and small woods on either side of the Helmand River, bordered by arid desert.

HEAT: High Explosive Anti-Tank. An explosive shaped charge that on impact creates a very high-velocity jet of metal in a state of superplasticity that can punch through solid armour.

HEDP Rounds: High Explosive Dual Purpose 30mm cannon rounds.

HEISAP: High Explosive Incendiary Semi-Armour Piercing – kinetic rockets carried by Apache AH1.

HESCO Bastion: Square wire mesh cubes lined with Hessian. Filled with sand and/or rubble and used as defensive ramparts to protect bases from fire.

HLS: Helicopter Landing Site.

IDF: Indirect Fire. Term used for mortar and rocket attacks.

IED: Improvised Explosive Device.

Intel: Intelligence.

IRT: Incident Response Team consisting of aircrew, medical team, EOD (bomb disposal) team, and fire rescue team. The medical team is made up of an RAF Medic and RAF Emergency Care Specialist Nurse. In addition, the team is regularly augmented by an RAF aviation medicine doctor. All the components are protected on the ground by an RAF Regiment team. Flown in two Chinooks with an Apache AH1 providing overwatch.

ISAF: International Security Assistance Force. NATO multinational military force in Afghanistan.

ISTAR: Intelligence, Surveillance, Target Acquisition, and Reconnaissance, a practice that links several battlefield functions together to assist a combat force in employing its sensors and managing the information they gather.

JEngO: Junior Engineering Officer.

JTAC: Joint Tactical Air Controller, also known as FAC, or Forward Air Controller. A soldier responsible for the delivery of air ordnance on to a target by combat aircraft.

KAF: Kandahar Airfield.

KIA: Killed in Action.

Klick: Military slang for kilometres.

LAW: Light Anti-tank Weapon. A portable one-shot, disposable 66mm unguided anti-tank rocket launcher; pre-loaded w/ HEAT rocket.

Loadie: Loadmaster responsible for passengers and equipment in military helicopters or transport aircraft. Also responsible for manning weapons such as Minigun or M60.

Lockheed AC-130 Spectre: a heavily armed ground-attack aircraft based on the Hercules C130 airframe.

MERT: Medical Emergency Response Team or Combat Air Ambulance based at Camp Bastion.

Military Cross: Third-level decoration awarded in recognition of gallantry during active operations.

Minigun: 7.62mm, multi-barrel machine gun with a high rate of fire (over 3,000 rounds per minute), employing Gatling-style rotating barrels with an external power source. Fitted to forward side doors of RAF CH47 Chinooks.

MREs: Meal, Ready-to-Eat. A self-contained, individual field ration in lightweight packaging that can be eaten cold, or heated with a flameless heater (included within). For use in combat or other field conditions where organised food facilities aren't available.

NVG: Night Vision Goggles. Optical instrument that magnifies available light by 50,000 times.

OC: Officer Commanding – Wing Commander in charge of a squadron.

Operation Herrick: British codename for all military operations in Afghanistan.

Operation Telic: British codename for all military operation in Iraq.

Paradigm: Prime contractor for the Skynet 5 contract with the MoD. It enables military personnel deployed on two- to six-month tours to make 30 minutes of Government-funded phonecalls to any location in the world each week.

Pinzgauer: High-mobility all-terrain 4 x 4 and 6 x 6 military utility vehicles with open backs, covered by a canvas roof. Used alongside or in place of the Land Rover Defender as a patrol vehicle.

PTSD: Post Traumatic Stress Disorder.

RAF Regiment: The RAF's own infantry corps responsible for Force Protection, airfield defence, forward air control and parachute capability.

RIP: Relief in Place – one aircraft or unit replacing another over the battlefield.

Rock Ape: Colloquial term used within the RAF for members of the RAF Regiment.

RoE: Rules of Engagement. Laws set by a country's government, laying down rules for the use and proportionality of arms and military force.

RPG: Soviet-designed Rocket Propelled Grenade. Shoulder-launched rocket with a powerful grenade warhead.

Sangar: Army term for fortified look-out post.

SEngO: Senior Engineering Officer.

SF: Special Forces.

Shura: (Arabic) Consultation, meeting.

Tab: A fast march or run with full kit.

TACP: Tactical Air Control Party.

TADS: Target Acquisition and Designation System. The Apache AH1's targeting system.

Thermobaric: Enhanced blast Hellfire missile carried by the Apache AH1 and Reaper MQ-9.

Tracer: Bullets coated with phosphorous paint that burns with a red, orange, or green glow. Usually loaded every fourth round to check trajectory and accuracy of fire.

Wingman: The pilot who positions his aircraft outside and behind the leader of a flying formation.

WMIK: Weapons Mounted Installation Kit. Combat patrol variant of the Land Rover used principally for Force Protection and recce work. Agile, robust and powerful – mounted with GPMG and .50 cal.

Zeroing: Adjusting a weapon sight so it is properly aligned with the point of impact.

For further information about the people,
history, structure, role, equipment and
operations of the Royal Air Force, please
visit www.raf.mod.uk

Per Ardua Ad Astra

INDEX